With an introduction on **Learning Styles** and **Instructional Strategies** by Harvey F. Silver and Richard W. Strong

Styles and Strategies for Teaching High School Mathematics

Dr. Ed Thomas
Ph.D. Math Education

2nd Edition

27 Research-Based Strategies
for differentiating instruction and assessment in math

Design
Roberta Carswell-Panjwani

Cover
Bethann Carbone

All rights reserved. Permission to reproduce only those pages designated as "Reproducible" is extended to the purchaser for individual use only. No other part of this publication may be reproduced or transmitted in any form or by any means, electronic or mechanical, including photocopy, recording, or by any information storage or retrieval system, without written permission from the publisher.

© 2003 Thoughtful Education Press, LLC
(800) 962-4432
www.thoughtfuled.com

Printed in the United States of America
First printing March 2003

ISBN# 1-58284-048-2

Table of Contents

BUILDING THE 21ST-CENTURY MATH CLASSROOM:
AN INTRODUCTION BY HARVEY F. SILVER AND RICHARD W. STRONG............5

MASTERY STRATEGIES............17
Director............18
Convergence Mastery............24
Graduated Difficulty............29
New American Lecture............33
Proceduralizing............42

UNDERSTANDING STRATEGIES............47
Compare and Contrast............48
Concept Attainment............57
Concept Identification............63
Deductive Thinking............68
Pattern Finding............77
Mystery............83
Support and Refute............87

INTERPERSONAL STRATEGIES............93
Circle of Knowledge............94
Cooperative Learning............98
Game Competition............102
Paired Learner............109
Reciprocal Learning............115

SELF-EXPRESSIVE STRATEGIES............123
Inductive Learning............124
Divergent Thinking............131
Etch-a-Sketch............136
Metaphorical Expression............145
Modeling and Experimentation............150

META-STRATEGIES............163
Integrated Mathematical Engagement............164
Knowledge by Design............170
Math Notes............175
Task Rotation............179
Do You See What I See?............185

REFERENCES............189

ANSWERS AND SOLUTIONS TO SELECTED PROBLEMS............191

APPENDIX A: THE MATH LEARNING STYLE INVENTORY............197

ADDITIONAL RESOURCES............208

BUILDING THE 21ST-CENTURY MATH CLASSROOM

An Introduction by Harvey F. Silver and Richard W. Strong

Imagine yourself as a third grader. In math, you're adding, subtracting, multiplying, rounding, solving basic word problems, comparing fractions, even reading some rudimentary graphs. Someone asks you, "Are you good at math?" What do you think you would say? Flash forward to seventh grade. The math you're learning certainly has advanced, but so has your mind. How do you think you'd answer the question, "Are you good at math?" now? Now make one last jump. It's tenth grade. Sines, tangents, conic sections, matrices, you get the idea. Again, you're asked a simple question: "Are you good at math?" What's your answer this time?

The fact is, studies show that nearly all third graders and about three quarters of all seventh graders believe that they're good at math. But between seventh and tenth grade—just three short years—the number who say "yes" to the question, "Are you good at math?" shrinks down to a lowly 20%. That means that between middle and high school, more than half of all students lose their confidence when it comes to math. It also means that more than three quarters of all students graduate from high school entertaining the dangerous idea that math is a special realm for mathematicians and engineers, inscrutable to the average person and unnecessary for success in life.

This idea should give math teachers the shivers. For we know that math is at the heart of so many things that affect everyone from economics to technology, from the complexities of global marketing to the simple act of purchasing groceries. Math, as Howard Gardner (1983, 1999) has shown us, is a vital form of human intelligence. Math opens up career paths, empowers consumers, makes meaningful all kinds of data, from basketball statistics to political polls to the latest trends in the stock market. Quite simply, we cannot afford to have so many secondary students who dread math class. We cannot allow 80% of our graduates to walk out of school and into a fast-moving, technological society looking to avoid confrontations with math. For if we send an army of math-haters out into today's competitive global culture, we are short-changing millions of students by severely limiting their chances of future success.

And yet, we have met many math teachers who are wondering openly if students really can be successful in math. "My students are not very successful in mathematics. Half of them don't belong here." "We need more remedial math classes." "These kids don't know their times tables, how can they be expected to do algebra?" "The students in my math classroom are not motivated." These are just a few comments that are commonly made by math teachers in our high schools. So what is the truth? Do we believe our students can be successful in math?

How can we engage and motivate more students to meet the new and higher demands of the 21st Century, not to mention the challenges of expanding curriculums, state and national standards, school report cards, and greater expectations from colleges, government, and the public?

What is the status of math instruction, achievement, and attitudes in *your* classroom? Take a minute to rate the survey items below using a scale of 1 to 5. For each survey item, circle a score of 1 if the statement is far from indicative of your classroom. Circle a 5 if the statement is strongly indicative of your classroom. Assign values between 1 and 5 accordingly.

If your survey indicates that your math classroom has room for improvement, we would like to invite you to read this book and begin to transform your classroom into an exemplary learning environment. Of course, this is as good a place as any to ask: "With dozens of books on improving math instruction on the market, what makes this one different, better?" The answer can be summed up in two simple but deep principles that drive Ed Thomas's work in math:

1. **Effective instruction is *strategic*.**

2. **Different students have different *learning styles* and need different things from their math teacher.**

Survey of the Learning Environment in Your Math Classroom

The students in my math class:

1 2 3 4 5	1. view my class as purposeful, exciting, and fun.
1 2 3 4 5	2. actively participate in the learning process.
1 2 3 4 5	3. develop proficiency in the skills I teach.
1 2 3 4 5	4. communicate about math through reading, writing, and speaking on a regular basis.
1 2 3 4 5	5. are invited to use critical thinking skills.
1 2 3 4 5	6. understand the math they learn.
1 2 3 4 5	7. retain the math they learn (at least until the next school year).
1 2 3 4 5	8. have opportunities to be self-expressive as they learn math.
1 2 3 4 5	9. are given choices in levels of difficulty and problems to solve.
1 2 3 4 5	10. know that I will implement a variety of teaching strategies to help all students succeed.

PRINCIPLE 1:
Effective Instruction is Strategic

In what is the most comprehensive study of the research behind various teaching strategies and their impact in the classroom, Robert Marzano, Debra Pickering, and Jane Pollock (2001) demonstrate conclusively that teaching strategies have a real and pervasive effect on student learning. Indeed, the evidence is clear: Classroom strategies like comparing and contrasting, developing and testing hypotheses, working cooperatively, creating visual representations, organizing information graphically, and using higher-order questions result in better performance and deeper learning among students. But as most teachers know, asking students to compare and contrast two time-distance-rate problems, for example, or to work cooperatively to solve a particularly rigorous problem may not result in the kinds of deep learning the research points to. It is in moments like these—when we apply research-based techniques only to experience a roomful of blank faces when what we were expecting was active engagement—that the gap between research and practice seems wider than ever. So, the question becomes, "How can I put this research into classroom practice so that it leads to a positive change in student learning?" To answer this question, let's look in on a classroom.

> ### In the Classroom I
>
> **Situation:** Alesandra Ciccio, a high school mathematics teacher, has been teaching her students how to solve equations with one variable for one week. Every day, Alesandra reviews the process, answers questions, provides in-class practice time, and assigns appropriate homework. She believes there is not much more she can do. Every day, when her students return to class, Alesandra finds they are still making many of the same mistakes. She is ready to test, move to the next math unit, and admit that some of her students will never become proficient at the equation-solving process.
>
> **Applying a strategy:** If Alesandra had a working knowledge of how and when to use teaching strategies for mathematics, she might have incorporated the Convergence Mastery Strategy into her teaching. This strategy applied to Alesandra's situation would work as follows:
>
> Once Alesandra realized that her students had reached an apparent plateau of proficiency, she would inform her students that they were going to participate in a fun evaluation activity. She would prepare a series of five short quizzes on solving equations with one variable. Before each quiz, students would work cooperatively to review and perfect the equation-solving process. The review time would last approximately ten minutes. All students would be required to take the first quiz.
>
> At the end of the first quiz, students would cooperatively grade their solutions with Alesandra's help. Students who scored 100% would become permanent tutors and helpers and would exit the quiz-taking portion of the activity. Students who scored less than 100% would work cooperatively with the tutors and helpers to find their mistakes, correct them, and prepare for the next quiz. This process would continue until all five quizzes were taken. Since 100% success on a quiz is equivalent to an "A" in the grade book, students would communicate with each other, work cooperatively, and work hard to eliminate errors so they could take advantage of the immediate help and retake opportunities. As students progressed through this process, they would *converge toward mastery*.

What effect do you think the Convergence Mastery Strategy would have in your classroom? Do you think students' mastery of the equation-solving process would improve as a result of the strategy?

Let's look in on another classroom where the students are having a different kind of problem.

In the Classroom 2

Situation:
Robert Gould is trying to curb his algebra students' impulsivity as problem solvers. Too often, when Robert's students are faced with word problems, they will jump to solutions rather than engage in quality, pre-solution thinking and planning. This is especially worrisome to Robert since he knows that nearly one-half of the items on his state's math test are problems that students need to set up themselves.

Applying a strategy:
Robert selects the strategy known as Math Notes because it is designed specifically to help students:

1. Identify the facts of the problem
2. Determine exactly what the problem is asking
3. Represent the problem visually
4. List the steps that need to be taken to solve the problem.

He begins by presenting this problem to students:

Bookworm Problem

Volumes 1 and 2 of a 2-volume set of math books are next to one another on a shelf in their proper order (Volume 1 on the left, Volume 2 on the right). Each front and back cover is $\frac{1}{4}$" thick and the pages portion of each book is 2" thick. If a bookworm starts at Page 1 of Volume 1 and burrows all the way through to the last page of Volume 2, how far will the bookworm travel?

Answer:
_____
_____
_____
_____

Next, he asks students to take a minute and try to solve the problem as they normally do. As Robert suspects, nearly all the students answer either 5 inches ($2\frac{1}{2}$ inches for each book x 2) or $4\frac{1}{2}$ inches ($2\frac{1}{2}$ inches for each book minus $\frac{1}{2}$ inch for the front cover and back cover). That's when Robert introduces and models Math Notes. Using the same problem, Robert shows students how he thinks through and sets up the problem on a Math Notes Organizer.

Cont. on next page ...

In the Classroom 2 cont. ...

MATH NOTES ORGANIZER

The Facts:

Volumes 1 and 2 are next to each other:
- V1 is on the left
- V2 is on the right

Front and back covers $\frac{1}{4}$" thick
Pages 2" thick each book.
Bookworm starts at Page 1 and burrows to last page of V2.

The Steps:

1. The bookworm burrowed through two covers.

2. Each cover is $\frac{1}{4}$."

3. Burrows from Page 1 of V1 to last page of V2--**no pages burrowed through!**

4. $\frac{1}{4} + \frac{1}{4} = \frac{1}{2}$ inch

The Questions:

How far did the bookworm travel?

How many book covers did the bookworm burrow through?

How many pages?

The Diagram:

1st page of Volume 1
Last page of Volume 2

What students see very clearly is that without a strategy for breaking down and attacking difficult word problems, they are likely to miss essential information or misinterpret what the problem is asking them to do. Over the course of the year, students keep a notebook of problems they've solved using Math Notes. This way, they can refer back to their notebooks and look for models they can use whenever they come across new problems.

The Convergence Mastery Strategy and Math Notes are only two of the 27 effective teaching strategies that Ed Thomas lays out in this book. Convergence Mastery is, as its name suggests, a Mastery strategy—a strategy focused on helping students remember mathematical procedures and practice their computational skills. But math, of course, is about more than memory and practice. It is also about asking questions, making and testing hypotheses, thinking flexibly, visualizing concepts, working collaboratively, and exploring real-world applications. To accommodate this cognitive diversity, the strategies in this book are broken up into five distinct categories. Four of these categories—Mastery, Understanding, Self-Expressive, and Interpersonal—develop specific mathematical skills. The fifth category, the Meta-Strategies contain strategies like Math Notes, strategies that foster several kinds of mathematical skills simultaneously. The map on the next page explains these five categories.

STRATEGIES FOR TEACHING HIGH SCHOOL MATHEMATICS

Mastery Strategies help students *remember* mathematical *procedures* and *practice* their *computational skills*.

Interpersonal Strategies help students *discuss* mathematical ideas, *collaborate* to solve problems, and *explore the human connections* to mathematical content.

Meta-Strategies *combine* the thinking of Mastery, Understanding, Self-Expressive, and Interpersonal strategies to help students become *complete, multifaceted problem solvers*.

Understanding Strategies help students *uncover* and *explain* the *principles* and *big ideas* behind the math they learn.

Self-Expressive Strategies help students *visualize* math and *think flexibly* and *creatively* to solve *non-routine problems*.

Each of the strategies in these five categories represents a different kind of thinking, a different way of interacting with mathematical content, a different opportunity to grow as a learner and problem solver. Take just one of these ways of thinking away, and you really don't know math. Think about it: If you can't compute accurately (Mastery), explain mathematical concepts (Understanding), find ways to solve non-routine problems (Self-Expressive), or explore and discuss ideas with fellow problem solvers (Interpersonal), then you don't have the complete picture, and without a complete picture you don't really know math. This simple but often overlooked idea—that mathematical learning and problem solving require the cultivation of different kinds of thinking—brings us to the second way that this book will help you and your students achieve higher levels of success: *learning styles*.

PRINCIPLE 2:
Different Students Have Different Learning Styles

Let's listen in on two high school students who were asked the same question: "Who was your favorite math teacher and why?"

> **ALISHA:** I'm a junior now and my favorite math teacher so far has definitely been Ms. Tempiano. She really teaches, and by that I mean she's very clear about explaining what we're learning and about showing us exactly how to do it. Whenever we learned a new skill or a new technique, not only would she review the steps, she would work with us to develop an acronym to help us remember how to apply the steps, like "Please Excuse My Dear Aunt Sally" for remembering order of operations.
>
> Then, once we had our acronym, she would let us practice the steps to different problems—sometimes alone and sometimes in groups—while she walked around the room and worked with us like a coach. I loved the instant feedback. That really helped me when she would walk around and watch what we were doing and help us with any problems we were having.

> **ETHAN:** I didn't really think I liked or was good at math before I had Mr. Hollis for Algebra I. He did this thing called "Problem Solving Fridays." Every Friday, we focused on what he called "non-routine" problems, which were basically these really cool problems about things like building bridges or developing a new lottery game, problems that didn't have simple answers. So we had to experiment, try different things out—you know, get creative—to see how we might be able to find a solution.
>
> Actually, I knew I would like Mr. Hollis on the first day of class. I was a freshman and math was first period. I walked in expecting the same old thing: worksheets, the odd problems, quizzes. But instead, Mr. Hollis spent the first day on *metaphors!* He challenged us to create a metaphor for the problem-solving process. I showed how each step in the problem-solving process was like one of the stages in human digestion. It was really cool—I showed how you "chew" and "break down" and "process" both equations and food. The class loved it. And you know what else? I never forgot the steps in solving equations after that.

Almost immediately we can see that Alisha and Ethan treat math very differently. Alisha is attracted to problems that have clear solutions. Ethan, on the other hand, gets excited about non-routine problems where finding a solution requires experimentation and flexibility. Alisha solves problems by selecting an algorithm and applying it step by step, while Ethan's problem-solving process is one of generating and exploring alternatives.

As far as math teachers go, Alisha prefers one who is clear about expectations and who models new skills, allows students to practice the skills, and who provides regular feedback and coaching along the way. From Ethan's point of view, an ideal math teacher allows students to explore mathematics through the imagination and creative problem solving. Finally, and most significantly, each student sees different purposes for learning and using math. For Alisha, math represents structure and stability, a set of fail-safe procedures that can be used again and again to find correct solutions. Ethan, of course, would disagree. For him, math is a medium for expressing powerful ideas and creating new and interesting products—a kind of intellectual playground full of possibilities, unseen connections, and fascinating applications. The differences in how these two students experience and approach math are the result of *learning styles*.

Learning styles come from psychologist Carl Jung's seminal work on the human mind (1923). What Jung discovered is that the way we take in information and then judge the importance of that information develops into different personality types. Working from Jung's foundation, Kathleen Briggs and Isabel Myers (1962/1998) later expanded learning styles, turning them into a comprehensive model of human difference, which they made famous with their Myers-Briggs Type Indicator®. By applying the insights of Jung, Myers, and Briggs specifically to mathematics, we have identified four separate styles of math students, which are shown on the next page.

THE FOUR TYPES OF MATH STUDENTS*

Mastery Math Students ...

Want to ... learn practical information and set procedures

Like math problems that ... are like problems they have solved before and that use algorithms to produce a single solution

Approach problem solving ... in a step-by-step manner

Experience difficulty when ... math becomes too abstract or when faced with non-routine problems

Want a math teacher who ... models new skills, allows time for practice, and builds in feedback and coaching sessions

Interpersonal Math Students ...

Want to ... learn math through dialogue, collaboration, and cooperative learning

Like math problems that ... focus on real-world applications and on how math helps people

Approach problem solving ... as an open discussion among a community of problem solvers

Experience difficulty when ... instruction focuses on independent seatwork or when what they are learning seems to lack real-world application

Want a math teacher who ... pays attention to their successes and struggles in math

Understanding Math Students ...

Want to ... understand why the math they learn works

Like math problems that ... ask them to explain, prove, or take a position

Approach problem solving ... by looking for patterns and identifying hidden questions

Experience difficulty when ... there is a focus on the social environment of the classroom (e.g. on collaboration and cooperative problem solving)

Want a math teacher who ... challenges them to think and who lets them explain their thinking

Self-Expressive Math Students ...

Want to ... use their imagination to explore mathematical ideas

Like math problems that ... are non-routine, project-like in nature, and that allow them to think "outside the box"

Approach problem solving ... by visualizing the problem, generating possible solutions, and exploring among the alternatives

Experience difficulty when ... math instruction is focused on drill and practice and rote problem solving

Want a math teacher who ... invites imagination and creative problem solving into the math classroom

---

*If you are interested in finding the learning styles of your math students, we suggest using the **Math Learning Style Inventory for Secondary Students**. A sample of the **Math Learning Style Inventory** is included in Appendix A of this book.

It is important to remember that no student—no person—is a perfect representative of a single style. Learning styles are not pigeonholes; it is neither possible nor productive to reduce this student to a Self-Expressive learner or that student to an Understanding learner. Various contexts and types of problems call for different kinds of thinking, and all students rely on all four styles to help them learn mathematics. However, it is equally true that people tend to have style preferences; like all people, each student will usually show strength in one or two styles and weakness in one or two others. What all this means is that learning styles are the key to motivating students and helping them experience higher levels of success in math. Tapping into the power of learning styles is a matter of building on students' strengths by accommodating their preferred styles while simultaneously encouraging them to stretch their talents and grow as learners by developing less-preferred styles.

So how do we accomplish this? Take another look at our map of strategies.

THE FIVE TYPES OF STRATEGIES IN THIS BOOK

Mastery Strategies help students *remember* mathematical *procedures* and *practice* their *computational skills*.

Interpersonal Strategies help students *discuss* mathematical ideas, *collaborate* to solve problems, and *explore the human connections* to mathematical content.

Meta-Strategies *combine* the thinking of Mastery, Understanding, Self-Expressive, and Interpersonal strategies to help students become *complete, multifaceted problem solvers*.

Understanding Strategies help students *uncover* and *explain* the *principles* and *big ideas* behind the math they learn.

Self-Expressive Strategies help students *visualize* math and *think flexibly* and *creatively* to solve *non-routine problems*.

What the map on the previous page shows us is how styles and strategies come together, the place where they meet. Accommodating students' strong styles and fostering their weaker styles requires little more than varying the strategies you select and use in your classroom. When you use a Self-Expressive Strategy, for example, not only are you inviting your creative students who think math is too black and white into the learning process, you are also challenging all of your "procedure whizzes" to step back and think about math in a new and illuminating way. The same is true for the Mastery, Understanding, and Interpersonal strategies: The different kind of thinking required by each style of strategy will engage some students and challenge others, while the Meta-Strategies combine the thinking of all four styles inside a single strategy.

*The key to making all of this work in the classroom is **rotation**.* Use all five types of strategies regularly. Keep track of what styles you use and when. Experiment: If a concept seems to be eluding students, try using a strategy like Metaphorical Expression (Self-Expressive) or Compare and Contrast (Understanding). If students of all styles need to work on complex problem-solving, try a Meta-Strategy like Do You See What I See? Remember that good problem solving requires all four styles of thinking; therefore, teaching students how to become good problem solvers will require you to rotate around the "wheel of style."

The 21st-Century Classroom: Within Our Reach

What Ed Thomas has found, through years of teaching math and conducting professional development seminars for math teachers, is that building a 21st-Century math classroom means making students as important as standards. But rhetoric is one thing; a math classroom that is humming with the thought of actively engaged students is quite another. What Ed shows is that getting the classroom we all wish for is not pie-in-the-sky idealism. Thankfully, building a 21st-Century math classroom does not require us to reinvent ourselves or our beliefs. By developing a working knowledge of the research-based strategies in this book and by rotating them so that you accommodate and grow the learning styles of all your students, you can increase significantly the power of your teaching and your students' learning.

We know this book will be an important tool in developing such a classroom.

Harvey F. Silver

Richard W. Strong

MASTERY STRATEGIES

**Director
Convergence Mastery
Graduated Difficulty
New American Lecture
Proceduralizing**

Mathematics, Styles, and Strategies
DIRECTOR

Wouldn't it be nice if you could command your students to do their math? Wouldn't it be nice if you could direct your students to be proficient at math? The Director Strategy enables you to do just that.

To be successful in math, students must be proficient in a variety of mathematical processes and routines. Many of the math routines we want our students to know consist of a fixed sequence of steps that all students must follow. By using the Director Strategy, the teacher can provide instruction to the entire class through a responsive engagement activity. As a result of the Director Strategy, students concurrently perform each step of a math process upon the command of the teacher. A math expression or term serves as the command cue.

No apology is necessary for the use of the Director Strategy. There are times when insisting on conformity to rigid standards is as appropriate and educationally useful as is responding to each student individually. Each teaching strategy has its own assets and liabilities. Knowing what the Director Strategy can and cannot do is central to making an informed judgment about when its use is educationally sound. The issue need not—indeed, should not—be an either/or.

Developing a Director Activity
Any math process that utilizes a routine, step-by-step thinking process is a candidate for a Director activity. To develop the activity, outline the steps involved in performing the math process. Develop *one* command term that will be used to initiate student engagement in each step of the process.

The director term and outline of the process steps for *finding averages* are listed on the next page.

Director Term: AVERAGE

Process Steps: For finding the average of the set of numbers
{ 12, 10, 22, 16 }.

1. Write the problem: "Find the average of the numbers 12, 10, 22, and 16."
   Average

2. Find the sum of the numbers 12, 10, 22, and 16.
   Average

3. Divide the sum from step two by 4. This quotient is the average.
   Average

4. Write "The average of 12, 10, 22, and 16 is 15."
   $(12 + 10 + 22 + 16) \div 4 = 15$.
   Average

Director: Obtaining Desired Student Behaviors
To optimize the power of the Director Strategy, students should be:

1. seated with clean paper and pencil with their attention directed to the teacher only.

2. told that the purpose of the activity is to help them to become proficient in an important math concept or skill.

3. instructed to listen carefully to the teacher's directions and to engage in thinking, doing, and writing when they hear the teacher give the command signal.

4. prepared to answer questions about their work.

5. ready to practice several examples.

TEACHER'S GUIDE:
DIRECTOR
Featured math concept: **Finding the Inverse of a Function**

Directions (to be read to students):
Today we are going to review the process for finding the equation for the inverse of a function. To help ensure that everybody is successful, I will communicate each step of the process to you. Following each step I will call out the command signal *Inverse*. When I pause and boldly say *Inverse*, you perform the step on your paper. I will circulate around the room to be sure that everybody is working correctly.

Introduction to Inverse Functions

In the type of problem you will do today, a function rule or equation will be given. Your goal is to perform some algebraic steps on the equation to find the equation of the inverse function. A function and its inverse function are related in the following way.

If a function f(x) generates ordered pairs of the form (a,b), then the inverse function $f^{-1}(x)$ generates ordered pairs of the form (b,a). In other words, the inverse of a function can be used to generate ordered pairs of the original function. When plotted on a Cartesian plane, the graphs of f(x) and $f^{-1}(x)$ are reflections of each other across the line y=x. Let's go through the process of finding an inverse function now.

- Write the given function f(x) = 2x + 4 on your paper.
Inverse

- Substitute x for f(x) and $f^{-1}(x)$ for x and rewrite the equation.
Inverse

Stages of Student Work

$f(x) = 2x + 4$

$x = 2(f^{-1}(x)) + 4$

Cont. on next page →

DIRECTOR: *Finding the Inverse of a Function cont. ...*

Stages of Student Work

- Now we are going to solve $f^{-1}(x)$. To begin the process of isolating $f^{-1}(x)$, we will apply the subtraction property of equality and subtract 4 from both sides of the equation. Subtract 4 from both sides of the equation. ***Inverse***

$$x = 2(f^{-1}(x)) + 4$$
$$\underline{-4 \qquad\qquad -4}$$
$$x - 4 = 2(f^{-1}(x))$$

- Your new equation should now read $x - 4 = 2f^{-1}(x)$. Since our goal is to solve for $f^{-1}(x)$, we will apply the division property of equality and divide both sides of the equation by 2. Divide both sides of the equation. ***Inverse***

$$\frac{x-4}{2} = \frac{2(f^{-1}(x))}{2}$$

$$\frac{x-4}{2} = f^{-1}(x)$$

- Your new equation should now read $(x - 4)/2 = f^{-1}(x)$. By convention, we usually write $f^{-1}(x)$ on the left side of the equation. This can be accomplished by applying the symmetric property of equality, which states that *if a = b then b = a*. Switch the left and right sides of your equation. ***Inverse***

$$f^{-1}(x) = \frac{x-4}{2}$$

- Your final equation should read $f^{-1}(x) = (x-4)/2$.

- Now check your solution by substituting $x=4$ (an arbitrary value from the domain of $f(x)$ into the original $f(x)$ equation and find $f(4)$. ***Inverse***
The value of $f(x)$ should be 12. Substitute 12 for x in the $f^{-1}(x)$ equation and find $f^{-1}(12)$. ***Inverse***
The value of $f^{-1}(x)$ should be 4. (Why?)

$$f(4) = 2 \cdot 4 + 4 = 12$$
(therefore) $f(4) = 12$

$$f^{-1}(12) = \frac{12-4}{2}$$

- Graph $y = 2x + 4$, $y = x$, and $y = (x - 4) / 2$ on a graphing utility. ***Inverse***

$$f^{-1}(12) = 8/2 = 4$$

- Verify that the graphs of the original function and the inverse function are reflections of each other across the line $y = x$. ***Inverse***

therefore $f^{-1}(12) = 4$

TEACHER'S GUIDE:
DIRECTOR
Featured math concept: **Pythagorean Theorem:**
Solving for the Missing Parts of a Right Triangle

Directions (to be read to students):
Today we are going to review the process of solving for the missing side of a right triangle. To help ensure that everybody is successful, I will communicate each step of the process to you. Following each step I will call out the command signal **Pythagorean**. When I pause and boldly say **Pythagorean**, you perform the step on your paper. I will circulate around the room to be sure that everybody is working correctly.

- Draw right triangle ABC, with C the right angle, and label sides a=4, c=5, and b=x.
Pythagorean

- In any right triangle the longest side is across from the right angle and is called the hypotenuse. The other two sides are called the legs. According to the Pythagorean theorem, the sum of the squares of the legs equals the square of the hypotenuse. Write an equation that reflects the Pythagorean theorem. Use 5, 4, and x in your equation.
Pythagorean

- Your equation should read $4^2 + x^2 = 5^2$ or $x^2 + 4^2 = 5^2$. Both equations are equivalent. (Why?) Rewrite the equation in a simpler form by substituting 16 and 25 for 4^2 and 5^2. (Why?)
Pythagorean

- Your new equation should read $16 + x^2 = 25$. Apply the subtraction property of equality by subtracting 16 from both sides of the equation. Write the resulting equation.
Pythagorean

Stages of Student Work

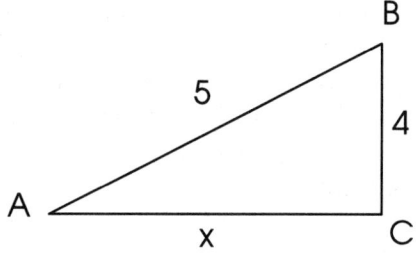

$4^2 + x^2 = 5^2$

$16 + x^2 = 25$

$16 + x^2 = 25$
$\underline{-16 \qquad -16}$

Cont. on next page →

DIRECTOR: *Pythagorean Theorem cont. ...*

Stages of Student Work

- Your new equation should read $x^2 = 9$. Our purpose for subtracting 16 from both sides of the equation was to isolate the x^2 term. This makes sense since we are solving the equation for x and since x represents the measure of the side of the triangle we are trying to find. To find the value of x, we will apply the square root principle. Take the square root of both sides of the equation.
Pythagorean

- When you apply the square root principle in an equation you get two answers for x. In this case you should have obtained $x = 3$ and $x = -3$. (Why?) Since the equation is only a math model for the geometry problem, you must use your reasoning skills to determine which value is the solution to the problem.
Pythagorean

- In this geometry problem, x represents the measure of a side of a right triangle. In this case it does not make sense to have a negative measure for the side of a triangle. Write $x = 3$ for your final solution.
Pythagorean

- Now check your solution by applying the Pythagorean theorem to the side measures 3, 4, and 5.
Pythagorean

$16 + x^2 = 25$
$\underline{-16 \qquad -16}$
$\qquad x^2 = 9$

$\sqrt{x^2} = \pm\sqrt{9}$

$x = \pm 3$

$x = 3$

$3^2 + 4^2 = 5^2$

$9 + 16 = 25$

$25 = 25$

Page 23

Mathematics, Styles, and Strategies
CONVERGENCE MASTERY

The Convergence Mastery Strategy can be used to lead students toward mastery of a particular math concept or skill. The strategy is most effective when used after the concept or skill has been introduced and partially mastered by students.

To implement the strategy, the teacher will ask students to practice or review the math concept or skill to be mastered with a learning partner. The practice time should last approximately 10 minutes. After the practice period, the teacher will ask the students to clear their desks and take the first of five quizzes prepared by the teacher. The quizzes should be timed (2-5 minutes), relatively short, and test only the concept or skill to be mastered.

At the completion of the first quiz, all papers should be quickly graded in class using the Paired Learner model. Students who perform without error on the first quiz will receive a 100% grade of mastery and exit the quiz-taking component of the Convergence Mastery activity. Students who commit one or more errors will receive a temporary incomplete grade. After the first quiz is graded, all students will participate in a short period (5 minutes) of error analysis, review, and practice with a learning partner. Students who scored 100% on the first quiz are expected to assist other students during the review and practice period. Following the review and practice period, the students who did not score 100% on the first quiz will participate in the second quiz in the series.

The process described in the preceding paragraph will continue until all five quizzes have been administered. Expect nearly all students to improve each time they take the next quiz. As the activity progresses toward the fifth quiz, the students will converge toward mastery.

If a few students do not master the concept or skill by the fifth quiz, maintain an open door policy for those students to practice and retake the quiz at a later date.

Developing a Convergence Mastery Activity

Selecting a Topic
Many math concepts and skills are candidates for a Convergence Mastery activity. Some of the topics appropriate for Convergence Mastery activities are listed below and categorized by grade level.

Elementary	Middle	High
Addition Facts	Multiplication Facts	Factoring
Multiplication Facts	Prime Factorizations	Solving Equations
Place Value	GCF and LCM	Geometry Proofs
Reading Numbers	Solving Equations	Law of Sines
Writing Numbers	Finding Percents	Law of Cosines
Renaming Fractions	Fraction Operations	Differentiation

Be sure that the topic you select is one that the students are familiar with and have partially mastered. For example, if a teacher knows that students have had experience adding fractions, but have made many mistakes in the process, addition of fractions would be an appropriate topic for a Convergence Mastery activity.

Preparing for the Quizzes
The quizzes for a Convergence Mastery activity should be short and only contain problems that directly reflect the concept or skill to be mastered. To save paper and time, the five quizzes can be written on a transparency or displayed to the entire class through a multimedia device. A sample of five quizzes for addition of fractions is shown here.

Quiz 1	Quiz 2	Quiz 3	Quiz 4	Quiz 5
1. $1/2 + 3/4$	1. $1/5 + 1/4$	1. $3/4 + 3/4$	1. $5/6 + 2/5$	1. $1/5 + 2/4$
2. $4/5 + 3/7$	2. $2/5 + 1/6$	2. $1/2 + 2/5$	2. $2/7 + 5/7$	2. $2/3 + 3/3$
3. $2/3 + 1/8$	3. $4/7 + 1/2$	3. $5/6 + 3/8$	3. $7/8 + 5/7$	3. $6/7 + 1/2$

CONVERGENCE MASTERY

Student Activity

Featured math concept: **Trigonometric Identities**

Student Name: _____

Directions:
Study the trigonometric identities listed to the right. Memorize them with help from your learning partner. Be prepared to write the identities correctly on a series of Convergence Mastery quizzes. The only possible grades on the quiz are **Mastery (100%)** or **Still Needs Improvement (Incomplete Grade)**. An incomplete is given if any errors occur. You will have up to five chances to earn a mastery grade.

$\sin(x+y) = \sin x \cos y + \cos x \sin y$
$\sin(x-y) = \sin x \cos y - \cos x \sin y$
$\cos(x+y) = \cos x \cos y - \sin x \sin y$
$\cos(x-y) = \cos x \cos y + \sin x \sin y$

$\tan(x+y) = \dfrac{\tan x + \tan y}{1 - \tan x \tan y}$

$\tan(x-y) = \dfrac{\tan x - \tan y}{1 + \tan x \tan y}$

$\sin x \cos y = \tfrac{1}{2}(\sin(x+y) + \sin(x-y))$
$\sin x \sin y = \tfrac{1}{2}(\cos(x-y) - \cos(x+y))$
$\cos x \cos y = \tfrac{1}{2}(\cos(x+y) + \cos(x-y))$

Quiz 1
Write the trigonometric identities for each expression below.

$\sin(x-y)$

$\cos(x+y)$

$\sin x \cos y$

$\tan(x+y)$

$\sin(x+y)$

Quiz 2
Write the trigonometric identities for each expression below.

$\sin(x+y)$

$\cos(x-y)$

$\sin x \sin y$

$\tan(x-y)$

$\cos(x+y)$

Quiz 3
Write the trigonometric identities for each expression below.

$\cos(x-y)$

$\tan(x+y)$

$\sin x \cos y$

$\tan(x-y)$

$\cos x \cos y$

Quiz 4
Write the trigonometric identities for each expression below.

$\cos x \cos y$

$\cos(x-y)$

$\sin x \cos y$

$\tan(x-y)$

$\sin x \sin y$

Quiz 5
Write the trigonometric identities for each expression below.

$\sin(x+y)$

$\cos(x-y)$

$\sin x \cos y$

$\tan(x+y)$

$\sin(x-y)$

CONVERGENCE MASTERY
Featured math concept: **Properties of Numbers**

Student Name: _____

Directions:
Study the properties listed to the right. Practice writing them using math notation. Be prepared to write the properties correctly on a series of Convergence Mastery quizzes. The only possible grades on the quiz are **Mastery (100%)** or **Still Needs Improvement (Incomplete Grade)**. An incomplete is given if any errors occur. You will have up to five chances to earn a mastery grade.

Properties of Real Numbers

Closure + $\forall\, a, b, \in R,\, a + b \in R$
Closure • $\forall\, a, b, \in R,\, a \cdot b \in R$
Commutative + $\forall\, a, b, \in R,\, a + b = b + a$
Commutative • $\forall\, a, b, \in R,\, ab = ba$
Associative + $\forall\, a, b, c \in R,\, (a + b) + c = a + (b + c)$
Associative • $a, b, c \in R,\, (ab)c = a(bc)$
Distributive •/+ $\forall\, a, b, c \in R,\, a(b + c) = ab + bc$
Distributive •/- $\forall\, a, b, c \in R,\, a(b - c) = ab - bc$
Identity + $\forall\, a \in R,\, \exists\, 0 \in R \,|\, a + 0 = a$
Identity • $\forall\, a \in R,\, \exists\, 1 \in R \,|\, a(1) = a \neq 0$
Inverse + $\forall\, a \in R,\, \exists\, {-a} \in R \,|\, a + {-a} = 0$
Inverse • $\forall\, a \in R,\, \exists\, (1/a) \in R \,|\, a(1/a) = a \neq 0$

Quiz 1
Write the following properties using math notation.

Commutative +

Associative •

Identity +

Closure •

Inverse •

Quiz 2
Write the following properties using math notation.

Identity +

Closure •

Distributive •/+

Commutative •

Associative •

Quiz 3
Write the following properties using math notation.

Associative +

Distributive •/-

Commutative +

Identity +

Identity •

Quiz 4
Write the following properties using math notation.

Commutative •

Associative +

Identity •

Closure +

Inverse +

Quiz 5
Write the following properties using math notation.

Distributive •/+

Commutative +

Closure +

Closure •

Identity •

CONVERGENCE MASTERY

Student Activity

Featured math concept: **Perfect Squares**

Student Name: _____

Directions:

Study the perfect squares listed below. Memorize them with help from your partner. Be prepared to write the perfect squares correctly on a series of Convergence Mastery quizzes. The only possible grades on the quiz are **Mastery (100%)** or **Still Needs Improvement (Incomplete Grade)**. An incomplete is given if any errors occur. You will have up to five chances to earn a mastery grade.

Table of Perfect Squares for Number 1 - 25

n	n²	n	n²	n	n²	n	n²	n	n²
1	1	6	36	11	121	16	256	21	441
2	2	7	49	12	144	17	289	22	484
3	9	8	64	13	169	18	324	23	529
4	16	9	81	14	196	19	361	24	576
5	25	10	100	15	225	20	400	25	625

Quiz 1
Write the perfect squares of the numbers shown below.

14 ___
21 ___
11 ___
24 ___
18 ___
19 ___
23 ___

Quiz 2
Write the perfect squares of the numbers shown below.

12 ___
21 ___
14 ___
25 ___
17 ___
13 ___
22 ___

Quiz 3
Write the perfect squares of the numbers shown below.

16 ___
23 ___
15 ___
22 ___
14 ___
17 ___
24 ___

Quiz 4
Write the perfect squares of the numbers shown below.

19 ___
20 ___
15 ___
23 ___
19 ___
16 ___
21 ___

Quiz 5
Write the perfect squares of the numbers shown below.

17 ___
23 ___
13 ___
25 ___
12 ___
15 ___
24 ___

Mathematics, Styles, and Strategies
GRADUATED DIFFICULTY

In the mathematics classroom, students function at different levels of understanding. Some students might not be ready for the most challenging problems and others might become bored with problems that are too easy. The Graduated Difficulty Strategy is based on the influential work of Muska Mosston (1972) on differentiating student assessment. The strategy enables teachers to address the diverse levels of their students by offering problems of varying difficulty levels and allowing students to begin at the most appropriate level. Upon successful completion of one level, students will be prepared to advance to the next level.

Developing a Graduated Difficulty Activity

Virtually every math concept and skill can be made more or less difficult by modifying the numbers in the problems of an activity. In the example below, the difficulty levels of three *statistical average* problems were adjusted by modifying the numbers of each problem.

Problem A
Find the average of:

2, 4, 8, and 12

Problem B
Find the average of:

$3\frac{1}{2}$, $4\frac{1}{2}$, 6 and 8.5

Problem C
Find the average of:

3x, 4x, 6x, and 7x

The difficulty level of a problem can also be modified by including a secondary concept in the problem. Each statistical average problem below has a difficulty level that corresponds to the difficulty level of the secondary concept incorporated into the problem.

Problem A:
Find the average of the first ten whole numbers that are perfect squares.

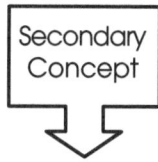

Perfect squares

Problem B:
Find the average of the first ten prime numbers.

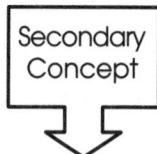

Prime numbers

Problem C:
Find the average of the first 200 whole numbers.

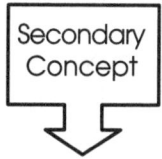

$\Sigma = n(n+1)/2$

Graduated Difficulty: Observable Student Behaviors

To optimize the power of the Graduated Difficulty Strategy, students should be:

1. offered a choice of three levels of difficulty.
2. encouraged to begin working at the highest level at which they can experience success. The choice should be dependent on students' strengths, weaknesses, and levels of understanding.
3. taught to evaluate their work and build on their successes.
4. encouraged to advance to the highest level problem.

Graduated Difficulty: A Sample Problem Experience

Student Problem:
In each problem, the task is to find the total distance around the outside edges of the figure. Problems A, B, and C increase in their respective levels of difficulty. Begin with the highest level problem that you can successfully solve. If you start with problem A or B, once you successfully solve the problem examine the differences between it and the problem at the next level. Plan how you might solve the next problem, then try to solve it. Continue this process until you successfully solve the highest-level problem.

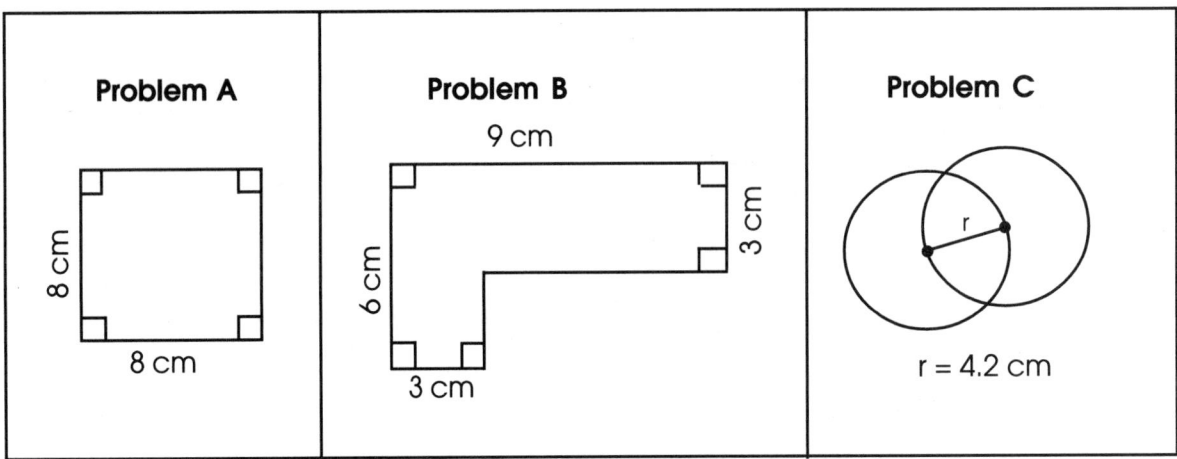

The Student's Choice:
Students who are just beginning to comprehend perimeter might choose to solve Problem A. Students who have a handle on the perimeter concept might choose to solve Problem B. In this figure, students will have to make additional calculations to find the measures of unmarked segments. Students who desire a real challenge can tackle the circle problem. If students find that their initial choice was too difficult or too easy, they can advance or drop to a more appropriate level. Since students are not penalized for choosing an easier level problem, the Graduated Difficulty Strategy contributes to a nonthreatening and success-oriented learning environment.

GRADUATED DIFFICULTY
Featured math concept: **Trigonometric Identities**

Student Name: _____

Directions:
Solve each of the warm-up problems below. Then examine each of the three trig identity problems. All three problems are challenging, but Problem 2 is more challenging than Problem 1, and Problem 3 is more challenging than Problem 2. Begin with the highest-level problem that you can successfully solve. If you start with Problem 1 or 2, once you successfully solve the problem, examine the differences between it and the problem at the next level. Plan how you might solve the next problem, then try to solve it. Continue this process until you successfully solve the highest-level problem.

Warm-up: Evaluate each of the following:

1. $\sin \pi/4$
2. $\cos \pi/4$
3. $\sin \pi/6$
4. $\cos \pi/6$
5. $\sin^2 \pi/4 + \cos^2 \pi/4$
6. $\sin^2 \pi/6 + \cos^2 \pi/6$

Choose one of the following and solve:

Problem 1: Prove the following trigonometric identity:

$(\csc x + \cot x)(1 - \cos x) = \sin x$

Problem 2: Prove the following trigonometric identity:

$\cos^4 x - \sin^4 x = \cos 2x$

Problem 3: Prove the following trigonometric identity:

$\left(\dfrac{1 + \tan \theta}{1 - \tan \theta}\right)^2 = \dfrac{1 + \sin 2\theta}{1 - \sin 2\theta}$

Page 31

GRADUATED DIFFICULTY

Student Activity

Featured math concept: **Complex Fractions**

Student Name: _____

Directions:
Solve each of the warm-up problems below. Then examine each of the three complex fraction problems. All three problems are challenging, but Problem 2 is more challenging than Problem 1, and Problem 3 is more challenging than Problem 2. Begin with the highest-level problem that you can successfully solve. If you start with Problem 1 or 2, once you successfully solve the problem, examine the differences between it and the problem at the next level. Plan how you might solve the next problem, then try to solve it. Continue this process until you successfully solve the highest-level problem.

Warm-up: Perform the indicated operations:

1. $\dfrac{1}{2} + \dfrac{1}{3}$
2. $\dfrac{3}{5} + \dfrac{2}{3}$
3. $\dfrac{3}{4} - \dfrac{2}{5}$
4. $\dfrac{1}{2} \cdot \dfrac{1}{3}$
5. $4\dfrac{3}{5} + 2\dfrac{1}{2}$
6. $2\dfrac{1}{2} \div 2\dfrac{1}{2}$

Choose one of the following and solve:

Problem 1: Simplify the following:

$$\dfrac{\dfrac{3}{4} + \dfrac{3}{2}}{\dfrac{1}{2} - \dfrac{1}{4}}$$

Problem 2: Simplify the following:

$$\left[\dfrac{\dfrac{3}{4} + \dfrac{3}{2}}{\dfrac{1}{2}}\right]^2$$

Problem 3: Simplify the following:

$$\left[\dfrac{\dfrac{3}{5} + \dfrac{3}{2}}{\dfrac{1}{2} - \dfrac{1}{4}}\right]^2$$

Mathematics, Styles, and Strategies
NEW AMERICAN LECTURE

I recently had an opportunity to watch some college professors' lectures broadcast on satellite television. The professors were representatives of several universities. I assumed that they must be very good lecturers since they were selected for worldwide broadcast. But after watching the lectures, I concluded that there must be a teaching strategy that I didn't know about called the *Old American Lecture*. Based on what I saw, its purpose was to bore students, confuse students, and provide information that was disconnected from what students already knew.

The New American Lecture Strategy provides a positive, brain-based twist on the traditional lecture by incorporating a hook, a visual organizer, and effective questioning in all four learning styles. The purpose of the hook is to help students to build a bridge between what they already know and new concepts and skills presented through the lecture. The purpose of a visual organizer is to provide students with a non-linguistic framework that shows the relationship between the various "chunks" of information. Effective questioning in all four learning styles motivates students and provides more opportunities for all students to better understand new concepts and skills.

Developing a New American Lecture Activity

Selecting a Topic
Since the New American Lecture is used to provide students with information, this strategy is ideal for introducing new math topics. Since most mathematics is progressive and connected, students almost always have prerequisite knowledge that can be the basis for an effective hook. Since most new math topics include titles, definitions, theorems, and examples, visual organizers can easily be made for lectures that introduce new topics. When introducing a new math topic, it is important to help students understand the new concepts. Questions in all four learning styles can help students to build that understanding. To demonstrate how the components of a New American Lecture Strategy can be developed, let's use the concept of integers as an example.

Designing a Hook
A well-designed hook encourages students to recall and share previous experiences and knowledge and will connect smoothly to the focus of the lecture. For the topic of integers, one of the fundamental concepts is the idea of opposites. The following activity is a candidate for an effective hook: *In the real world, some actions can be considered opposites of other actions. When performed consecutively, opposite actions often cancel each other's effect. For example, the processes of turning on a light and turning off a light are opposites. When both of these processes occur consecutively, one cancels the effect of the other. Work with a learning partner to identify another pair of opposite actions that are common in the real world.* It is highly probable that all students will have some previous experiences with opposite actions that cancel each other's effect. Since the students will have generated the information, they will be eager to share. Be sure to give students an opportunity to share their opposite actions. They will now be hooked and interested in the upcoming lecture.

Creating a Visual Organizer

A well-prepared visual organizer will assist students in the notetaking process and help them stay on task during the lecture. The visual organizer should provide the title of the lesson and framework for taking notes on new terms, definitions, postulates, theorems, diagrams, and sample problems. For the topic of integers, the visual organizer can contain a place for students to define key vocabulary, such as *integer, positive, negative, opposite, sign, origin, number line, graph, coordinate,* and *absolute value,* as well as a section for diagramming a number line. The organizer can also contain sections for explaining the inverse property of addition and for creating sample problems involving the task of combining integers. A sample visual organizer for introducing integers is displayed below.

Questions in All Four Styles

Effective questioning in all four styles will provide an opportunity for all students to learn and understand the information conveyed through the lecture. Throughout the lecture, it is essential to stop every 2-5 minutes and ask style-based questions to help students review and process the information. For the introductory topic of integers, Mastery questions might ask students to identify numbers as positive or negative, combine integers, or find the opposites of integers. Interpersonal questions might ask students to work in pairs to graph integers on a number line and combine integers using two-sided counters. Understanding questions might ask students to explain why the sum of two negatives is a negative and why two negative signs in front of a number make the number positive. Self-Expressive questions might ask students to invent a new way of modeling the process of combining two integers. Sample integer questions in all four styles are shown below.

Integers Visual Organizer

Words to Know
whole number
integer
positive
negative
origin
sign
absolute vale

The Number line

⟵┼┼┼┼┼┼┼┼┼┼┼┼┼┼┼⟶
          0

The Additive Inverse Property

Sample
1.
2.
3.

Assignment for tomorrow:

Integer Questions in All Four Styles

Mastery
Find the opposite of each integer.
-5   6   0   -1

Combine the following integers.
-4 + 7 =   9 + 9 =   10 - 11 =   -4 -5 =

Interpersonal
Work with a partner and:
1. Plot the numbers from the first part of the Mastery problem on a number line.
2. Use 2-sided counters to model the problems in the second part of the Mastery problem.

Understanding
Explain why two negative signs in front of a counting number result in a positive number.

Self-Expressive
Create a new way, other than the number line and 2-sided counters, to model the process of combining two integers.

NEW AMERICAN LECTURE

Featured math concepts: **Parabolas, Translations & Reflections**

Student Name: _____

One of the beauties of mathematics is the variety of ways mathematical ideas can be represented to show inherent patterns. For example, a function can be represented as a set of ordered pairs, an equation with two variables, and a two-dimensional graph. This lesson challenges you to examine graphs of functions of the form $f(x) = a(x + b)^2 + c$ and to look for patterns in the graphs as a, b, and c change their values.

Hook

In sports, a team can take on a different personality when one particular player is in *or* out of the lineup. The outcome of a sporting event can also change, pending the success or failure of an individual play. Can you think of an example where the outcome or product of something can change when one small element is changed? Write about it on your visual organizer.

Parabolas, Translations, and Reflections

The graph of a function of the form $f(x) = a(x + b)^2 + c$ is a parabola. The function $f(x) = a(x + b)^2 + c$ is equivalent to $f(x) = x^2$ when $a = 1$, $b = 0$, and $c = 0$. The graph $f(x) = x^2$ contains the points { (-4, 16), (-3, 9), (-2, 4), (-1, 1), (2, 4), (3, 9), (4, 16) } and any point of the form (x, x^2) for any real number x. The graph of $f(x) = x^2$ is shown to the right.

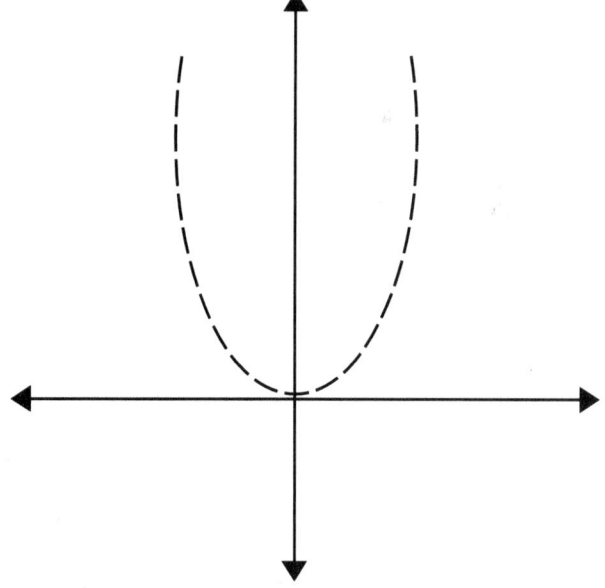

If any of the values of a, b, and c are changed, the graph of the new function will be a new parabola. The new parabola will differ in size and/or position from the graph of $f(x) = x^2$.

VISUAL ORGANIZER:
Parabolas, Translations, & Reflections

 Hook:

 Math vocabulary relevant to $f(x) = a(x + b)^2 + c$:

function _____
ordered pair _____
graph _____
parabola _____
translation _____
reflection _____

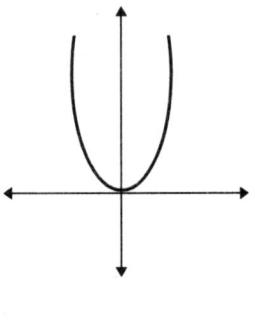 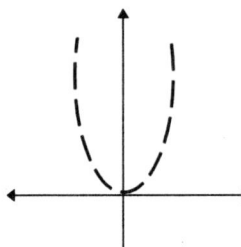 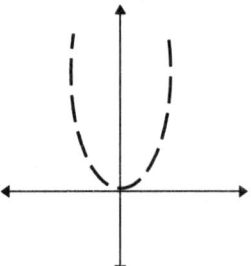

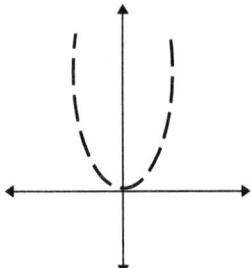 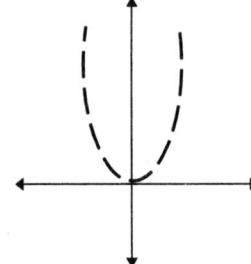 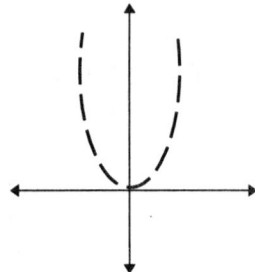

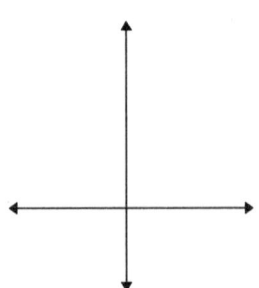 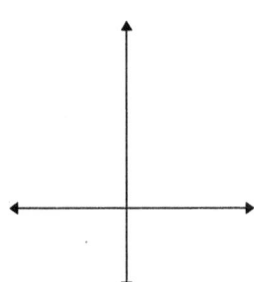 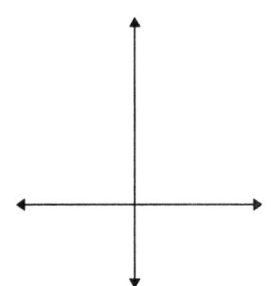

NEW AMERICAN LECTURE: *Parabolas; Translations, & Reflections* cont. ...

Directions:

The **graph** of a **function** of the form $f(x) = a(x + b)^2 + c$ is a **parabola**.

1. On your Visual Organizer, work with your learning partner to define the terms **function**, **ordered pair**, and **graph**.

2. Define the terms **parabola**, **translation**, and **reflection**.

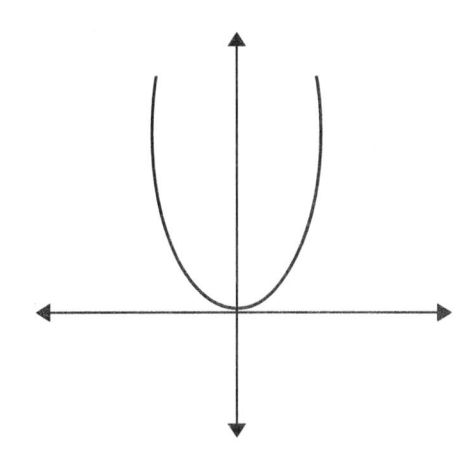

3. The graph of $f(x) = x^2$ is shown on your Visual Organizer. Using a graphing calculator or utility, graph $f(x) = x^2$ using the window $-10 < x < 10$ and $-10 < y < 10$. Graph each function below and compare each graph with the graph of $f(x) = x^2$. Sketch and label the graph of each function on your Visual Organizer. Determine the effect of the numbers a, b, and c in $a(x + b)^2 + c$.

    a. $f(x) = x^2 + 2$ $f(x) = a(x + b)^2 + c$ where $c = 2$

    b. $f(x) = x^2 - 4$ $f(x) = a(x + b)^2 + c$ where $c = -4$

    c. $f(x) = (x - 2)^2$ $f(x) = a(x + b)^2 + c$ where $b = -2$

    d. $f(x) = (x + 4)^2$ $f(x) = a(x + b)^2 + c$ where $b = 4$

    e. $f(x) = .5x^2$ $f(x) = a(x + b)^2 + c$ where $a = .5$

    f. $f(x) = -x^2$ $f(x) = a(x + b)^2 + c$ where $a = -1$

    g. $f(x) = (x-2)^2 + 2$ $f(x) = a(x + b)^2 + c$ where $b = -2, c = 2$

    h. $f(x) = -x^2 + 4$ $f(x) = a(x + b)^2 + c$ where $a = -1, c = 4$

Review the questions/exercises in all four styles on the next page.

Questions in All Four Styles:
GRAPHING PARABOLAS

Mastery
Use graph paper and pencil to sketch the graphs of the following equations.

1. $y = x^2 + 4$
2. $y = x^2 - 4$
3. $y = (x + 4)^2$
4. $y = (x - 4)^2$
5. $y = -(x - 4)^2 + 4$

Interpersonal
Work with a partner and find six equations of parabolas whose graphs create the picture below. Verify your results with a graphing calculator or utility.

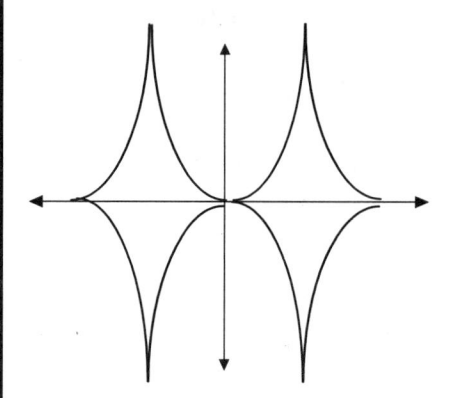

Understanding
The graph of $y = x^2 + a$ is the same as the graph of $y = x^2$ translated 'a' units in the positive direction of the y-axis.

The graph of $y = (x + a)^2$ is the same as the graph of $y = x^2$ translated 'a' units in the negative direction of the x-axis.

Explain why this is so.

Self-Expressive
Explain ways that the graph of $y = x^2$ and its translated and reflected images can be used to generate designs that can be used in art, engineering, fashion, or advertising.

Example:

Student Activity

NEW AMERICAN LECTURE
Featured math concept: **Introduction to Solving Equations with One Variable**

Student Name: _____

Directions:
This lesson on solving equations makes use of a visual organizer for the information and challenges below. Use your organizer as you answer questions and record important information about equations.

Hook
1. Write a sentence which reveals an interesting and true personal fact about yourself. For example, a student might write, "Last year I hiked to the bottom of the Grand Canyon." Be prepared to share your statement with the class.

2. Rewrite your statement, and put an underlined blank space in place of your name.

3. Fill in the blank with your learning partner's name. Evaluate the new statement as True or False.

Personal statements, like the one you wrote, are either True or False depending on the name of the person that is written into the sentence. The same concept is true for algebraic sentences. In an algebraic sentence (or equation), the variable x represents the blank space. Evaluate the sentence below as True or False when the number 5 is substituted for x.

$$2x + 24 = 16$$

Evaluate the sentence as True or False when the number -4 is written into the algebraic sentence.

Solve each completion statement and equation on your visual organizer.

Work with your learning partner and find definitions of the following terms associated with solving equations: **equation, variable, equal sign, unequal sign, solution set, order of operations, properties of equality,** and **substitution**.

Assignment
Solve each equation

1. $5x + 1 = 26$

2. $.5a = 11$

3. $\sqrt{x+1} = 9$

4. $b^2 + 5 = 49$

5. $2y - 10 = 30$

6. $x - x = 0$

VISUAL ORGANIZER

Solving Equations (An Introduction)

Hook:

$$2x + 24 = 16$$

An equation is: _____
_____
_____

Find solutions to the following factual sentences.

1. The capital of the state of California is: _____ .

2. The element known as water is made of ___ parts of hydrogen and ___ parts of oxygen.

3. The planet Jupiter is the ___th planet from the sun.

4. The third President of the United States was _____ .

5. The sun is approximately ____ miles from Earth.

Find solutions to the following algebraic equations.

1. $5x + 20 = 40$

2. $(4 - t) = 10$

3. $n^2 - 1 = 48$

4. $|x - 2| = 8$

5. $a(a + 1) = 56$

Math vocabulary relevant to solving equations:

equation _____
variable _____
equal sign _____
unequal sign _____
solution set _____
order of operations _____

properties of equality _____

substitution _____

Assignment for tomorrow: _____
_____
_____

Page 40

Questions in All Four Styles: SOLVING EQUATIONS

Mastery
Solve each equation for x.

1. $2x + 10 = 32$
2. $.4 + x + .5 = 1$
3. $5 - 2x = 10 - 7$
4. $x - 1/4 = 1/2$

Interpersonal
The geometry equations below each have two or more variables. Work with a partner and find two numbers that make each equation true.

perimeter	$20 = 2l + 2w$
area	$100 = lw$
surface area	$60 = 2lw + 2wh + 2lh$
area	$36 = .5\,bh$
volume	$30 = (1/3)\,bh$

Understanding
Sometimes, equations in algebra have no solution. Written below is an example of an equation with no solution.

Work with a partner and determine why the equation has no solution.

$$2(x - 4) = 5 + 2(x - 4)$$

Self-Expressive
Work with a learning partner and create three *different* equations that all have the same solution.

Mathematics, Styles, and Strategies
PROCEDURALIZING

The study of mathematics is very well known for its procedures: completing the square, long division, differentiating a product, finding the greatest common factor, finding the least common multiple, just to name a few. Often, the difference between successfully and unsuccessfully internalizing math procedures proves the difference between high and low achievers in math.

The Proceduralizing Strategy is used to represent important procedures as a series of clear and concise steps so students can learn them, understand them, and retain them for future use. Through this strategy, the teacher identifies the steps of the procedure, communicates and models the steps of the procedure, and carefully supervises directed practice as students work toward proficiency.

Developing a Proceduralizing Activity

While many mathematical procedures can be the basis of a Proceduralizing activity, teachers should refrain from teaching every math concept as a step-by-step procedure. Too many procedures can confuse students' thinking and cause them to mistakenly apply procedures in the wrong context. Most mainstream mathematical procedures can be the basis of an effective proceduralizing activity. The steps in the Proceduralizing Strategy are as follows:

Step 1
Select a math procedure that you want your students to learn. The procedure should be one that students can successfully learn with reasonable effort. The math procedure should also be one that is relevant in terms of applications and future studies. For example, the procedure for finding the area of a rectangle is a relevant process that students can learn with reasonable effort.

Step 2
List the steps of the procedure that are needed for students to complete the math task. Keep the list of steps succinct by eliminating secondary or prerequisite procedures. The steps on the next page on the left side are essential and succinct for finding the area of a rectangle. The steps to the right include steps for secondary processes and are too numerous.

Succinct

Finding the Area of a Rectangle

1. Determine or identify the length and width of the rectangle.

2. Choose the proper formula $A = lw$.

3. Substitute the values for l and w into the formula.

4. Evaluate the formula.

Too Numerous

Finding the Area of a Rectangle

1. Determine or identify the length and width of the rectangle.

2. Choose the proper formula, $A = lw$.

3. Substitute the values for l and w into the formula.

4. If the length and width of the rectangle are whole numbers, simply multiply the whole numbers together.

5. If the length and width of the rectangle are fractions, write the fractions side by side and multiply the numerators together and the denominators together.

6. If the length and width of the rectangle are decimals, write the decimals vertically and use the multiplication algorithm.

Step 3
Display the procedure where students can see it. Ask them to write it down, study it, and visualize themselves implementing the procedure.

Step 4
Model the procedure using one or more sample problems. Ask students to work through the sample problems with you. Through questioning, ask students to review the steps aloud as you practice together(guided practice).

Step 5
After guided practice, engage students in independent practice until you see that they have become automatic and proficient in the procedure.

PROCEDURALIZING

Student Activity

Featured math concept: **Solving a Quadratic Equation by Completing the Square**

Student Name: _____

Directions:
To successfully solve a quadratic equation by completing the square, procedural steps must be followed. The steps below clearly outline the correct procedure for completing the square of a quadratic equation. Use the steps to solve the equation $12x + 1 = 2x^2$.

Prerequisite Skills
Write a polynomial in descending order • Apply the properties of equality • Halve and square a number • Apply the square root principle • Factor a polynomial

Step 1
Write the equation so the nonvariable term is on the right side and the variable terms (x) are written in descending order on the left side of the equation.

$2x^2 + 12x = -1$

STEP 2
If the coefficient of the variable squared term is ≠ 1, divide all the terms of the equation by the coefficient and simplify.

$\frac{2x^2}{2} + \frac{12x}{2} = -\frac{1}{2}$

$x^2 + 6x = -\frac{1}{2}$

Step 3
Add the square of half the coefficient of the unit variable term to both sides of the equation.

$x^2 + 6x + 9 = 9 - \frac{1}{2}$

Step 4
Factor the perfect square trinomial (left side of the equation) and combine the numbers on the right side as a single fraction.

$(x + 3)^2 = \frac{17}{2}$

Step 5
Apply the square root principle.

$(x + 3) = \pm \sqrt{\frac{17}{2}}$

Step 6
Solve the equation for x.

$x = -3 \pm \sqrt{\frac{17}{2}}$

Step 7
Simplify your answer.

$x = -3 \pm \frac{\sqrt{34}}{2}$

PROCEDURALIZING

Student Activity

Featured math concept: **Analytic Geometry: Graphing a Parabola**

Student Name: _____

Directions:
To successfully graph the solution set of an equation of the form $y = ax^2 + bx + c$, procedural steps must be followed. The steps below clearly outline the correct procedure for graphing a parabola. Use the steps to sketch the graph of $y = 2x^2 + 12x + 16$.

Prerequisite Skills
Complete the square • Plot points • Halve and square a number • Apply the properties of equality • Apply the square root principle

Step 1
Prepare the quadratic side of the equation by sliding the c term to the right. This will create a space for the new term created by completing the square.

$x = 2x^2 + 12x \qquad +16$

Step 2
Factor the 2 from $2x^2 + 12x$.

$y = 2(x^2 + 6x) \qquad +16$

Step 3
Complete the square of the $x^2 + 6x$ terms in the parentheses. Since + 9 (half of 6 squared) is added inside the parentheses, -18 will have to be added outside the parentheses to keep the equation balanced. (Why?)

$y = 2(x^2 + 6x +9) - 18 + 16$

Step 4
Factor the perfect square trinomial and combine the numbers on the right side.

$y = 2(x + 3)^2 - 2$

STEP 5
Plot the graph. The vertex of the parabola is (-3, -2). The opposite of the addend to x is the x coordinate of the vertex, and the constant on the right side of the equation is the y coordinate. Choose a few arbitrary values for x, and plot. Then sketch the curve.

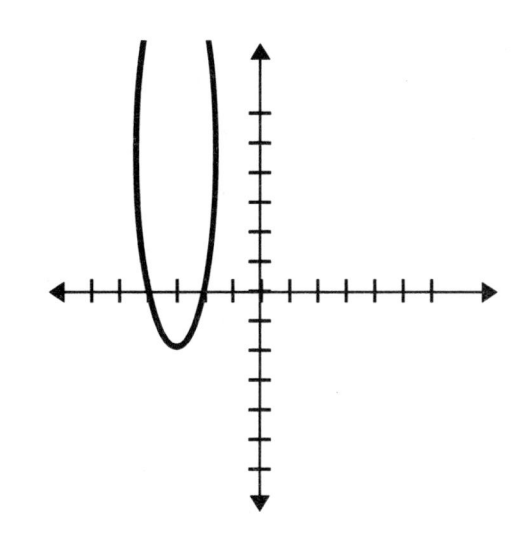

PROCEDURALIZING

Student Activity

Featured math concept: **Graphing the Solution of y = mx + b**

Student Name: _____

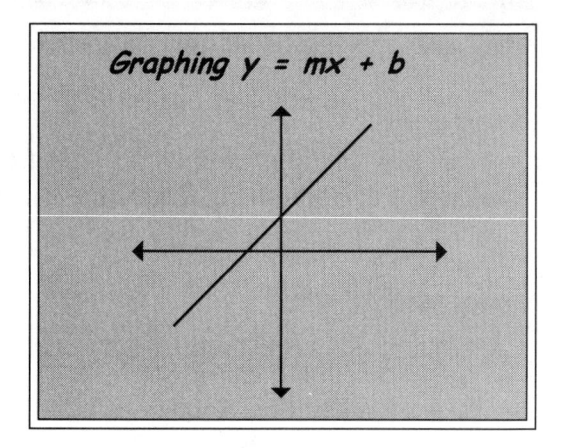

Directions:
To successfully graph the solution set of a linear equation, procedural steps must be followed. The steps below outline the procedure for graphing a linear equation.

Prerequisite Skills:
Solve an equation for a specified variable • Plot points on a Cartesian Plane • Draw a line using a straight edge • Write any number in fraction form

Graphing y = mx + b

Sketch the graph of the equation $4x + 2y = 12$.

$y = -2x + 6$

Step 1
Write the problem.

Step 2
Solve the equation for 'y' and write the equation in y = mx + b form.

Step 3
Plot the number b on the y-axis. This point is the y-intercept of the graph.

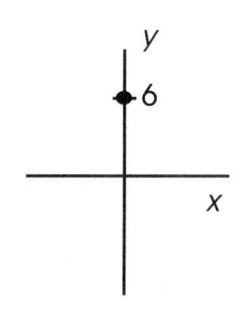

Step 4
Write the slope m as a fraction $\frac{\Delta y}{\Delta x}$.

$$m = \frac{-2}{1} = \frac{\Delta y}{\Delta x}$$

Step 5
From the y-intercept, move Δx units horizontally and Δy units vertically on the Cartesian Plane. Plot a point at this location.

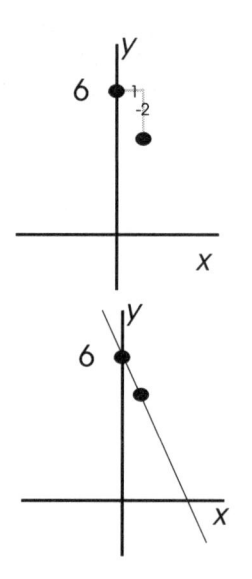

Step 6
Draw a line through the two points plotted in steps 3 and 5. The line, and all its points, represent the infinite set of (x, y) ordered pair solutions of the linear equation $4x + 2y = 12$.

UNDERSTANDING STRATEGIES

Compare and Contrast
Concept Attainment
Concept Identification
Deductive Thinking
Pattern Finding
Mystery
Support and Refute

Mathematics, Styles, and Strategies
COMPARE AND CONTRAST

Because of the abstract nature of mathematics, so much of the content that students learn is *invisible*—impossible to see, hear, smell, taste, or touch—as well as "confusable," or easily mixed up with other abstract ideas. One of the most effective ways to avoid the pitfalls of the invisible and the confusable is to double students' ability to "see" the content they are learning. For example, if you want students to understand logarithms, double their insight into logarithms by setting exponents against them. This juxtaposition of ideas that have some critical aspects in common and other critical aspects that are strikingly different will bring students' understanding of each into much sharper focus. Comprehension moves from the superficial to the deep. The chance for making insightful connections increases significantly; remembering key information about both logarithms and exponents when it is needed for a test, project, or class discussion becomes much easier.

So, if comparing and contrasting can increase mathematical understanding, insight, and retention, why do students have a difficult time making comparisons? Research (Mullis, Owen, and Phillips, 1990) shows that a majority of American students lack the skills needed to make sophisticated comparisons. We have all probably experienced a time in our teaching when a comparison strategy did not result in deeper understanding of a topic. The question to ask ourselves then, is, "If comparing and contrasting information is so important to learning, what can we do to improve the results of a comparison learning strategy in our classrooms?"

Developing a Compare and Contrast Activity
In order to get the most out of comparing and contrasting, the strategy has been broken into four distinct phases. Each phase in the strategy helps build student comphrehension layer by layer.

**THE FOUR PHASES OF THE
COMPARE AND CONTRAST STRATEGY**

1. Description
- Establish purpose
- Provide sources of information
- Identify criteria for description
- Generate information using the criteria

2. Comparison
- Use a visual organizer to collect data
- Identify important similarities
- Identify important differences

3. Conclusion
- Decide whether the two ideas are more like or different from each other
- Explore cause for differences or effects of differences
- Decide what generalizations you can make about both examples

4. Application
- Provide an assessment activity that helps students arrive at the purpose of the activity.

To see how these phases deepen learning, let's look at each phase in a sample lesson on solving problems involving objects dropped from various heights and accelerating according to gravity.

TEACHER'S GUIDE:
COMPARE AND CONTRAST
Featured math concept: **Falling Object Model**

Description Phase
(To be read to students):
"It turns out the biggest problem students face in solving word problems is not in making careless errors, but rather in rushing to solve problems before they really understand what the problem is asking for. Think of your own experiences with word problems. Why do you think so many students rush to solutions?

"Today we are going to do two things. First, we are going to introduce a new kind of word problem that has its own formula, namely, falling object problems. *(Note: Teacher reviews the equation and the terms for falling object problems.)* Second, we are going to use a strategy called Compare and Contrast to help us learn how to read word problems more analytically so that we know exactly what the problem is asking us to do before we try to solve it.

"Here are two word problems. Using the organizer on the next page, describe what each problem is asking you to do. Draw a diagram showing each problem situation. Then, solve the problem showing both the work and the thinking you used to solve the problem."

Problem 1:

A worker is standing on top of a 100-foot building when he accidentally drops his hammer. How long will it take for the hammer to hit the ground?

Problem 2:

While working on a different building, the worker drops his hammer again. This time, the hammer takes four seconds to hit the ground. How high is the building?

COMPARE AND CONTRAST: *Falling Object Model cont. ...*

"Next, team up with your partner and share your work and solutions. Describe each problem using the criteria listed on the organizer below."

Sample Student Work/Organizer

How is the problem written? (What needs to be found out?)	The problem is asking me to find out how long it will take for the dropped hammer to hit the ground.	The problem is asking me to determine how high the building is.
What models can be used to solve the problem?	Falling Object Model (Based on increase in speed caused by gravity.) $h = -16t^2 + s$ h = height in feet of object at given point t = # of seconds object falls s = initial height in feet	Same as Problem 1.
What does the diagram look like?	100 ft. (s) / 0 ft. (h)	? ft. (s) / 4 seconds (t) / 0 ft. (h)
How did you go about solving the problem? (Describe your thinking and show your work.)	1. Reviewed formula for falling objects: $h = -16t^2 + s$ 2. Substituted 100 for s, because that's the height from which hammer was dropped. 3. Substituted 0 for h because the height of the ground is 0 feet. 4. Solved the problem: $h = -16t^2 + s$ $0 = -16t^2 + 100$ $16t^2 = 100$ (added $16t^2$ to both sides) $t^2 = 6.25$ (divided both sides by 16) $t = \sqrt{6.25}$ $t = 2.5$ seconds	1. Used same formula: $h = -16t^2 + s$. 2. Substituted 4 for t. 3. Substituted 0 for h. 4. Solved the problem $h = -16t^2 + s$ $0 = -16(4^2) + s$ $0 = -256 + s$ $s = 256$ feet

COMPARE AND CONTRAST: *Falling Object Model cont. ...*

Comparison Phase:
"Next, compare the two problems. Using the criteria from the Description Phase, complete the comparison organizer below."

Sample Student Work/Organizer

How is Problem 1 different from Problem 2?	How is Problem 2 different from Problem 1?
· Height of the building (s) is given.	· Number of seconds object falls (t) is given.
· Number of seconds object falls (t) is missing.	· Height of the building (s) is missing.
· Problem is asking us to find how long until the hammer hits the ground.	· Problem is asking us to find the height of the building.
· Answer will be in seconds.	· Answer will be in feet.

Similarities

· Both problems use falling object model.

· Both problems involve the time it takes for an object to fall from a height to the ground.

· Both problems set h at 0 since 0 is the height of the ground.

· Both diagrams look similar.

COMPARE AND CONTRAST: *Falling Object Model cont. ...*

Conclusion Phase:
"With your partner, develop a brief that explains your findings. Be sure to discuss what causes the differences in how you go about solving each type of problem."

Application Phase:
"To show what you know, create two problems like Problem 1 and two problems like Problem 2. Then, since we noticed that Problem 1 asks you to solve for t and Problem 2 asks you to solve for s, create two more problems that are looking for you to solve for h. Come up with some creative ways to make sure $h \neq 0$, or the height of the ground."

Note: This lesson is duplicated on the following pages with all organizers left blank for student use.

Student Activity

COMPARE AND CONTRAST
Featured math concept: **Falling Object Model**

Student Name: _____

Directions:
Think about the ways in which you approach word problems. Do you take your time to think about the problem and strategies for solving it or do you rush through?

You are going to use the Compare and Contrast Strategy to solve a type of problem that has its own formula: falling object problems. This will help you to learn how to read word problems more analyitically in order to know exactly what the problem is asking you to do before you try to solve it.

Read the following two word problems. Using the organizer on the next page, describe what each problem is asking you to do. Draw a diagram showing each problem situation. Then, solve the problem showing both the work and the thinking you used to solve the problem."

Problem 1:

A worker is standing on top of a 100-foot building when he accidentally drops his hammer. How long will it take for the hammer to hit the ground?

Problem 2:

While working on a different building, the worker drops his hammer again. This time, the hammer takes four seconds to hit the ground. How high is the building?

COMPARE AND CONTRAST: *Falling Object Model cont. ...*

Next, team up with your partner and share your work and solutions. Describe each problem using the criteria listed on the organizer below.

Student Organizer

How is the problem written? (What needs to be found out?)		
What models can be used to solve the problem?		
What does the diagram look like?		
How did you go about solving the problem? (Describe your thinking and show your work.)		

COMPARE AND CONTRAST: *Falling Object Model* cont. ...

Comparison Phase:
Next, compare the two problems. Using the criteria from the Description Phase, complete the comparison organizer below.

Student Organizer

How is Problem 1 different from Problem 2?	How is Problem 2 different from Problem 1?

Similarities

COMPARE AND CONTRAST: *Falling Object Model* cont. ...

Conclusion Phase:
With your partner, develop a brief that explains your findings. Be sure to discuss what causes the differences in how you go about solving each type of problem.

Application Phase:
To show what you know, create two problems like Problem 1 and two problems like Problem 2. Then, since we noticed that Problem 1 asks you to solve for t and Problem 2 asks you to solve for s, create two more problems that are looking for you to solve for h. Come up with some creative ways to make sure $h \neq 0$, or the height of the ground.

Mathematics, Styles, and Strategies
CONCEPT ATTAINMENT

So many essential concepts in math are taught in the least memorable and most passive of ways: through textbook definitions or bald statements. To tell students, "A function is a mathematical relation in which each element of the domain is paired with exactly one element of the range," is practically to guarantee that their interest will be low, that their understanding will be superficial, and their retention short. But having students compare examples and non-examples of functions in order to develop a set of critical attributes has an opposite effect: Learning becomes an active search; comprehension grows in light of new discoveries.

The Concept Attainment Strategy is based on the work of Jerome Bruner (1968), and his research into how humans develop conceptual understanding. What Bruner found is that no matter how many times a concept's definition is repeated, without an active process of testing and refining that concept, students never get a firm grasp on new concepts. They might very well be able to recite the glossary definition for a quadratic equation, but their understanding will have neither experiential nor analytical depth behind it. Their definition will not provide them with a clear way to determine the difference between a quadratic equation and a non-quadratic equation that can be expressed in quadratic form, for example. When it comes time for students to apply their understanding, they will likely flounder. Even worse, students will not have an adequate foundation on which to build future understandings—a situation that compounds itself with each new lesson and leaves the student further and further behind.

In response, Bruner developed Concept Attainment. In using this strategy, the teacher selects a concept to be studied and presents examples and non-examples—which have some but not all of the critical attributes—of the concept. Students must compare and contrast the examples and non-examples, develop a working hypothesis that lists the critical attributes, test their hypothesis against further examples and non-examples, and articulate the concept.

Developing a Concept Attainment Lesson

1. Select a concept with clear critical attributes (e.g. prime numbers, conic sections, linear equations) that you want students to understand deeply.
2. Provide students with examples, which contain all the critical attributes of the concept, and non-examples which contain some but not all the attributes.
3. Ask students to identify what all the examples have in common and how the examples differ from the non-examples. Students should generate an initial list of critical attributes of the concept.
4. Provide more examples and non-examples for students to use in testing and refining their initial list of attributes.
5. As a whole class, review the examples and non-examples and generate a final set of critical attributes.
6. Ask students to apply their understanding of the concept by completing an activity.

Concept Attainment: Observable Student Behaviors

In a typical Concept Attainment lesson, five behaviors should be present. Students should:
- observe attributes carefully
- compare and contrast examples with non-examples
- generate and test hypotheses
- define the concept according to the essential attributes
- generate additional examples

In the classroom* ...

To see these behaviors in action, let's look in on a middle school classroom where Dr. Mattine is introducing her students to the concept of prime numbers.

Dr. Mattine begins by telling her students: "I have an idea that is important to our work. I would like us to work together as a group to build up a description of this idea so that we can use it correctly when we need it. Here's how I would like us to work— I'll give you positive examples of the idea, and we'll call these the YES ideas; I'll give you negative examples of the idea, and we'll call these the NO ideas. I want you all to observe the examples carefully and really think about them. Let's see if we can use these examples to help us describe my idea."

Dr. Mattine divides the board into two narrow columns and one wide column. She labels the two narrow columns YES and NO. She labels the wide column DESCRIPTIONS. Then she lists the first several examples.

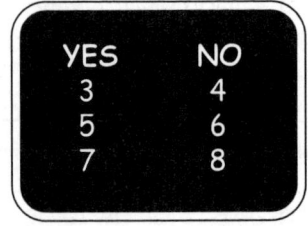

YES	NO
3	4
5	6
7	8

She waits; then she asks the students to write down three ideas that occur to them as they study the examples. Groans. Robert says, "I know the answer already. Why do I need three?" Chorus of agreement.

Dr. Mattine explains that she's not sure there's enough evidence yet and that they should try to get at least one other possibility in case they're wrong. After waiting a few minutes or more, she asks Robert to say what his idea was. Robert says, "Odd numbers. They're all odd." Dr. Mattine asks for a description, and records it in the Descriptions column: "All odd. Even numbers are NO."

"Now," says Dr. Mattine, "here is 9, which is a NO." Disbelief. "What did you just learn?"

"Our idea is wrong," says Robert. "If 9 is a NO, and 9 is odd, then YES can't be all of the odd numbers. Maybe some odd numbers belong, but not all of them. Why is 9 a NO?"

"Good question, Robert," says Dr. Mattine. "Let's look at the lists and see if we can figure out why 9 is a NO and not a YES."

*Adapted with permission from Silver, et al 1996

In the classroom cont. ...

As students propose ideas, Dr. Mattine writes them in the Descriptions column without passing judgment. If the students are in agreement that a previously suggested idea is not correct, she insists that they provide evidence from the list and then cross it out, but she does not erase it. When student ideas falter, she offers additional examples.

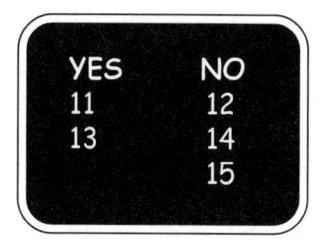

YES	NO
11	12
13	14
	15

Finally, "What is a 2?" Dr. Mattine asks the students. "How many of you think it is a YES? How many of you think it is a NO? The 2 is a YES. Why?"

As the lesson continues, Dr. Mattine encourages her students to observe the characteristics of the numbers in each list. What do you notice about these numbers? What do you know about them? She encourages them to brainstorm ideas with their neighbors.

Finally, one of the students tentatively offers, "I don't think there is anything that will go into any of the YES numbers, but you can divide all of the NO numbers." Dr. Mattine writes that description on the board, and then asks students to check the evidence. Everyone agrees that the description is accurate until another student said, "What about 1? Every number can be divided by 1." Dr. Mattine suggests that the students list the numbers in the YES column and the NO column, and write their factors next to each to check this idea. There is great excitement as the students begin to see a pattern: all of the numbers in the YES column have exactly two factors, 1 and the number itself; the numbers in the NO column have those same factors, but they have additional factors as well.

Dr. Mattine announces that the class has correctly identified the idea, and asks them to suggest a definition for the YES column. The agreed-upon definition reads: *Our idea is a number that can be divided by exactly two factors, one and itself.* At this point, Dr. Mattine tells the class that these numbers are called PRIMES, and asks that they find the four primes between 15 and 30 for homework.

Student Activity

CONCEPT ATTAINMENT
Featured math concept: **Difference of Perfect Squares**

Student Name: _____

Directions:
This lesson is about an important mathematical concept. You will examine a number of examples which show this important concept and a number of non-examples which may contain some of the attributes of this concept, but not all of them. As you examine the examples and non-examples, try to determine what the critical attributes of the concept are. Pay close attention to the similarities and differences between the examples and non-examples as well as to any patterns you notice.

Let's Begin
Identify the concept represented by the expressions in the **yes** column. Expressions in the **no** column do not conform to the concept in the **yes** column, but will help in your thinking process.

YES	YES
$a^2 - b^2$	$(rs)^2 - (tu)^2$
NO	**NO**
$a^2 + (2)^2$	$x^3 - 49$

What did you notice about the examples? Were there any similarities between them? Did you notice any patterns? Do you think you might know what the attributes of the concept are? Write down your hypothesis in the box below.

_____
_____
_____
_____
_____
_____
_____
_____

Concept Attainment cont. ...

Here are some more examples:

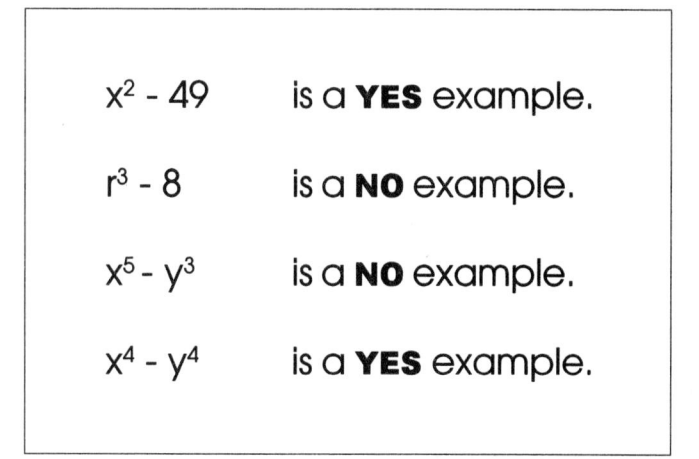

$x^2 - 49$ is a **YES** example.

$r^3 - 8$ is a **NO** example.

$x^5 - y^3$ is a **NO** example.

$x^4 - y^4$ is a **YES** example.

Study these new examples carefully and make observations. Look back at your previous ideas. Has anything changed? If so, what are your new ideas? Do you know what the attributes of the concept are now? Explain below.

Concept Attainment cont. ...

Now, let's see how you do.

1. Mark these examples according to whether they are YES or NO examples.

$1 - d^2$	YES/NO	$9b^2 - 4$	YES/NO
$18y^2 - 21y^2 - 9$	YES/NO	$r^3 - (2)^3$	YES/NO

2. Try to develop a few examples of your own in the spaces below.

YES	NO

3. Can you find the example that doesn't belong in each of the following sets? Mark it with an X and be able to explain why it does not belong.

$x^2 - 4$	$(ab)^2 - (2)^2$	$1 - x^2$	$z^2 + 4$

$a^2 - b^2$	$x^6 - y^6$	$x^3 - y^2$	$4 - s^2$

$9a^2b^2$	$x^2 - 100$	$b^2 - 9$	$9 - b^2$

Mathematics, Styles, and Strategies
CONCEPT IDENTIFICATION:
A VARIATION ON CONCEPT ATTAINMENT

The Concept Identification Strategy is a simplified version of Concept Attainment. Rather than teaching new concepts, Concept Identification helps students practice skills and review their understanding. Through this strategy, teachers can make practice far more fun and interesting than simply assigning problems and listening to student groans: Practice becomes a search for an answer, a mini-puzzle to be solved.

The teacher presents two sets of practice problems to students. One set of problems, labeled **yes**, has solutions which conform to a specific math concept or criteria. The other set of problems, labeled **no**, has solutions that do not conform to the specific math concept or criteria. The students are challenged to work alone or with a learning partner to solve both sets of problems. Once both sets of problems are solved, the students must analyze the solutions of the **yes** problems to identify the concept represented by those solutions. The solutions of the **no** problems can be used to verify the students' thinking.

Developing a Concept Identification Activity

Selecting a Math Skill for Students to Practice
To develop a Concept Identification activity, select a math skill you want your students to practice. A math skill that produces numerical answers will work well. For the purpose of demonstration, simplifying integer expressions will be the selected math skill for students to practice.

Determining a Concept for Students to Identify
In the Concept Identification activity, the answers to all the problems in the **yes** column conform to a specific math concept or set of criteria. A wide range of math concepts and criteria can be used for students to identify. Several possibilities are listed below:

- Prime numbers
- Odd numbers
- Even numbers
- Perfect squares
- Perfect cubes
- Multiples of a specific number
- Factors of a specific number
- Fractions that are repeating decimals
- Composite numbers
- Numbers that are one less or one more than perfect squares

In our example, students will be asked to simplify integer expressions. The concept students will try to identify will be numbers that are one less than a perfect square.

Creating YES and NO Problems

In most cases, the **yes** and **no** problem should contain 5 - 10 problems each. If the math concept is hard to identify, more than five problems may be needed. In our example, five problems in the **yes** and **no** sets should be sufficient.

	YES		NO
1.	20 - 5 + 35 - 2	1.	20 - 6 +3
2.	1 - 8 + 3 + 4	2.	15 - 20 + 20 - 8
3.	10 + 10 - -4	3.	-10 + 20 -1
4.	12 - 2 - 2	4.	12 - 2 + 1
5.	-5 + 8 + 12	5.	-5 + 58 - 3

Before the actual problems are created, the final answers must be determined. The numbers 48, 0, 24, 8, and 15 will serve as the answers for the **yes** column and the numbers 17, 27, 9, 11, and 50 will serve as the answers for the **no** column. The integer problems in the yes and no columns shown here were developed so their solutions would match the numbers above.

Concept Identification: Observable Student Behaviors

Concept Identification activities serve as ideal paired learner activities. If a learning pair works to solve the Concept Identification activity below, one student may choose to solve the problems in the **yes** column while the other student solves the problems in the **no** column. When both students complete their problems, they can work together to check the solutions. When the students are certain their solutions are correct, they work to identify the selected math concept.

	YES		NO
1.	20 - 5 + 35 - 2	1.	20 - 6 +3
2.	1 - 8 + 3 + 4	2.	15 - 20 + 40 - 8
3.	10 + 10 - -4	3.	-10 + 20 -1
4.	12 - 2 - 2	4.	12 - 2 + 1
5.	-5 + 8 + 12	5.	-5 + 58 - 3

As the students work to identify the math concept represented by the answers in the **yes** column, they may first guess that the concept in the **yes** column is *even numbers*. But the solution to problem 5 in the **yes** column is inconsistent with *even numbers* and the solution to problem 5 in the **no** column could not be even, since the **no** column's solutions must not conform to the **yes** column. So after rechecking and verifying the solutions to those problems, students would rule out the *even number* idea. Eventually, students would identify the concept in the **yes** column as *one less than a perfect square*.

While many students may not initially think of the concept of *one less than a perfect square*, further experiences with Concept Identification activities will help students to broaden their thinking. In the meantime, teachers should feel free to provide helpful hints. Over time, students will become pros at using practice as a means of solving a challenge--the challenge of identifying a hidden math concept. Use this strategy with your students to build proficiency, teach concepts, and make reviewing math more fun.

CONCEPT IDENTIFICATION

Student Activity

Featured math concept: **Evaluating Derivatives**

Student Name: _____

Directions:
In each problem below you will solve two sets of problems. The solutions of the **yes** set have something in common regarding a specific math concept. The solutions of the **no** set are not representative of that math concept. Your challenge is to solve the problems in both sets and see if you can identify the math concept represented by the solutions of the **yes** set.

Problem 1
Given $f(x) = 3x^2 + 2x + 2$, identify the concept represented by the derivative expressions in the **yes** column. Solutions in the **no** column do not conform to the concept in the **yes** column, but will help in your thinking process.

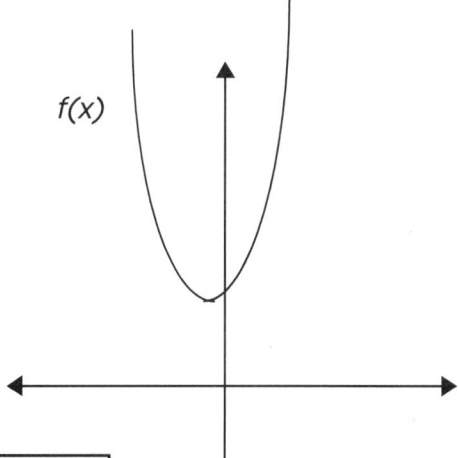

f(x)

YES	NO
$f'(1)$ _____	$f'(\frac{1}{2})$ _____
$f'(\frac{11}{3})$ _____	$f'(0)$ _____
$f'(\frac{-1}{3})$ _____	$f'(\frac{5}{6})$ _____
$f'(\frac{1}{6})$ _____	$f'(3)$ _____
$f'(\frac{13}{6})$ _____	$f'(\frac{7}{3})$ _____

Identified concept: _____
_____
_____

CONCEPT IDENTIFICATION

Featured math concept: **Algebraic Expressions**

Student Name: _____

Problem 1

Let $a = -2$, $b = 4$, $c = 1$, and $d = .5$.
Identify the concept represented by the values of the expressions in the **yes** column. Solutions in the **no** column do not conform to the concept in the **yes** column but will help in your thinking process.

YES	NO
$(-a)^{(b-2c)}$	$b - c$
$2dc\,(b^{-a})$	$b\,(b + c)$
$b(d^2)$	$c + 4d + 8b$
$2d\,|ab|$	$ad + (b + c) + 10$
$cb + a$	$b\,(-a + c)$

Problem 2

Solve each problem for x. Identify the concept represented by the solutions of the equations in the **yes** column. Solutions in the **no** column do not conform to the concept in the **yes** column but will help in your thinking process.

YES	NO
$x - 8 = -4$	$x + 4 = 17$
$2x - 1 = 23$	$5x + 11 = 61$
$\dfrac{x}{6} = 7$	$\sqrt{x} = 8$
$.5x - 10 = 20$	$2(x - 1) = 78$
$4 + 2x = x + 10$	$2x - 10 = 20$

Student Activity	**CONCEPT IDENTIFICATION**
	Featured math concept: **Geometry**
	Student Name: _____

Directions:

The geometric figures in the **yes** column have something in common regarding a specific numerical characteristic of the figures. The figures in the **no** column do not have that specific numerical characteristic. Your challenge is to identify the numerical characteristic that is common to the figures in the **yes** set. *(Hint: Look at the diagonals.)*

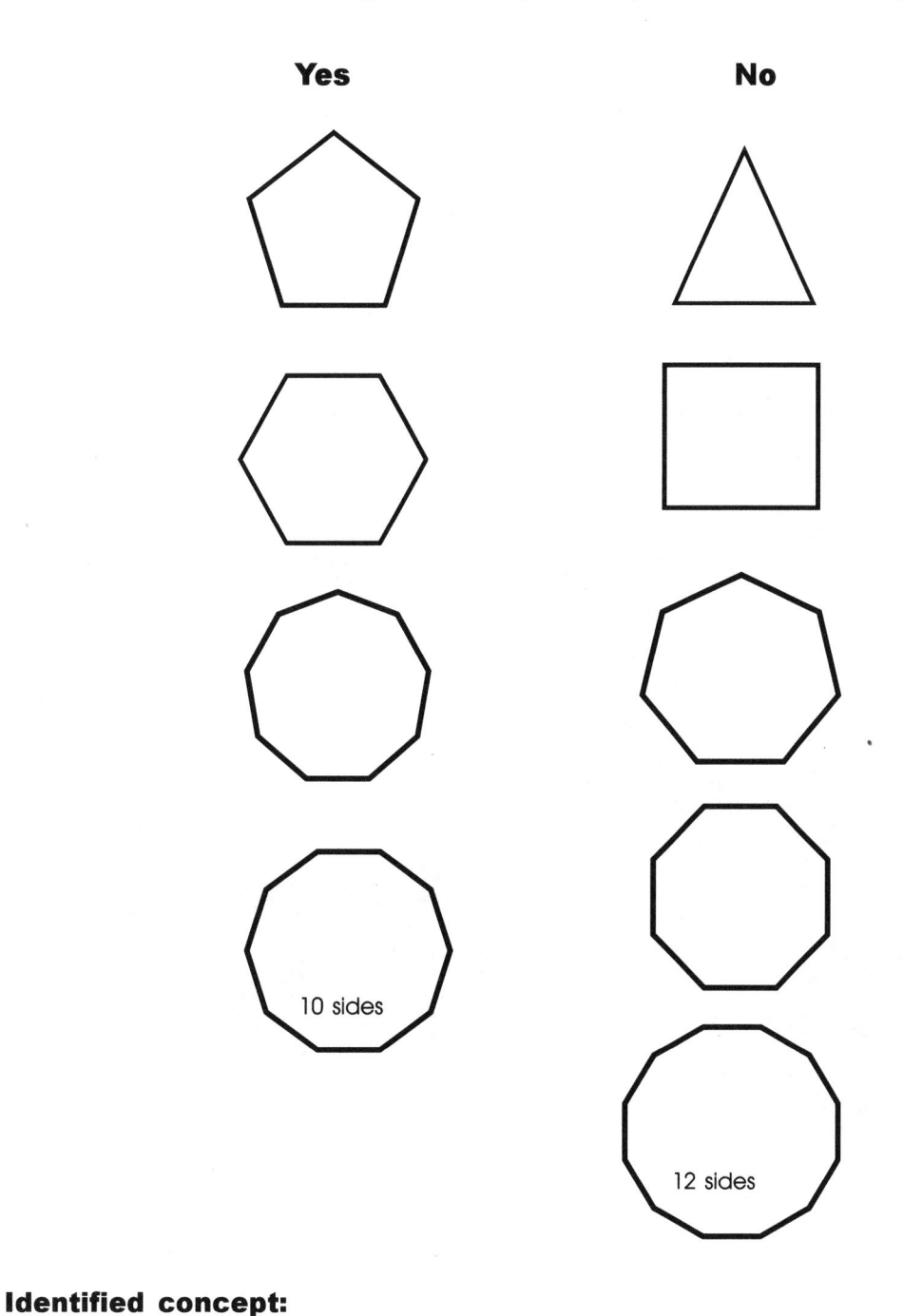

Yes   **No**

10 sides

12 sides

Identified concept:
_____
_____

Mathematics, Styles, and Strategies
DEDUCTIVE THINKING

In a study of instructional differences among math classrooms in different countries, high praises were given to teachers who frequently challenged their students to think deductively. Deductive Thinking is an essential part of the thinking process needed to solve higher-level math problems. Given any higher-level math problem, students must use their thinking skills to determine what is given, determine what is asked, use deductive reasoning to generate and gather more information, engage problem-solving skills, and decide on a solution.

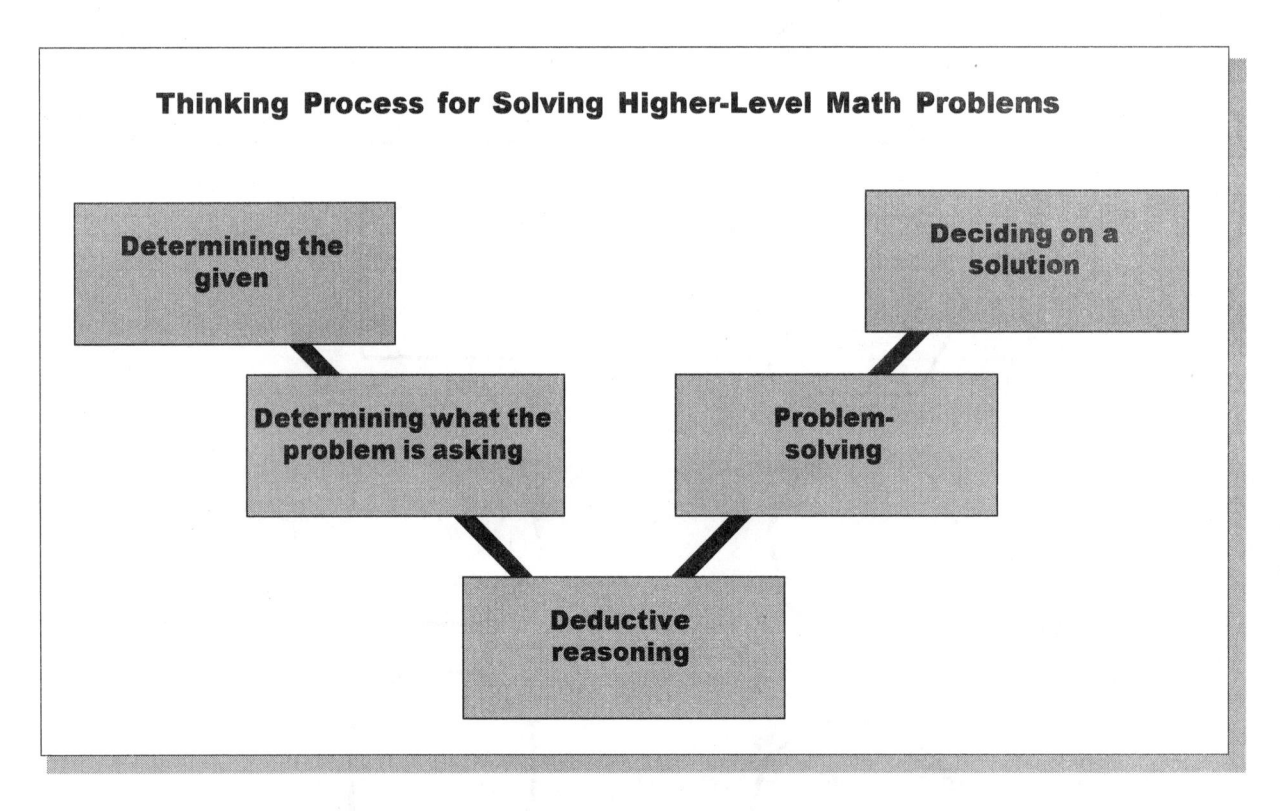

Thinking Process for Solving Higher-Level Math Problems

- Determining the given
- Determining what the problem is asking
- Deductive reasoning
- Problem-solving
- Deciding on a solution

For most students, the ability to think about mathematics deductively is not automatic, but is an application of mathematics that has to be taught and learned. In some classrooms, teachers avoid activities that require students to think deductively. They know that teaching simple math concepts, skills, and algorithms is easier than teaching students to think deductively. In the best math classrooms, teachers engage their students in Deductive Thinking activities on a regular basis and model deductive reasoning to help students learn and grow as problem solvers.

Developing a Deductive Thinking Activity

To develop a Deductive Thinking activity, create a math problem that:

1. provides given facts and information
2. asks students to find, prove, or verify a math solution
3. requires that students deduce essential information from the given
4. enables students to check their answer to determine if it is reasonable or correct

Creating a Sample Deductive Thinking Problem
The sample problem that follows focuses on geometry and features three parallel lines cut by a transversal.

- **Providing given facts and information**
    Given: Line 1 is parallel to line m
    Line m is parallel to line n
    Line t is a transversal
    m∠2 = 135°

- **Asking students to find, prove, or verify**
    Students will be asked to find the m∠12.

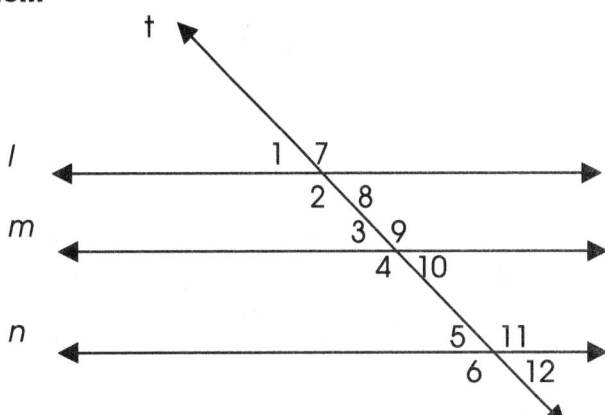

- **Requiring students to use deductive reasoning**
In this problem students will be asked to find the m∠12. In order to do so, they will have to determine a series of relationships among angles based on the given and known geometry theorems. In this example, m∠2 = m∠4 (*if two parallel lines are cut by a transversal, corresponding angles are congruent*) and m∠4 = m∠11 (*if two parallel lines are cut by a transversal, alternate interior angles are congruent*). By the transitive property of equality, m∠11 = m∠2 = 135°.

- **Applying the given information and facts from deductive reasoning**
Since ∠11 and ∠12 are a linear pair, they are supplementary. Thus, m∠11 + m∠12 = 180° and 135° + m∠12 = 180°. Therefore, m∠12 = 45°.

- **Determining the reasonableness of the answer**
From the picture, it can be seen that ∠12 is an acute angle. Therefore, the conclusion that m∠12 = 45° is reasonable.

DEDUCTIVE THINKING

Featured math concept: **Geometry and Volume**

Student Name: _____

Student Challenge: "The Bowling Ball Problem"

Katherine bought a bowling ball for her father's birthday. The bowling ball will be packaged and wrapped snugly into a box the shape of a cube. The ball will be protected by filling the open spaces of the box with spherical styrofoam pellets. Each pellet has a diameter equal to 2 centimeters. The bowling ball has a circumference equal to 27 inches.

1. Find the dimensions of a cubical box needed to snugly hold the bowling ball.

2. Find the volume of the space which remains in the box after a bowling ball is placed in it (ignore the space created by the finger holes in the ball).

3. Approximate the number of styrofoam pellets needed to fill the remaining space in the box.

DEDUCTIVE THINKING

Featured math concept: **Exchange of Money**

Student Name: _____

Student Challenge: "The Missing Dollar Problem"

Three traveling salesmen stopped at a restaurant for dinner. They paid $30.00 ($10.00 each) for the dinner buffet. While they were eating, the restaurant owner/chef realized he charged too much for their meal. He gave the waitress $5.00 and asked her to give it back to the salesmen. As she approached the table, she did not know how to divide $5.00 evenly among three people. So she decided to keep $2.00 and return $3.00, giving each of the salesman $1.00.

Since each salesman originally paid $10.00 and now got $1.00 back, they each actually paid $9.00. But three salesmen times $9.00 equals $27.00. And $27.00 plus the $2.00 the waitress kept adds up to $29.00.

Our story began with $30.00. What happened to the missing dollar?

DEDUCTIVE THINKING

Student Activity

Featured math concept: **Analytic Geometry**

Student Name: _____

Directions:

1. Find the shortest distance between the graphs of y = x and y = x - 4.

    Repeat for y = .5 and y = .5x - 4.

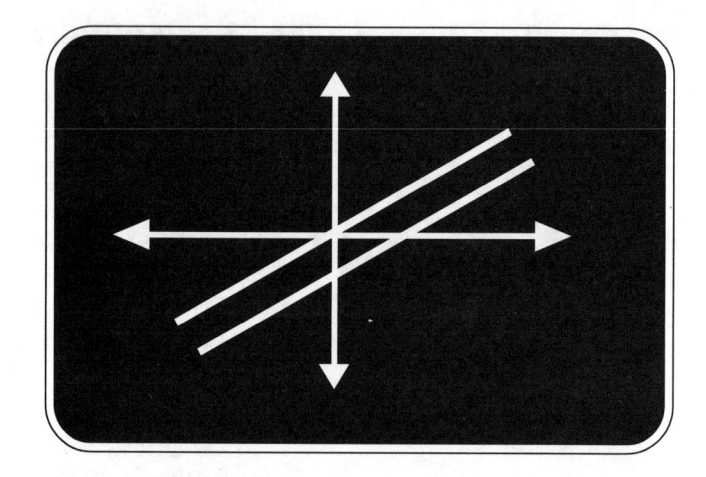

2. Find the exact values of the coordinates of the point of intersection, in the first quadrant, between the graphs of y = .5 (x - 2)² -4 and y = x + 1.

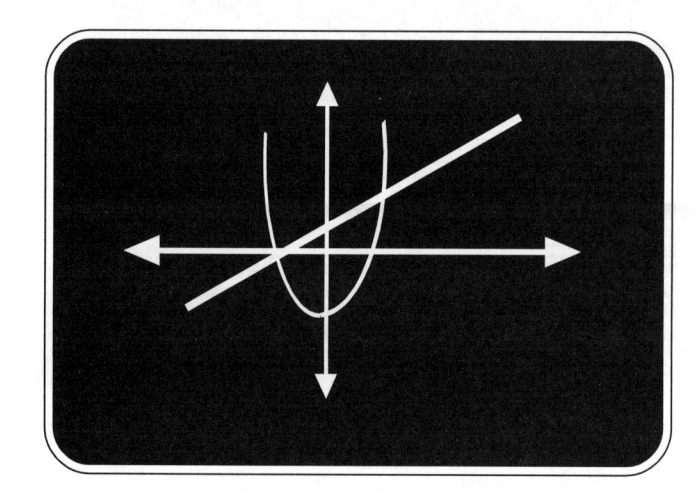

3. Repeat Problem 2 for y = (x + 1)² - 4 and x - y + 2 = 0.

DEDUCTIVE THINKING

Student Activity

Featured math concept: **Analytic Geometry**

Student Name: _____

Directions:

1. Solve the following problems for the hexagons graphed on the coordinate system below.

 a. Find linear equations, with proper domain restrictions, that represent the sides of the partially shaded regular hexagon pictured below. Verify your findings using a graphing calculator or utility.

 b. Find the perimeter and area of the partially shaded hexagon.

 c. Find the dimensions of the shaded rectangle in the partially shaded hexagon.

 d. Find the perimeter and area of the shaded rectangle in the partially shaded hexagon.

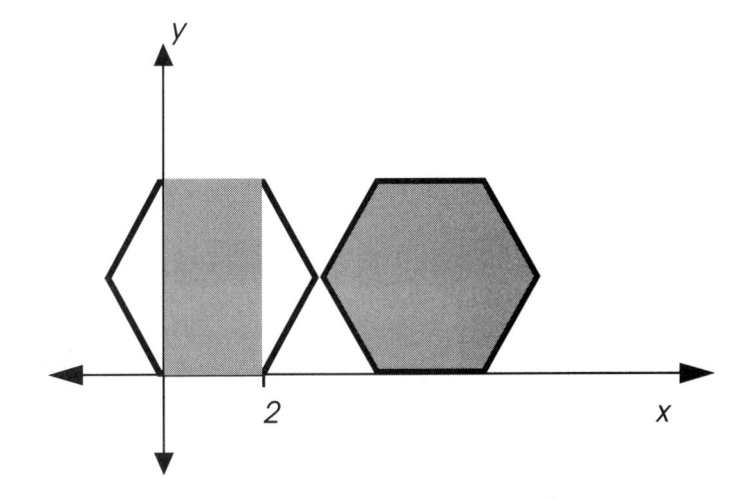

2. a. The shaded hexagon is congruent to the non-shaded hexagon. Find the coordinates of the vertices of both hexagons.

 b. Modify your equations from Problem 1a so they represent the shaded hexagon in the picture. Verify your findings using a graphing calculator or utility.

DEDUCTIVE THINKING

Student Activity

Featured math concept: **Sums of Whole Numbers**

Student Name: _____

Directions:

1. The sum $1 + 2 + 3 + 4 + 5 + ... + n$ is equal to $\dfrac{n(n+1)}{2}$

   Use this formula to calculate the following:

   a. $1 + 2 + 3 + ... + 19$

   b. $1 + 2 + 3 + ... + 99$

   c. $2 + 4 + 6 + 8 + ... + 100$ *(Hint: Factor out 2.)*

   d. $101 + 102 + 103 + ... + 200$ *(Hint: Think subtraction!)*

$$\Sigma$$

2. The sum $1 + 3 + 5 + ... + n$ is always a perfect square.
   For example, $1 + 3 + 5 + 7 = 16 = 4^2$.
   Use the formula from Problem 1 to prove that $1 + 3 + 5 + ... + n$ is always a perfect square.

DEDUCTIVE THINKING
Featured math concept: **Geometric Relationships**

Student Name: _____

Student Challenge: "Segments Cubed"

The volume of the cube below is 1 cubic unit.

1. Find the length of SV.

2. Find the length of SY.

3. Find the ratio of the area of the triangle VXS to the area of triangle VYS.

4. What kind of figure is STYV?

5. Find the area of STYV.

6. Name a triangle with vertex V that is congruent to triangle SVT.

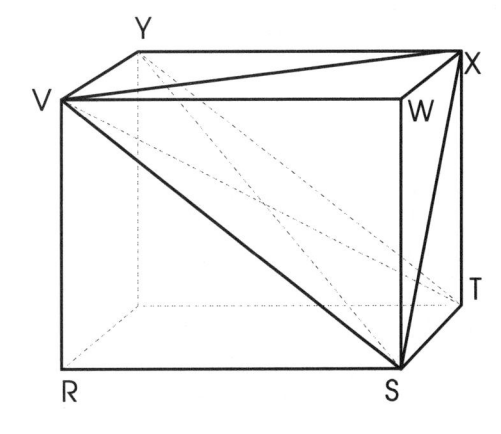

DEDUCTIVE THINKING

Featured math concepts: **Math Facts and True Values**

Student Name: _____

Directions:

1. Let p: The sum of the prime factors of 210 is 17.
    q: If U = integers, A = odd whole numbers, B = even integers, and c = integer multiples of 7, then the Venn diagram below is correct.
    r: (2 + 3) + 5 = 5 + (2 + 3) is an example of the associative property.

   Find the truth value of:

   $((\sim r \lor \sim q \lor \sim p) \to (q)) \to (p \land r)$.

   [Venn diagram: Universe U as rectangle, divided diagonally with A in upper-right triangle and B in lower-left region. Circle C straddles the dividing line.]

Logical Truth Tables

p	q	p ∨ q
T	T	T
T	F	T
F	T	T
F	F	F

p	q	p ∧ q
T	T	T
T	F	F
F	T	F
F	F	F

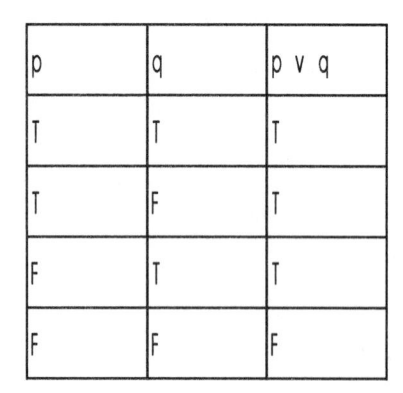

p	q	p → q
T	T	T
T	F	F
F	T	T
F	F	T

Mathematics, Styles, and Strategies
PATTERN FINDING

Mathematics is often referred to as the queen of all sciences. This title stems from the inherent beauty of mathematics. Much of the beauty of mathematics can be attributed to the patterned behavior of numbers and geometric shapes. Many important classes of numbers, including even and odd numbers, can be described by patterns. Once identified and understood, a mathematical pattern can be used to solve a variety of math problems. The Pattern Finding Strategy encourages and challenges students to use the power of patterns to solve problems, discover new knowledge, and make generalizations. In the study of formal mathematics, students can use the power of patterned thinking to prove integer theorems through a process called proof by mathematical induction.

Developing a Pattern Finding Activity

Many mathematical patterns are well documented in math textbooks. For example, the Fibonacci Sequence 1, 1, 2, 3, 5, 8, 13, ... appears in many general math, algebra, and geometry texts. With a little bit of creativity, a teacher can pose many questions that relate to the Fibonacci Sequence or a teacher-generated sequence. For example,

1. Find the sum of the first 10 terms of the sequence 1, 6, 11, ...
2. Find the 20th term of the sequence 8, 18, 28, 38, ...
3. Write a program that computes the limiting quotient of the (n +1)th and nth terms of the Fibonacci Sequence.
4. Research the relationship between the Fibonacci Sequence and nature.
5. Prove that for any four consecutive terms of the Fibonacci Sequence, the positive difference of the perfect squares of the inside terms equals the product of the outside terms.

Pattern Finding: Observable Student Behaviors

The power of the Pattern Finding Strategy is found in its versatility, simplicity, and its natural relation to the problem-solving and reasoning processes. Students should be encouraged to:

1. Understand the problem to be solved
2. Communicate how a pattern might help to solve the problem
3. Discover and identify the pattern and related patterns
4. Follow and implement the pattern to solve the problem
5. Make a generalization whenever possible
6. Communicate their findings with the class

A Sample Pattern Finding Activity:

Problem
Complete the gray portion of the table below. In each table, identify a pattern of answers in the gray boxes and use the pattern to determine the value of the number with the zero exponent. Use your findings to make a generalization.

Data Tables

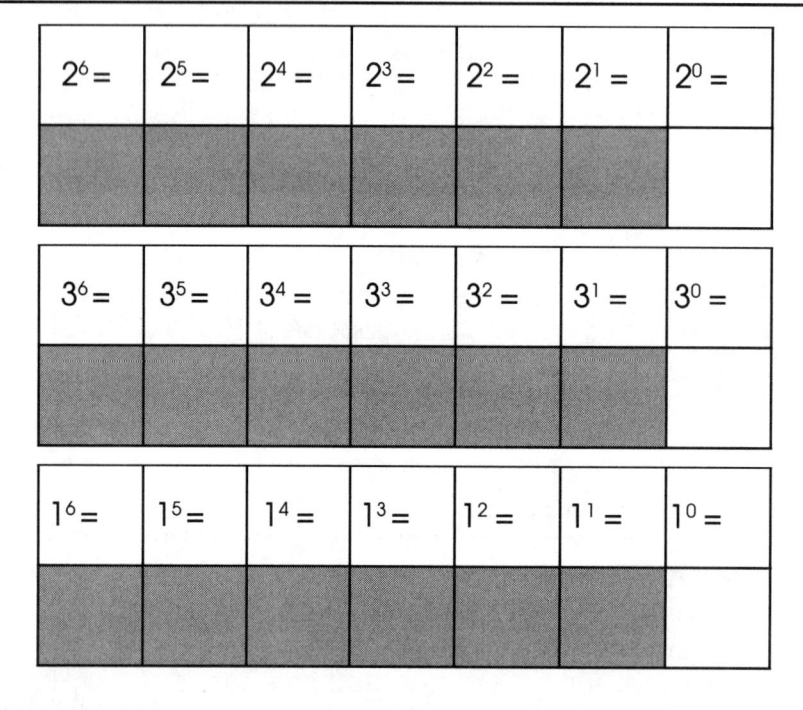

$2^6=$	$2^5=$	$2^4=$	$2^3=$	$2^2=$	$2^1=$	$2^0=$

$3^6=$	$3^5=$	$3^4=$	$3^3=$	$3^2=$	$3^1=$	$3^0=$

$1^6=$	$1^5=$	$1^4=$	$1^3=$	$1^2=$	$1^1=$	$1^0=$

Apply Patterned Thinking

Students should compute the powers and generate the following sequences 64, 32, 16, 8, 4, 2, ___, 729, 243, 81, 27, 9, 3, ___, and 1, 1, 1, 1, 1, 1, ___ .

For the first sequence, students should recognize the halving pattern and follow the pattern to determine $2^0 = 1$. Students should discover the pattern of thirds and the constant pattern of ones and follow those patterns to determine $3^0 = 1^0 = 1$.

Finally, students should make the conjecture that, in general, $n^0 = 1$, $n \neq 0$.

PATTERN FINDING

Featured math concepts: **Surface Area and Volume**

Student Name: _____

Problem 1

A series of congruent rectangular rods are stacked on top of each other and staggered by 1 cm. The rods are all the same size. The length, width, and height of one of the rods are 10 cm, 2 cm, and 2 cm respectively. Determine the total surface area and volume of the stacked rods for the number of rods shown in the table. Use the patterns of the progressive surface areas and volumes to find a general formula for the surface area and volume when n rods are used.

Number of rods	Surface area	Volume
1		
2		
3		
4		
5		
n		

Student Activity

PATTERN FINDING
Featured math concepts: **Zero Exponent and Negative Exponents**

Student Name: _____

Problem 1
Use mental math or pencil and paper to evaluate each number under the gray bar in the first row of the table. Write your answers in the boxes in the bottom row. When you finish evaluating the gray box numbers in a table, look for a pattern in the progression of the answers. Continue the progression of the pattern and write the values of the numbers with the zero and negative exponents.

2^4	2^3	2^2	2^1	2^0	2^{-1}	2^{-2}	2^{-3}

3^4	3^3	3^2	3^1	3^0	3^{-1}	3^{-2}	3^{-3}

10^4	10^3	10^2	10^1	10^0	10^{-1}	10^{-2}	10^{-3}

Based on the pattern you discovered, write a general rule for raising any natural number n to a negative or zero power.

PATTERN FINDING
Featured math concepts: **Surface Area and Volume**

Student Name: _____

Problem 1
A series of congruent rectangular rods are stacked directly on top of each other. The rods are all the same size. The length, width, and height of one of the rods are 10 cm, 2 cm, and 2 cm respectively. Determine the total surface area and volume of the stacked rods for the number of rods shown in the table. Use the patterns of the progressive surface areas and volumes to find a general formula for the surface area and volume when n rods are used.

Number of rods	Surface area	Volume
1		
2		
3		
4		
5		
n		

PATTERN FINDING
Featured math concept: **Fibonacci Sequence**

Student Name: _____

Problem 1
A set or list of numbers that follow a pattern is often called a sequence. A famous sequence in mathematics is the Fibonacci sequence developed by the Italian mathematician Leonardo Fibonacci. Part of the Fibonacci sequence is listed below.

The Fibonacci Sequence

Term	1st	2nd	3rd	4th	5th	6th	7th	8th
Value	1	1	2	3	5	8	13	21

a. Work with a partner to discover the pattern of the Fibonacci sequence.

b. Find values of the 9th, 10th, 11th, 12th, and 20th terms of the sequence.

c. If x_n represents the value of the nth term of the sequence, write an expression, in terms of x and n, for the value of the (n + 1)th term of the sequence.

d. For any four consecutive terms of the Fibonacci sequence, prove that the positive difference of the perfect squares of the inside terms is equal to the product of the outside terms.

Mathematics, Styles, and Strategies
MYSTERY

Most students love a good riddle to solve. Math is full of riddling opportunities. For example,

I know a number that loses all its value when its digits are rearranged. The digit sum and the digit product of the number are very famous elements themselves. Find the number.

The Mystery Strategy provides students with a puzzle to be solved, riddle to be unraveled, or improbable phenomenon to be explained. Since it is human nature to be captured by a good puzzle or mind teaser, a Mystery activity can engage students in a complex and fun problem that requires problem-solving, reasoning, communication, and logic.

The Mystery Strategy is adapted from J. R. Suchman's (1966) Inquiry model and it plays on humans' natural curiosity—that desire to understand our universe and the millions of mysteries that ripple through it. According to Suchman, when students investigate a problem or question under their own impelling curiosity, they are more likely to retain the information they gather along the way.

In the example above, the culprit number is 10. When rearranged, the digits 1 and 0 can become ∅, which is the empty set (no value). The digit sum and digit product of 10 are 1 + 0 = 1 and 1 • 0 = 0 which are the multiplication and addition identity elements respectively.

MYSTERY

Student Activity
Featured math concept: **Geometric Proof**
Student Name: _____

Directions:

In the problem below the steps and reasons of a geometric proof are shown, but are out of order and scattered about the page. Work with a partner to determine the original given statement and the prove statement. Arrange all the steps and reasons in the proper order.

- ∠BDA and ∠BDC are right angles.
- ∠BDA and ∠BDC are congruent.
- The base angles of an isosceles triangle are congruent.

Given: _____
Prove: _____

Statements	Reasons
1.	1.
2.	2.
3.	3.
4.	4.
5.	5.
6.	6.

- Perpendicular lines form four right angles.

- ∠A and ∠C are congruent.
- Angle-Angle-Side
- Right angles are congruent.
- Given
- $\overline{BD}$ is congruent to $\overline{BD}$.
- Reflexive property of congruence
- △ABC is isosceles and $\overline{BD}$ is perpendicular to $\overline{AC}$.
- △BDA and △BDC are congruent.

Student Activity

MYSTERY
Featured math concept: **Creative Thinking**

Student Name: _____

Directions:

In the problem below, a well-known math concept or principle is cleverly described by clues that are facts or, in some cases, plays on words. To identify the Mystery math principle, you will have to apply your mathematical knowledge to information implied by the clues.

Problem
Work with a learning partner. Study the clues below. Identify the Mystery math family.

1. Many of the members of the family serve as the focus of many problems.

2. The two youngest in the family are the only ones ever home.

3. The youngest in the family is only three and always tries.

4. Each of the members of the family is multifaceted.

Solution:

MYSTERY

Student Activity

Featured math concept: **Creative Thinking**

Student Name: _____

Directions:

In the problem below, a well-known math concept or principle is cleverly described by clues that are facts or, in some cases, plays on words. To identify the Mystery math principle, you will have to apply your mathematical knowledge to information implied by the clues.

Problem

Work with a learning partner. Study the clues below. Identify the Mystery math family.

1. Its starting point is neither prime nor composite.

2. Only three players determine the fate of many.

3. While the world teaches not to ASSUME, the exception is its rule.

4. Its purpose can be found on some beverages preceded by a percentage.

Solution:

Mathematics, Styles, and Strategies
SUPPORT AND REFUTE

Every day students hear questionable claims that are made on television, in advertisements, in the news, or in personal conversations. Many people who make claims incorporate mathematics to motivate buyers, change the attitudes or opinions of voters, or change the way people think or behave. Unfortunately, some of the numbers used in some claims are misleading or even untrue. The Support and Refute Strategy challenges students to move beyond automatic acceptance of a given claim and use their mathematical problem-solving and reasoning skills to make sense of the claim or to challenge the claim. In the Support and Refute thinking process, students will form their own hypothesis, gather data, analyze the data, and perform math operations whose solutions will either support or refute the claim.

Developing a Support and Refute Activity

Ideas for Support and Refute activities abound in the media. In one week, dozens of claims can be heard from news reporters, advertisers, politicians, and magazine authors. To prepare an activity for students:

1. Determine a catchy title;
2. Communicate the claim and the context in which it was heard (communicate by transparency, video display, handout, or verbal delivery); and
3. Challenge your students to support or refute the claim.

Support and Refute: Observable Student Behaviors

The power of the Support and Refute Strategy is dependent upon students' degree of involvement in the problem-solving and reasoning processes. Students should be encouraged to:

1. Identify the claim;
2. Develop a hypothesis of their belief or disbelief in the claim;
3. Collect, organize, and display real relevant data;
4. Perform and display appropriate calculations;
5. Draw an appropriate conclusion; and
6. Communicate their findings with the class.

Support and Refute: A Sample Problem-Solving Plan

Claim
Over one billion gallons of water can be saved in the U.S. if people turn their faucets off while brushing their teeth.

Hypothesis
Upon discussion with a learning partner, a student might choose to disagree with that claim.

Gathering Data
Students might plan to perform an experiment at home by letting the water run into a measured container while brushing their teeth. They might ask other family members to participate in the experiment.

After approximating the amount of water lost to running water, they would bring their data to school and share it with their partner. Partners might gather more data by polling classmates to determine how often people brush their teeth and check the U.S. population through the media center.

Calculations
Students might multiply the population by the number of times people brush, times the average amount of water lost in a teeth-brushing session. Subtractions might be made for infants and elderly with no teeth.

Conclusions
Students will compare their comprehensive numbers with the numbers in the claim and draw a conclusion. Students will communicate their findings to the class.

SUPPORT AND REFUTE

Featured math concepts: **Estimation and Measurement**

Student Name: _____

Directions:
Each problem below describes a real-world or problem-solving situation that includes a startling claim. The claim is written in *italics*. Work with a learning partner to produce a thorough argument that **supports** or **refutes** the claim. Be sure to include mathematical hypotheses, experiments, data, calculations, and summaries that justify your solution.

Problem 1
The city of Atlanta, Georgia has approximately 3,000,000 residents in its metropolitan area. Transportation is supported by four main interstate roads: the outer perimeter I-285, the East/West Interstate I-20, and two north-south interstates, I-75 and I-85.

During rush hour, all the interstates in the Atlanta area are heavily traveled but allow traffic to move about 65 mph. In a 9:00 a.m. morning radio traffic report, the announcer claimed that *a wreck had just occurred at a point on I-85 South, 5 miles south of the perimeter and that by 9:10 a.m., traffic would be jammed bumper to bumper from the point of the wreck back to the perimeter.*

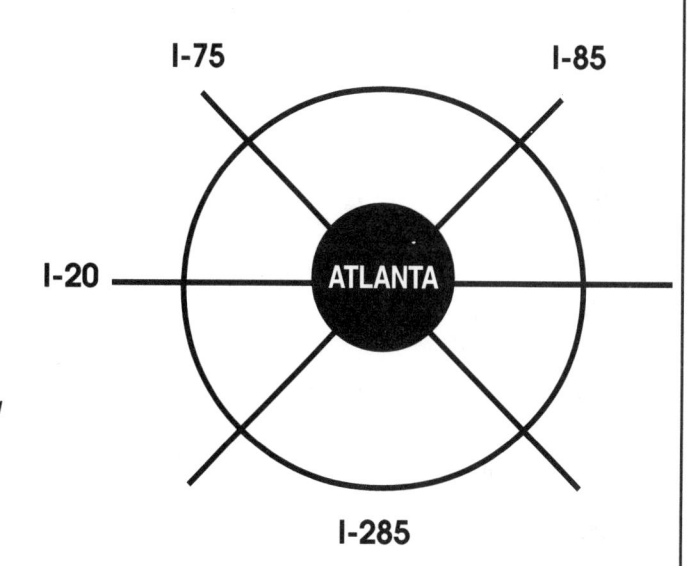

Support or refute the announcer's claim.

Problem 2
Regarding the interstate system described in Problem 1, a report on the evening news made the following claim: *On a given day, the sum total of miles driven on the Atlanta interstate system is more than 400 trips to the moon.*

Support or refute the announcer's claim.

SUPPORT AND REFUTE

Featured math concepts: **Estimation and Measurement**

Student Name: _____

Directions:
Each problem below describes a real-world or problem-solving situation that includes a startling claim. The claim is written in *italics*. Work with a learning partner to produce a thorough argument that **supports** or **refutes** the claim. Be sure to include mathematical hypotheses, experiments, data, calculations, and summaries that justify your solution.

Problem 1
Tiny Tim loved to play with tin foil. He particularly enjoyed folding and creasing it. One day, while folding and creasing his tin foil, he made the following claim: *If I had a super large sheet of tin foil that was just 1 millimeter thick and folded it in half 100 times, the measure of the thickness of the folded stack would be greater than the distance of 100 round trips from the Earth to the sun.*

Support or refute Tiny's claim.

Problem 2
Sally, who recently took up the game of golf, played a round of golf and walked the golf course. The course consists of 10 par-four holes, 4 par-five holes, and 4 par-three holes. Sally played all 18 holes and shot a 104. At the end of the game, Sally made the following claim: *I am so tired, I know I walked at least five miles.*

Support or refute Sally's claim.

Student Activity	**SUPPORT AND REFUTE**
	Featured math concept: **Personal Finance**
	Student Name: _____

Directions:
Each problem below describes a real-world or problem-solving situation that includes a startling claim. The claim is written in *italics*. Work with a learning partner to produce a thorough argument that **supports** or **refutes** the claim. Be sure to include mathematical hypotheses, experiments, data, calculations, and summaries that justify your solution.

Problem 1

A local radio station ran an advertisement that featured the following dialogue.

John: I can't believe the prices I'm seeing in this newspaper. Everything is going up!

Mary: Tell me about it. I was at the grocery store yesterday and noticed that bread and milk each went up 11 cents. Will it ever stop?

John: Wait a minute. Here's something that actually went down. You know how most banks charge prime rate plus one percent on interest for home improvement loans?

Mary: Yes, that's why we haven't been able to do any improvement projects around here.

John: Well, I found a bank that actually charges prime rate minus one percent. Just go to the bank, complete a simple application, and we're on our way.

Mary: That's great! *Now we can do those projects we've put off!*

*Disclaimer by third announcer: The prime minus one percent rate is good for the first six months of the loan. After six months, interest will be calculated at prime plus 3.5 percent. Loans can be obtained for up to ten years.

INTERPERSONAL STRATEGIES

Circle of Knowledge
Cooperative Learning
Game Competition
Paired Learner
Reciprocal Learning

Mathematics, Styles, and Strategies
CIRCLE OF KNOWLEDGE

Some of the best work in mathematics has occurred after the right questions were asked. New fields of mathematics have blossomed from questions like "Can a salesman find a travel path that minimizes mileage and time required for visiting companies in fifteen cities?" The mathematician Euler spent several years trying to answer his own question, "Is the number 1000009 really prime?"

By asking the right questions, any math teacher can spark interest among students and motivate them to engage in mathematics. The focus of the Circle of Knowledge Strategy, based on Adler's Socratic Seminar (1982), are the key questions that spark student interest, lead to rich discussion, and engage students in critical thinking and learning.

Developing a Circle of Knowledge Activity
When it comes to wondrous discoveries, facts, and relationships, mathematics is a world of plenty. For example,

- Discovery: *What is the sum of the angles of any triangle?*

- Fact: *The number of counting numbers is infinite.*

- Relationship: *The pattern of the Fibonacci Sequence can be found in the growth patterns of plants and trees in nature.*

Any mathematical concept can be the basis of questioning that incites student interest and motivation for learning. The key, however, is in how the questions are posed, arranged, and asked. The examples below show how questions can be formed to spark student interest, lead students to rich discussion, and engage students in critical thinking and learning.

Sparking Student Interest
When implementing the Circle of Knowledge Strategy, the first questions should be thought-provoking and capture the interest of all students. Initially, students must be encouraged to internalize the question and think deeply about their responses before communicating their thoughts. From the examples above, sparking questions might be as follows:

1. Draw a 90 degree angle on a sheet of paper. Since an angle has two sides, only one more is needed to make a triangle. I want you to draw a third side so the triangle you make has a second 90 degree angle in it. If you experience difficulty doing this, don't give up quickly. Think through the process carefully and be ready to answer the question, "Is this possible?"

2. How many people are in our classroom? How many people are in our school (you can approximate from this point on)? How many people are in our state? How many people are in our country? How many people are in our world? Is it certain that this last question has an exact answer? Is it possible to find the exact answer?

3. The other day I was looking at an evergreen tree. I noticed that it was symmetric and mathematically proportional. While the shape and size of the tree is mathematical, I have never seen a math formula that can be used to find the width of a tree at a given height. Perhaps you can invent one. I have a transparency of an evergreen superimposed on a graphing grid. What do you think?

Leading Students to Rich Discussion

After students have an opportunity to internalize the sparking questions and think about their responses, ask them to share their ideas with a learning partner. Talking to a fellow student is far less threatening than sharing initial thoughts with the entire class, and is therefore a great place to test ideas. After students have an opportunity to share with a partner, ask student volunteers to share what was said between them. As various students share, encourage their partners to verify or add to the discussion.

At this point, a new level of questions can be asked to generate further discussions. For this stage of questioning, cooperative learning groups can be formed by uniting two sets of learning pairs. Examples of cooperative group questions might be as follows:

1. Since it appears to be impossible to draw a triangle that has two 90 degree angles, maybe the sum of the angles of a triangle can never be greater than 180 degrees (2 x 90 = 180). I would like each member of your group to use a straight edge and pencil to draw an arbitrary triangle. I want each member of the group to use a protractor to measure the angles of your original learning partner's triangle. Find the sum of the angles. Work as a group to answer the question, "What is the sum of the angles of any triangle?"

2. Our initial discussion has lead us to believe that, even though it may be impossible to count all the people in our world, there is a finite number of people in our world. But what about the set of counting numbers? Is the set of counting numbers countable? Is the set of counting numbers finite or infinite? Work as a group to answer the question, "Can you develop a believable argument or proof that would convince everyone?"

3. We have discovered that some elements of nature display growth patterns that are mathematical. The Fibonacci Sequence contains the numbers 1, 1, 2, 3, 5, 8, 13, 21 ... . After the second term, each term is the sum of the preceding two terms. Work as a cooperative group to answer the question, "How do the numbers representing the terms of the Fibonacci Sequence fit the growth pattern of an evergreen tree? Be prepared to share your ideas with the class.

Engaging Students in Critical Thinking and Learning

To ensure that your students are engaging in critical thinking, ask them to show their responses in writing, diagrams, charts, graphs, or pictures. Encourage students to use their written responses as they participate in the group and class discussions. To ensure that they are learning, record students' responses on flip charts, transparencies, or poster boards. Summarize the students' responses frequently and invite the authors of the ideas to critique your understanding of their ideas.

Student Activity

CIRCLE OF KNOWLEDGE
Featured math concept: **Sets of Infinite Magnitude**

Student Name: _____

Today's Question for Consideration
If two sets each contain an infinite number of elements, can one set have more elements than the other set?

∞

Background Information
A set is infinite if the number of elements in the set has no bound.

Initial Discussion
If you could travel in space an infinite distance from Earth, how far would that be? Is it true that, however far from Earth one could travel, there is always a distance from Earth that is greater than the original distance? Have you ever had an experience in life that seemed of great magnitude, only to find a related situation, later in life, of even greater magnitude? Did the incidence of greater magnitude ever make the first incident seem less significant by comparison? Explain.

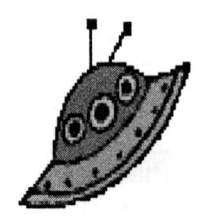

Focus Questions for Small Group Discussions
The set of even whole numbers is infinite. The set of odd whole numbers is infinite. The set of whole numbers (both odd and even) is infinite. Even though all three of these sets are infinite, does the set of whole numbers have more elements than either the set of even or odd whole numbers? Do the sets of even whole numbers and odd whole numbers have an equal number of elements?

Sharing Through Whole Group Discussion
Share your answers and thinking process to the focus questions with the whole group.

Synthesizing the Discussion
Based on what you learned today, write and complete the following statement in your journal: *Even though two sets can be described as infinite, ...*

Student Activity

CIRCLE OF KNOWLEDGE
Featured math concept: **Evaluating 2^n**

Student Name: _____

Today's Question for Consideration
How powerful is the process of doubling?

$2^3 = 8$

$2^4 = 16$

$2^5 = 32$

Background Information
In an exponential expression, the exponent indicates the number of times the base is used as a factor.

$$a^b = \underbrace{a \cdot a \cdot a \cdot \ldots \cdot a}_{b \text{ times}}$$

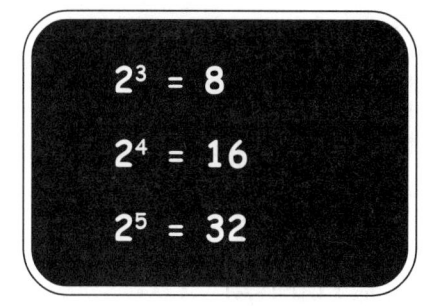

Initial Discussion
The other day a student named Kristine and her family went to a restaurant for dinner. Kristine and her dad ordered a nachos appetizer, two salads from the salad bar, chicken fingers, and barbecued ribs. Kristine's mom ordered a burger platter. Kristine and her parents each ordered a large soda. While the individual prices of items seemed reasonable, the total bill grew rapidly. Kristine's parents were surprised at how quickly the total bill accumulated. Did you ever have an experience that involved rapid growth beyond belief? Explain.

Focus Questions for Small Group Discussions
If the value of a penny is doubled, the resulting value is 2 cents. If the 2 cents are doubled, the resulting value is 4 cents. If this doubling process continues 98 more times, what base 2 exponential expression would be representative of the final amount of money? Find an approximation of a single number for this amount. Convert this number to an amount the average person could understand.

Sharing Through Whole Group Discussion
Share your answers and thinking processes with the whole group.

Synthesizing the Discussion
Based on what you learned today, write and complete the following statement in your journal: *When the base is two or more, exponential growth is ... because ....*

Mathematics, Styles, and Strategies
COOPERATIVE LEARNING

When members of companies and corporations are asked to describe the core skills that today's high school graduates will need to be employable in the business world, they often respond by stating that students will need to have the ability to:

1. Read, write, and communicate through the English language.

2. Practice mathematical proficiency in the areas of general math, algebra 1, and geometry.

3. Define a problem, hypothesize a solution, collect experimental data, analyze the data, and draw a conclusion.

4. Work collaboratively with others on a problem-solving task.

5. Use technology in the problem-solving process.

Based on a large body of research supporting the idea that cooperative and group interaction maximizes learning (Johnson and Johnson, 1999; Slavin, 1987, 1991), the Cooperative Learning Strategy integrates social skills objectives with mathematical content.

Cooperative Learning challenges students to work together, in cooperative groups or teams, toward a common learning task or goal. The cooperative groups usually consist of three to five students who complement each other's learning styles or levels of understanding. Cooperative Learning tasks are multifaceted so each group member can be assigned a specific task that contributes to the group's goal. To help maintain an orderly environment, individual group members often assume roles such as team leaders, record keepers, time keepers, materials managers, and reporters.

COOPERATIVE LEARNING

Student Activity

Featured math concept: **Word Scramble Geometry**

Student Name: _____

Directions:

Listed below are nine geometry problems which need to be solved. Divide the problems among the members of your cooperative group. The whole-number solution of each problem corresponds to one of the letters of the alphabet and one letter of the word. For example, 1 = a and 26 = z.

```
a b c d e      (1 - 5)
f g h i j      (6 - 10)
k l m n o      (11 - 15)
p q r s t      (16 - 20)
u v w x y      (21 - 25)
z              (26)
```

Use the solutions of the problems to find key letters of the mystery math word. All the letters of the word are given in scrambled form. Assign two possible starting letters to each member of the group. Each member should use trial and error to test various permutations of the remaining letters with their assigned starting letters. See who finds the mystery math word.

1. Find the number of diagonals in a hexagon.

2. Find the number which corresponds to the phrase 'one less than the number of faces in a cube.'

3. Given a line l in a plane and a point p in the plane but not on the line, state the number of lines in the plane which contain the point p and are parallel to line l.

4. Find the number of sides in a dodecagon.

5. Find the coefficient of π in the area of a circle with circumference = $4\sqrt{3}\,\pi$.

6. Find the number of angles in an equilateral triangle.

7. Find the perimeter of a pentagon with side = 3.6.

8. Find one half of the measure of the smallest angle in a right triangle if one of its acute angles equals 60°.

9. Find the measure of the complement of an angle whose measure is 76°.

Mystery Word: _____

COOPERATIVE LEARNING

Featured math concepts: **Classroom Volume and Algebra**

Student Name: _____

Directions:
The purpose of this activity is to work as a cooperative group of three or six students to measure the volume of your classroom and use algebra to verify your measure. Members of each cooperative group should perform the following tasks.

Step 1 — *Each group member (for groups of 3) or each pair in the group (for groups of 6):*
  a. Measure the length and width of your classroom in feet and inches
  b. Measure the height of your classroom in feet and inches
  c. Round your measures to the nearest foot
  d. Confirm answers with other group members

Step 2 — *Each group member:*
  a. Calculate the volume using the formula V = lwh. Check answers with other group members

Step 3 — *Each group member (for groups of 3) or each pair in the group (for groups of 6):*
  a. Roll a six-sided die and randomly obtain a unique number in the range 1 - 6
  b. If the number is 1 or 2, let x = the value of the length
  c. If the number is 3 or 4, let x = the value of the width
  d. If the number is 5 or 6, let x = the value of the height

Step 4 — *Each group member (for groups of 3) or each pair in the group (for groups of 6):*
  a. Write the measures of the length, width, and height in terms of x. For example, if l = 22 ft., w = 20 ft., h = 15 ft., and the group's random number = 2, then assign x = 22 and l = x, w = x - 2 and h = x - 7. (Why?)

Step 5 — *Each group member (for groups of 3) or each pair in the group (for groups of 6):*
  a. Calculate algebraic volume by multiplying lwh. Using the example from Step 4, v = x(x-2)(x-7) = $x(x^2 - 9x + 14) = x^3 - 9x^2 + 14x$.

Step 6 — *Each group member:*
  a. Use algebraic volume to calculate and verify the volume calculated in Step 2. Do this by substituting the value of x into the algebraic volume formula and simplifying. Using the example from Step 4, since $v = x^3 - 9x^2 + 14x$ and x = 22, $v = 22^3 - 9(22)^2 + 14(22) =$ 6600 cubic feet. Compare results with other group members and discuss.

Page 100

Teams, Games, and Tournaments
A Variation on Cooperative Learning

The purpose of the Teams, Games, and Tournaments Strategy is to involve all students in a fun and systematic game of competition and learning. The game requires students to work collaboratively within their team and competitively among several teams. Teams, Games, and Tournaments is an ideal cumulative review activity. The steps that follow explain how to organize this activity.

Pre-Competition
1. Rank your students by grade average or performance level.
2. Pair the student at the top of the list with the student at the bottom. Pair the student second from the top with the student second from the bottom. Continue that process until all the students are paired.
3. The first and last pairing will form a four-person team. The second from top and second from last pairing will form another four-person team. Continue that process until all the teams are formed.
4. Each team will practice and review a specific set of concepts so that all members are proficient at the math concepts and skills.
5. Before the team competition begins, each team should identify the number 1, 2, 3, and 4 players according to levels of proficiency.

Competition
1. Set up four competition tables numbered 1 - 4. On each table, place a stack of index cards with math questions or problems, one per card. All tables have the same questions and cards. The questions might be review questions for an upcoming test.
2. The number 1 members from all teams should report to table 1. The number 2 members of all teams should report to table 2, etc.
3. In a clockwise manner, the players take turns drawing a card from the stack. When a card is drawn, the question is read so all students at the table can solve the problem. The player who drew the card gets to share his/her answer. The next student in the clockwise direction can challenge the card drawer's answer (a challenge does not have to occur). If the card drawer's answer is correct, s/he keeps the card and the challenger loses a card to the card drawer. If the card drawer's answer is wrong and the challenger's answer is correct, the challenger gets the card. If the first clockwise student does not want to challenge, the next student in the clockwise rotation can challenge. That process can continue until all the players at a table are exhausted. Regardless of which player challenged last, when a new card is drawn, the next player in the clockwise direction has the first option to challenge.

Declaring a Winning Team
1. At the end of the competition, each team declares a first, second, third, and fourth place winner. Those players receive 40, 30, 20, and 10 points respectively.
2. All players return to their home team. Each team totals the points brought back to the team by the first, second, third, and fourth place winners. The team with the highest total wins the tournament. Appropriate prizes can be awarded.

Mathematics, Styles, and Strategies
GAME COMPETITION

One attribute that separates a master teacher from an unsuccessful teacher is the ability to motivate students to participate gladly in the learning process. Teachers who do not experience optimal success will often complain that their students demonstrate an "I don't care" attitude and choose not to participate. So what is the secret of the master teacher? Master teachers of mathematics motivate students to participate and learn by being positive advocates for their students and by being enthusiastic about the mathematics they teach. The belief that learning is important and fun is reflected in the teaching strategies they implement. Perhaps no single teaching strategy motivates more students or more strongly conveys the fact that learning can be fun than the Game Competition Strategy.

This strategy engages students in fun and challenging games that require them to solve math problems in order to win. While students focus on the fun of the game and the spirit of competition, significant learning takes place.

Developing a Game Competition Activity

When creating a Game Competition activity teachers should select model games that are popular with students. Effective math games can be modeled after successful game shows on television, popular family and children's games, and even sports games. The structure of the game should allow for a variety of levels of difficulty. In a game of questions and answers, questions might be categorized as 100 point, 200 point, 300 point, 400 point, and 500 point questions. The 100 point questions should be the easiest questions to answer and the 500 point questions should be the most difficult, but not impossible, to answer.

The format and rules of the game should be designed to adapt well to the classroom. For example, a game format that allows several teams to compete against each other would be highly adaptable to a classroom that utilizes cooperative groups. In team competition activities, it can be helpful to designate a team captain, leader, or spokesperson.

The scoring procedure for teams or game contestants must be one that a teacher can maintain with relative ease. The rules of the game should include conduct rules that remind students to behave appropriately and penalties for students who demonstrate poor conduct. The rules must be consistent to ensure that order is maintained in the classroom.

A Sample Creation of a Game Competition Activity
The steps that follow were used to create a specific math game designed for the classroom.

Selecting a Game Title
Since baseball is one of America's favorite pastimes, the sample math game will be called Math Baseball.

Developing the Game's Rules
Most students already know how to play baseball. Therefore, the rules of Math Baseball will incorporate many of the same rules as baseball.

While regular baseball is played between two teams, Math Baseball will accommodate multiple teams. The teams can be represented by cooperative groups or rows of students. The members of the groups will be batters. The teacher will be a constant pitcher for all teams and batters. Each pitch will be in the form of a math question. The various difficulty levels of the questions will be categorized as follows:

Pitch Category
90 mph fastballs
Curve balls
Change-ups

Hit Category
Single
Double
Triple
Homerun

In Algebra, 90 mph fastballs might be equations to solve, curveballs might be inequalities to solve, and change-ups might be equations involving absolute value. The hit value should be proportional to the difficulty of the question.

When a batter successfully answers a question, the batter makes the designated hit, and a runner will be posted for his/her team on a team diamond drawn and maintained on the front board. When a hit occurs, the runners advance the number of bases equal to the hit (one base for a single, two bases for a double, etc.). Each time a team's runner crosses homeplate, that team earns one run. When a batter misses a question, an out is recorded. Each team continues batting until three outs are recorded.

TEACHER'S GUIDE:
GAME COMPETITION
Featured math concept: **What It Is**

Directions:
To play this fun game, create five questions and answers for each category. Divide your class into 5 - 7 teams. Appoint a captain for each. The captain from Team 1, the focus team, begins by selecting the category. The teacher rolls a die or spins a spinner to see if the team is playing for 100, 200, 300, 400, or 500 points. The teacher reads the **answer**. All teams have one minute to generate a correct corresponding **question**. Once team consensus is reached, each team captain must record the team's question on paper. After one minute, the teacher calls "all pencils down."

The captain from Team 1, the focus team, has first try at a correct response. A correct response wins the point amount. An incorrect response results in the team losing the point amount. If Team 1 answers incorrectly, the first team (in consecutive order), that has the correct written response wins the points. Non-focus teams cannot lose points on a rebound. If Team 1 responds correctly, they can opt to go again. After two correct responses or a miss, Team 2 becomes the focus team. Play continues until all the questions and answers are exhausted. The team with the most points wins the game.

WHAT IT IS

Points:
- 100
- 200
- 300
- 400
- 500

Categories:
- ALGEBRA
- GEOMETRY
- DEFINITIONS
- APPLICATIONS
- MENTAL MATH

TEACHER'S GUIDE:
GAME COMPETITION
Featured math concepts: **Mental Math, Integers, and Perfect Squares**

Game 1: Integers Review
The Integer WAR Game (2 or 3 players)

Shuffle and divide evenly, among the members of your group, a deck of poker cards. Designate one member of your group as the caller and calculator judge. On the command of your group caller, each group member places a card face up on the table. The first group member to correctly state the combined sum of the number values of the cards wins all the cards (red = − , black = + , ace = 1, face cards = 10, number cards = their own number). In the event of a tie, the cards are pushed aside and awarded to the winner of the next card toss. The calculator judge can use a calculator *only* to settle disputes over correct answers.

Game 2: Perfect Squares Review
The *Perfect Squares* WAR Game (2 players)

Shuffle and divide evenly, among two players, a deck of poker cards. Designate one player as the caller and the other player as the calculator judge. On the command of the caller, each player places a card face up on the table. The first player to state correctly the perfect square of the combined sum of the number values of the cards wins all the cards (red = − , black = + , ace = 1, face cards = 10, number cards = their own number). In the event of a tie, the cards are pushed aside and awarded to the winner of the next card toss. The calculator judge can use a calculator *only* to settle disputes over correct answers.

TEACHER'S GUIDE:
GAME COMPETITION
Featured math concept: **Integrated Mathematics**

Directions: Math Bingo

In Math Bingo, each student plays one bingo card. Bingo cards can be made on the computer or purchased at a local toy store. The cards have 25 random numbers ranging from 1 to 75. The teacher calls random math problems from a list of 75 problems whose answers correlate with the numbers 1 - 75. The problems should review important concepts and not require too much time to solve. (A sample list of problems is provided on the next two pages.)

When a problem is called, each student can work with a learning partner to solve the problem. There is a two-minute time limit for each problem. If a student has the answer to the problem on his/her bingo card, he/she can X the number out. If the learning pair cannot solve the problem, they miss the opportunity to X a number out on that turn. The first student who completely Xs out a horizontal, vertical, or diagonal row wins the game. Problem sets can be developed for various math units.

B	I	N	G	O
1	26	37	50	71
3	28	33	53	73
2	22	free	57	68
9	21	34	46	70
13	29	37	52	63

Math Bingo

1. The number of straight lines that can be drawn through two distinct points.
2. The length of the diagonal of a square with a side length of $\sqrt{2}$.
3. The number of regular polygons that will tessellate a plane.
4. The number of sides in a quadrilateral.
5. The number of diagonals in a regular pentagon.
6. The number of faces in a rectangular solid.
7. The height of a triangle whose base is 8 and area is 28.
8. The number of edges on a square-based pyramid.
9. The number of diagonals in a regular hexagon.
10. The measure of one side of a regular decagon with perimeter 100.
11. The number of sides of a polygon whose interior angles add to 1620 degrees.
12. The number of edges on a cube.
13. One more than the number of sides of a dodecagon.
14. The length of a rectangle with perimeter 42 and width 7.
15. The area of a parallelogram with base 5 and height 3.
16. The positive square root of 256.
17. The value of x if 50 - 2x = 16.
18. 25% of 72.
19. The twin prime of 17.
20. The number of degrees in the complement of a 70 degree angle.
21. The eighth term of the Fibonacci sequence.
22. One third of 66.
23. The square root of 529.
24. 4!
25. The hypotenuse of a right triangle if the leg measures are 7 and 24.
26. The value of $a^2 + 1$ when a = -5.
27. Two more than the perimeter of a regular pentagon with side length = 5.
28. The area of a circle with a radius 2 $\sqrt{7/\pi}$.
29. The value of f(5) if f(x) = 6x - 1.
30. Arc sin (.5) (degrees)
31. Three more than the perimeter of a rhombus with side length = 7.
32. The circumference of a circle with radius $16/\pi$.
33. The slope of the line 66x - 2y + 24 = 0.
34. The ninth term of the Fibonacci sequence.
35. The number of diagonals in a 10-sided polygon (decagon).
36. The y-intercept of the line representing the graph of y = 2x + 36.
37. One more than the square of 6.
38. 50% of 76.
39. The number of degrees in the complement of a 51 degree angle.
40. Two less than seven times the total surface area of a cube with edge length = 1.

Math Bingo cont. ...

41. One more than the area of a parallelogram with base 10 and height 4.
42. Twice the square root of 441.
43. The measure of a base angle of an isosceles triangle with vertex angle = 94°.
44. 25% of 176.
45. The measure of an acute angle in an isosceles right triangle.
46. Two more than four times the average of the first 21 counting numbers.
47. Three less than half of 100.
48. The value of f(2) if $f(x) = 3x^4$.
49. The square of x if $3x - 5 = 16$.
50. The median of the set { 0, 1, 2, 3, ... , 100 }
51. The smallest whole number with factors 3 and 17.
52. The volume of a sphere with $r = \sqrt[3]{39/\pi}$
53. 25% of 212.
54. The number of diagonals in a dodecagon.
55. The sum of the first 10 counting numbers.
56. The mode of the set { 50, 41, 56, 42, 56, 50, 56, 49 }.
57. The LCM of 3 and 19.
58. Two less than the measure of an interior angle of an equilateral triangle.
59. Two less than half the measure of an interior angle of a regular hexagon.
60. $\cos^{-1}(\frac{1}{2})$ (answer in degrees)
61. The hypotenuse of a right triangle with leg lengths 11 and 60.
62. $2^6 - 2$
63. The area of a rectangle with length 9 and width 7.
64. $8^5 / 8^3$
65. Five more than five times the number of edges of a hexagonal pyramid.
66. The volume of a cylinder with base area 11 and height 6.
67. Seven more than the number of minutes in 1 degree.
68. 200% of 34.
69. Two digit multiple of 3 with rotational symmetry.
70. Ten times the greater twin prime of five.
71. One less than twice the square of six.
72. $2^3 \cdot 3^2$.
73. f o g (4) if $f(x) = 4(x + 2) - 7$ and $g(x) = x^2 + 2$.
74. One cent less than $\frac{3}{4}$ of a dollar.
75. LCM of 15 and 25.

Mathematics, Styles, and Strategies
PAIRED LEARNER

Being in a math class where new concepts are taught almost everyday can be a stressful and scary experience for students. Math concepts and algorithms that are second nature to the teacher can be confusing to a student who experiences them for the very first time. Students experience even more difficulty if they have to learn alone, with minimal support from the teacher. So how can a caring teacher provide comforting support to twenty-five or more students? The Paired Learner Strategy enables teachers to design activities that encourage students to work in pairs so they can support each other in the learning process.

To implement the Paired Learner Strategy, students can be paired in a variety of ways. Three common ways of pairing students are as follows:

1. pairing a student of a higher level of understanding with a student of a lower level of understanding;

2. pairing students who have the same level of understanding; or

3. simply pairing students who sit next to each other.

When the Paired Learner Strategy is used as a short-term alternative or supplement to direct instruction, pairing students without regard to their levels of understanding can be quick, easy, and effective. Students in the Paired Learner Strategy can receive additional support when two adjacent learning pairs are united to form a cooperative support group. This added feature is important because, during an activity, if a learning pair encounters difficulty that is beyond their combined knowledge and understanding, they can request help from the other learning pair in the cooperative support group. When the Paired Learner Strategy is implemented, the math classroom becomes a more relaxed place where students can enjoy productive learning experiences.

Developing a Paired Learner Activity

A Paired Learner activity can be developed for a daily warm-up activity, homework check, skill reinforcement exercise, critical thinking activity, and/or a math assignment or project.

The Paired Learner Activity and the Daily Warm-up and Homework Check

To get students started off on the right foot, many teachers have a daily warm-up problem ready for students upon entering class. A simple way to implement the Paired Learner model is to encourage students to solve the warm-up problems with their learning partner. When it comes to checking homework, paired learners can confirm correct solutions with each other and work to correct improper solutions when differences in answers occur.

The Paired Learner Strategy and Skill Reinforcement Exercises

When direct instruction and new learning take place in class, students can greatly benefit from immediate Paired Learner reinforcement activities. The teacher can easily engage paired learners by providing one to three math examples for students and asking them to solve them with their partners and check their solutions with another learning pair. The teacher can also ask students to create their own examples and answer key, so that their learning partners can solve their problems. When students finish working on their partner's problems, they can return their problems and solutions to each other and check their work using the pre-made keys. Expect enriching conversation to take place during this Paired Learner activity.

The Paired Learner Strategy and P3CR

Perhaps the best way to implement the Paired Learner Strategy and promote learning and understanding is to develop printed problem-solving, collaboration, communication, connections, and reasoning (P3CR) activities for students. P3CR activities include one to three problems that tie directly to the content and require students to think critically. When solving a P3CR activity, students work in class with their learning partner and receive a grade for correct solutions. Since the emphasis is on learning and understanding, the P3CR activity grade should emphasize participation. For the sample P3CR activity shown on the right, students might receive 70 points for participation and 10 points for each correct solution. At the end of the grading period, the average of the P3CR grades for each student might carry the weight of one major test grade. With this kind of fair grading leverage and support from a learning partner, students will be motivated to participate and learn for understanding.

Algebra II: P3CR #1

Directions: Work with a learning partner and solve the following problems.

1. Find the inverse function of $f(x) = 2 + x^2$, if $x \geq 0$.

2. Find an equation for f(x) if the graph of f(x) is shown to the right. Use your calculator to verify.

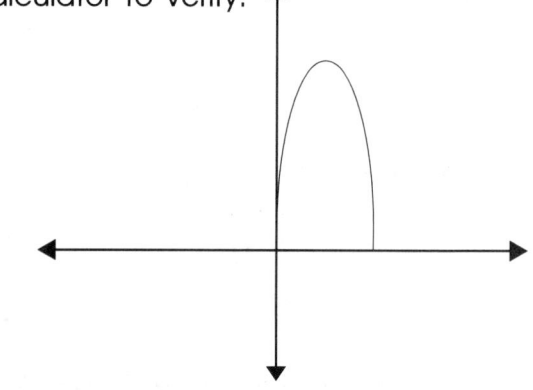

3. Explain why some functions do not have an inverse.

Paired Learners: Obtaining Desired Student Behaviors

When developing a Paired Learner activity, the teacher should consider how two students might work together and learn from each other. Will they be asked to make problems for each other, check each other's solutions, or plan and think together as they solve non-routine problems? The teacher should consider the proficiency of the students and the nature of the subject matter when designing the activity. For example, students who only have an introductory knowledge of a particular concept might not be able to make new problems for their partner. Instead, the Paired Learner activity might only consist of problems similar to examples worked recently by the teacher. To be effective, the purpose and objective of the activity should be well defined and support the objectives of the curriculum. The activity should contain clear and specific instructions for the students. When the Paired Learner Model is used as part of the daily routine, the expectations, time limit, and method of evaluation must be communicated to students on a regular basis. When a higher-level thinking activity is used, the task must be reasonable in difficulty, so students can successfully achieve the objectives of the activity.

Student Activity

PAIRED LEARNER
Featured math concept: **Constructing a Probability Model**

Student Name: _____

Directions:
Work with a learning partner. Open one pack of your favorite colored candies. Count the number of candies for each color represented in the pack. Record your data in the table below. Repeat the experiment for a second pack of the same kind of colored candies.

Colors	# pack one	# pack two	Average
Red			
Green			
Brown			
Yellow			
Orange			
Blue			
Total			

Create a bar graph that is representative of the average distribution of the colors in the two packs of candies. The colors of the bars should correspond to the colors of the candies.

```
15 |
   |
10 |
   |
 5 |
   |_____
   Red   Green   Brown   Yellow   Orange   Blue
```

Using your data, approximate the probability of selecting a candy of each color if the candy is randomly drawn from a typical pack. Use the formula:

$$p(\text{color}) = \frac{\text{average \# of candies of that color}}{\text{average \# of candies in one pack}}$$

PAIRED LEARNER
Featured math concept: **Introducing Functions**

Student Name: _____

Functions, Ordered Pairs, Equations, and Graphs

In many cases, a function can be defined as a rule. Define a function f as the rule "add four." As illustrated by the function diagram below, f was applied to the numbers in the oval on the left. Each outcome number was written in the oval to the right and geometrically connected with its initial value.

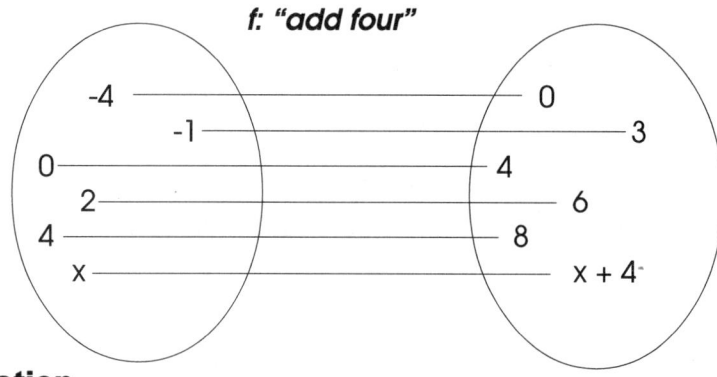

f: "add four"

```
   -4 ─────────────── 0
      -1 ──────────── 3
  0 ──────────────── 4
      2 ───────────── 6
  4 ──────────────── 8
      x ───────────── x + 4
```

Function Notation

The idea of applying the rule f to -4 and obtaining 0 can be expressed by writing $f(-4) = 0$. Similarly, $f(-1) = 3$, $f(0) = 4$, $f(2) = 6$, $f(4) = 8$, and $f(x) = x + 4$. This is called function notation.

Ordered Pairs

In the example above, line segments were used to connect each initial number with its outcome number. Another way to express the relationship between the initial numbers and outcome numbers for the rule f is to write the numbers as ordered pairs as follows:

(-4, 0), (-1, 3), (0, 4), (2, 6), (4, 8), and (x, x + 4)

Cont. →

PAIRED LEARNER: *Introducing Functions cont. ...*

Graphing a Function
The ordered pairs of a function f can be displayed geometrically as a graph on a rectangular coordinate plane. The ordered pairs of a function f from the previous page were (-4, 0), (-1, 3), (0, 4), (2, 6), (4, 8), and (x, x + 4). Notice that these points have been plotted on the x, f(x) plane below. Notice that these points lie in a straight line. This particular function is called a linear function.

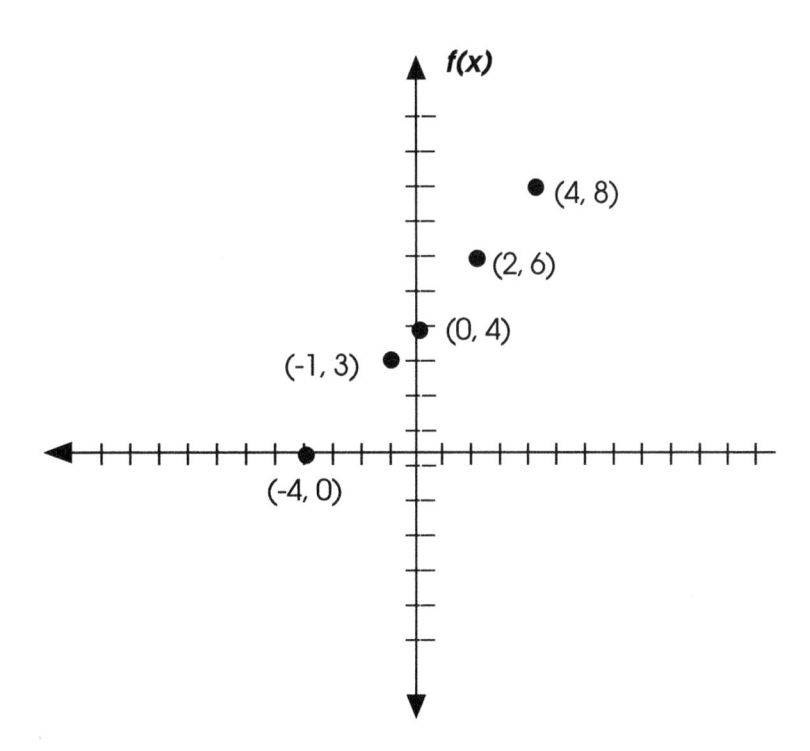

Understanding the Formal Definition of a Function
A function is a rule that can be applied to the numbers in a set of initial numbers (domain) and result in a set of outcome numbers (range). The rule must guarantee *one and only one* range number for each domain number.

The rule "add four" is a function because whatever number x we choose, we know there is going to be *one and only one* answer to the problem x + 4.

Work with a learning partner and complete the function activity on the next page.

PAIRED LEARNER: Introducing Functions cont. ...

Problem 1
a. Let the function g be defined by the rule "square and add 2." Apply the rule g to the domain numbers in the domain oval. Write the range numbers in the outcome oval. Connect the corresponding domain and range numbers using line segments.

b. Write each pair of corresponding domain and range values using ordered pair notation. Write each pair of corresponding domain and range values using function notation.

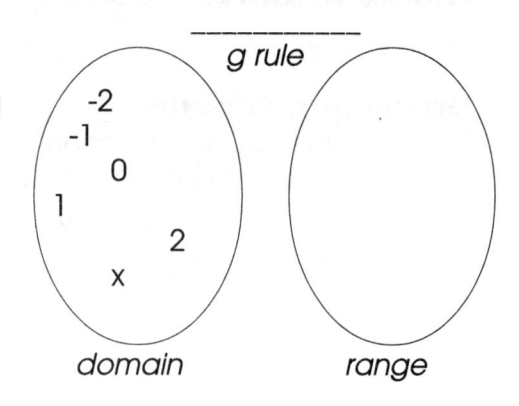

c. Plot each ordered pair on the coordinate plane shown to the right.

Problem 2
Three function diagrams are shown below. In this problem, the domain numbers and corresponding range numbers are given. Work with your learning partner and find the rule for each function diagram.

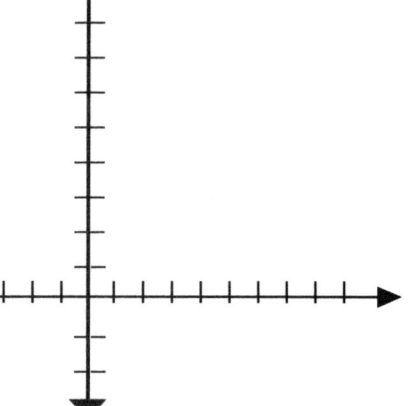

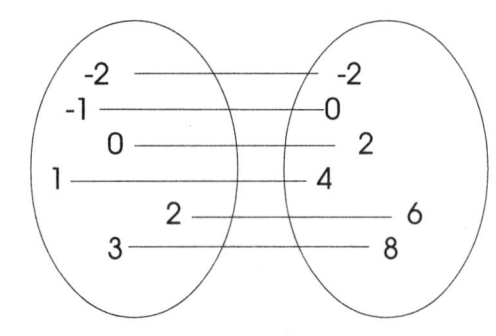

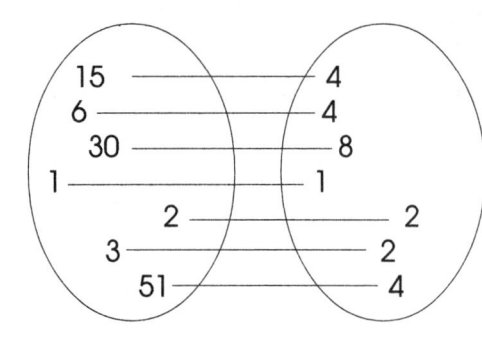

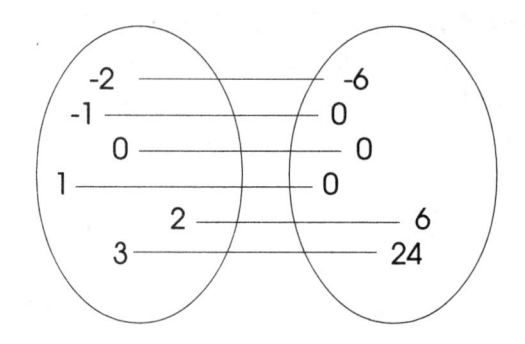

Problem 3
Create a function diagram for your learning partner. Swap diagrams with your partner. Guess your partner's rule. When you finish, swap back and work together to evaluate your results.

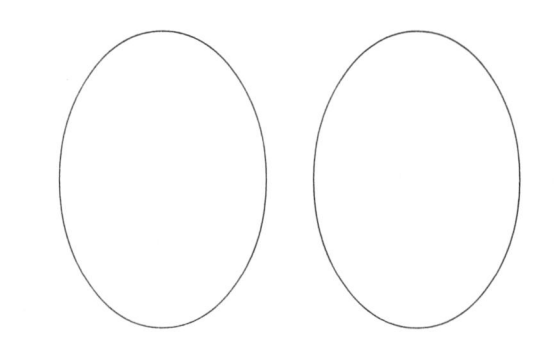

Mathematics, Styles, and Strategies
RECIPROCAL LEARNING

In the world of sports, players and participants depend on their coaches to watch their performance, make suggestions for improvement, and spark motivation in the learning process. Players learn to count on their coach to provide discipline, support, and encouragement. The role of the coach is integral to the practice and training routines that eventually lead players toward the mastery of an athletic skill or event.

The power of the coach and player relationship can also be captured with the Reciprocal Learning Strategy. In a Reciprocal Learning activity, students work collaboratively in pairs. One student plays the role of the coach and the other student plays the role of the player. Through modeling, the teacher helps students understand the roles of the coach and player, and provides math challenges with instructions and notes for the coach. During the challenge, the coach carefully watches the problem-solving steps of the player and provides reinforcing and helpful clues to the player throughout the process. The player is more inclined to participate in the math challenge knowing that support and help from the coach is part of the learning package. And by playing roles as both coach and player, students internalize math procedures as they simultaneously develop effective interpersonal skills.

Developing a Reciprocal Learning Activity
While there is no perfect way of developing a Reciprocal Learning activity, the steps which follow describe a simple way to construct a coach and player math activity.

Developing an Activity
Before beginning the strategy, the teacher should plan to provide students with an opportunity to share relevant experiences with their learning partners as an icebreaker and to create comfortable relationships. For example, if the focus is on students becoming proficient in rounding numbers, the teacher might invite students to discuss personal experiences when an answer derived with a calculator was too long to report. The teacher should ask students to share their experiences with rounding numbers.

Explaining and Assigning the Roles of Coach and Player
To ensure success in the Reciprocal Learning activity, the teacher should ask students if they have ever worked with a coach, and to share their experiences. The students' shared experiences can be used to explain the roles of the coach and player in the upcoming learning activity. The teacher should explain that the members of each learning pair will take turns playing the role of player and coach.

Developing the Coach's Dialogue and Notes
A page of problem-solving instructions, questions, and notes should be provided to the coach. The coach will read the instructions to the player and ask thought-provoking questions throughout the activity. As the coach observes the work of the player, the coach can refer to the coach's notes to be sure that the player is on the right track. This will ensure that proper and correct thinking skills are developed by the player. A sample set of coach's instructions, questions, and notes for rounding numbers is shown on the next page.

Problem: Round the number 7268 to the nearest thousand.

Coach's Guidelines for Helping Player:

- Write the problem on clean paper.

- What does the problem ask you to do?

- What digit is in the thousands place? Underline it.

- What do you think is the next step?

- Find the digit to the right of the 7. What is it?

- Tell me what you should do with this number.

- Is the number 2 greater than or equal to 5?

- Then what should you do?

- The problem is complete. Summarize the steps for rounding.

Coach's Notes:

- Round 7,268 to the nearest thousand.

- The digit in the thousands place is 7.

- Check the digit to the right of the 7. If the digit is 5 or higher, round the 7 up to 8. If the digit to the right of 7 is less than 5, do not adjust the number 7.

- The digit to the right of 7 is 2. Since 2<5, the digit in the thousands place will remain the same.

- Answer: 7,000

Implementing the Strategy and Summarizing the Learning Experience

Be sure to provide time for each member of each learning pair to play the role of coach and player. During the activity, the teacher should provide guidance and assistance to coaches and players as needed. To reinforce the process on rounding numbers, guided practice or homework should be provided by the teacher.

Student Activity	**RECIPROCAL LEARNING**
	Featured math concept: **Optimized Problems in Advanced Math and Calculus**
	Student Name: _____

Directions:
Students often cite word problems as a part of mathematics that give them trouble. Talk with your learning partner about your past experiences with word problems in math. Do you like them? What kind of success or difficulty have you had with them?

This learning activity will help you become a better problem-solver in math. You and your learning partner will take turns coaching each other through the problem-solving process. The learning activity will have two stages.

Stage 1
In Stage 1, Student A will play the role of the coach and Student B will be the player. The player will copy Problem 1 on clean paper and follow the directions of the coach. The coach should use the coach's notes to provide guidelines and hints for solving the problem, but should not provide the answer.

Stage 2
In Stage 2, Student B will play the coach and Student A will be the player. In this stage, the player will copy Problem 2 on clean paper and follow the directions of the coach. The coach should use the coach's notes to provide guidelines and hints for solving the problem, but should not provide the answer.

Problem 1
A cedar box is to be constructed in the shape of a rectangular solid so the height of the box is 1.5 feet and the volume of the box is 11.25 cubic feet. If the cost of the wood for the top/bottom and sides is $1.25 per square foot and $1.00 per square foot respectively, find the dimensions of the box that minimize the cost.

Problem 2
A cedar box is to be constructed in the shape of a rectangular solid so the length of the box is 5 feet and the volume of the box is 20 cubic feet. If the cost of the wood for the top/bottom and sides is $1.25 per square foot and $1.00 per square foot respectively, find the dimensions of the box that minimize the cost.

RECIPROCAL LEARNING

Coach's Role and **Coach's Notes**

Problem 1 & Coach's Notes

Coach's guidelines for helping player:

- Read the problem.

- What is given in the problem?

- What does the problem ask you to find?

- Draw and label all sides of the geometric figure referred to in the problem. Use the variables x and y for the unknown dimensions.

- Since the costs are written per square foot and the volume is given, what rectangular solid formulas will you need to solve this problem?

- Substitute the variables and values into the formulas.

- How can the surface area formula be written as a cost formula? How can the cost formula be written in one variable? (Hint: Use information from the volume formula.)

- Use the derivative to find the value that minimizes the cost.

- How can you find the value of the other variable?

- Do your answers make sense?

- Summarize the problem and the steps you used to solve the problem.

A cedar box is to be constructed in the shape of a rectangular solid so the height of the box is 1.5 feet and the volume of the box is 11.25 cubic feet. If the cost of the wood for the top/bottom and sides is $1.25 per square foot and $1.00 per square foot respectively, find the dimensions of the box that minimize the cost.

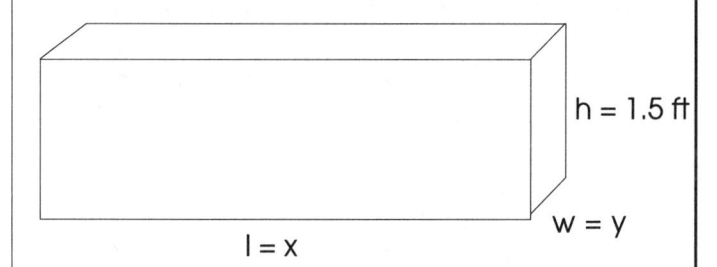

$l = x$, $w = y$, $h = 1.5$ ft

$V = lwh$ $SA = 2lw + 2hw + 2lh$
$11.25 = 1.5xy$ $SA = 2xy + 3y + 3x$

Cost = $1.25 (2xy) + $1(3y) + $1(3x)

Since xy = 11.25 / 1.5 and y = 11.25 / 1.5x
Cost = 1.25 (2)(7.5) + 1(3)(7.5/x) + 1(3x)

$C' = -22.5x^{-2} + 3$

Critical point of $C' = x = \sqrt{7.5} \approx 2.74$ ft.

The minimum cost occurs when $x \approx 2.74$ ft. and $y \approx 2.74$ ft.

Additional Problems
Repeat the problem above for:
1. v = 18 cubic feet, and w = 1 ft.
   Cost of wood: top/bottom: $2.00 per sq. ft.
                  sides: $1.50 per sq. ft.

2. v = 30 cubic feet, and h = 3 ft.
   Cost of wood: top/bottom: $4.00 per sq. ft.
                  sides: $1.50 per sq. ft.

3. v = 100 cubic feet, and l = 10 ft.
   Cost of wood: top/bottom: $2.00 per sq. ft.
                  sides: $1.50 per sq. ft.

RECIPROCAL LEARNING

Coach's Role and **Coach's Notes**

Problem 2 & Coach's Notes

Coach's guidelines for helping player:

- Read the problem.

- What is given in the problem?

- What does the problem ask you to find?

- Draw and label all sides of the geometric figure referred to in the problem. Use the variables x and y for the unknown dimensions.

- Since the costs are written per square foot and the volume is given, what rectangular solid formulas will you need to solve this problem?

- Substitute the variables and values into the formulas.

- How can the surface area formula be written as a cost formula? How can the cost formula be written in one variable? (Hint: Use information from the volume formula.)

- Use the derivative to find the value that minimizes the cost.

- How can you find the value of the other variable?

- Do your answers make sense?

- Summarize the problem and the steps you used to solve the problem.

A cedar box is to be constructed in the shape of a rectangular solid so the length of the box is 5 feet and the volume of the box is 20 cubic feet. If the cost of the wood for the top/bottom and sides is $1.25 per square foot and $1.00 per square foot respectively, find the dimensions of the box that minimize the cost.

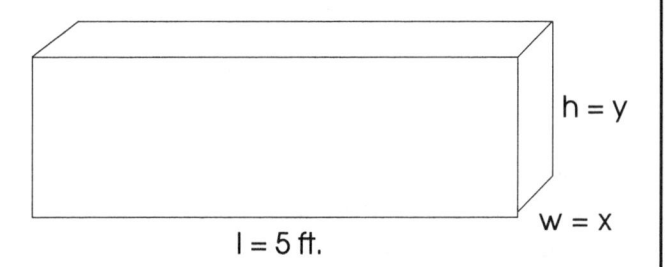

h = y
w = x
l = 5 ft.

V = lwh   SA = 2lw + 2hw + 2lh
20 = 5xy   SA = 10x + 2xy + 10y

Cost = $1.25 (10x) + $1(2xy) + $1(10y)

Since xy = 20 / 5 and y = 20 / (5x)
Cost = 1.25 (10x) + 1(2)(20) + 1(10)(4/x)

C' = 12.5 + 0 − 40x^{-2}

Critical point of C' = x = $\sqrt{3.2}$ ≈ 1.79 ft.
The minimum cost occurs when x ≈ 1.79 ft. and y ≈ 2.24 ft.

Additional Problems
Repeat the problem above for:

1. v = 10 cubic feet, and w = .5 ft.
   Cost of wood: top/bottom: $2.00 per sq. ft.
                 sides: $1.50 per sq. ft.

2. v = 40 cubic feet, and h = 4 ft.
   Cost of wood: top/bottom: $4.00 per sq. ft.
                 sides: $1.50 per sq. ft.

3. v = 200 cubic feet, and l = 10 ft.
   Cost of wood: top/bottom: $2.00 per sq. ft.
                 sides: $1.50 per sq. ft.

Student Activity

RECIPROCAL LEARNING
Featured math concept: **Optimized Problems in Advanced Math and Calculations**

Student Name: _____

Directions:
Students often cite word problems as a part of mathematics that gives them trouble. Talk with your learning partner about your past experiences with word problems in math. Do you like them? What kind of success or difficulty have you had with them?

This learning activity will help you become a better problem-solver in math. You and your learning partner will take turns *coaching each other* through the problem-solving process. The learning activity will have two stages.

Stage 1
In Stage 1, Student A will play the role of the coach and Student B will be the player. The player will copy Problem 1 on clean paper and follow the directions of the coach. The coach should use the coach's notes to provide guidelines and hints for solving the problem, but should not provide the answer.

Stage 2
In Stage 2, Student B will play the coach and Student A will be the player. In this stage, the player will copy Problem 2 on clean paper and follow the directions of the coach. The coach should use the coach's notes to provide guidelines and hints for solving the problem, but should not provide the answer.

Problem 1
The width of a rectangular solid is 10 inches.

The length is 5 inches more than the width and the height is 5 inches less than the width.

Find the surface area of the solid.

Problem 2
The length of a rectangular solid is 20 inches.

The width is 15 inches less than the length and the height has the same measure as the width.

Find the surface area of the solid.

RECIPROCAL LEARNING

Problem 1 & Coach's Notes

The width of a rectangular solid is 10 inches. The length is 5 inches more than the width and the height is 5 inches less than the width. Find the surface area of the solid.

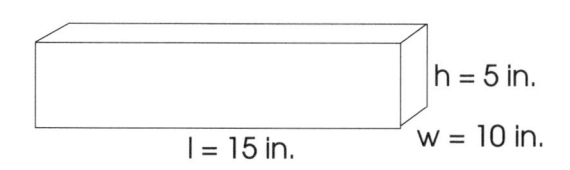

SA = 2lw + 2hw + 2lh
SA = 2(15)(10) + 2(5)(10) + 2(15)(5)
SA = 300 + 100 + 150
SA = 550 sq. in.

Additional Problems
Find the surface area of a rectangular solid if:
1. l = 12 cm., w = 5 cm., and h = 6 cm.
2. l = 10 in., w = 4 in., and h = 4 in.
3. l = 20 ft., w = 4 ft., and h = 4 ft.

h = 5 in.
l = 15 in.
w = 10 in.

Problem 2 & Coach's Notes

The length of a rectangular solid is 20 inches. The width is 15 inches less than the length and the height is the same as the width. Find the surface area of the solid.

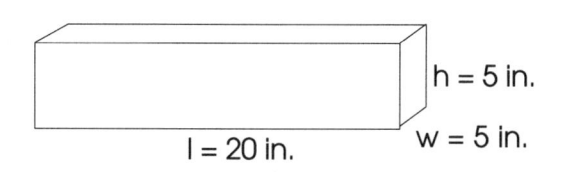

SA = 2lw + 2hw + 2lh
SA = 2(20)(5) + 2(5)(5) + 2(20)(5)
SA = 200 + 50 + 200
SA = 450 sq. in.

Additional Problems
Repeat the problem above for:
1. l = 14 cm., w = 6 cm., and h = 4 cm.
2. l = 24 in., w = 12 in., and h = 6 in.
3. l = 20 ft., w = 4 ft., and h = 2 ft.

h = 5 in.
l = 20 in.
w = 5 in.

SELF-EXPRESSIVE STRATEGIES

Inductive Learning
Divergent Thinking
Etch-a-Sketch
Metaphorical Expression
Modeling and Experimentation

Mathematics, Styles, and Strategies
INDUCTIVE LEARNING

Too often in mathematics classrooms, students learn formulas, problem-solving processes, and terms without a clear understanding of the big picture or the conceptual categories into which all these procedures and definitions fit. Without this all-important big picture, mathematics can seem to students like a hodgepodge of isolated facts with no conceptual "glue" to connect various ideas and hold their learning together. Instead, each topic becomes a new set of formulas to memorize instead of a twist that challenges or a layer that adds to their growing understanding of key mathematical concepts.

No strategy helps students to see the big picture in what they are learning better than Inductive Learning. The model for this strategy comes from the influential work of Hilda Taba (1971), who discovered that students' abilities to see big ideas and make generalizations could be greatly improved through a three-part process:

First, students examine key terms related to a particular topic or text;

Second, students organize these terms into meaningful groups and develop a simple label for each group that explains what the terms have in common; and

Third, students make predictions about the topic which they monitor and revise as they acquire relevant information.

In the secondary mathematics classroom, Inductive Learning lessons can be of three types:

1. **Term-Based Inductive Learning** containing the critical terms and definitions in a unit of study;

2. **Thinking-Based Inductive Learning** focused on "thinking words" or words related to the thinking processes that the students will use in the discipline or unit;

3. **Expression-Based Inductive Learning,** which asks students to examine, group, and label actual mathematical expressions that demonstrate key ideas.

An example of a thinking-based lesson appears on the following page. A ready-to-use expression-based example (focused on different types of polynomials) appears after the textual introduction to this strategy.

An Example of a Thinking-Based Inductive Learning Lesson

During the first week of Algebra 1, Amira Rosnan presents this list of words to her students:

abstract	double	guess	ratio
accelerate	effort	halve	reduce
addition	elaborate	increase	remit
amplify	equal	join	separate
amount	estimate	least	shape
apportion	extend	lose	share
attach	factor	loss	show
balance	figure out	mix	simplify
change	find	more	solve
chart	formulate	multiple	step
convert	further	odds	sum
decrease	grade	part of	total
deduct	gradual	product	trace
deposit	graph	propel	transform
difference	greatest	propagate	triple
diminish	gross	quadruple	value
divide	group	quantity	withdraw
			work

Amira wants her students to see the different kinds of mathematical categories that these words fit under and to see that math is not so daunting; in fact, it's made up of only a few related thinking processes. So, she begins by having students examine the words, review new words, and start to put common words together under descriptive headings. For example:

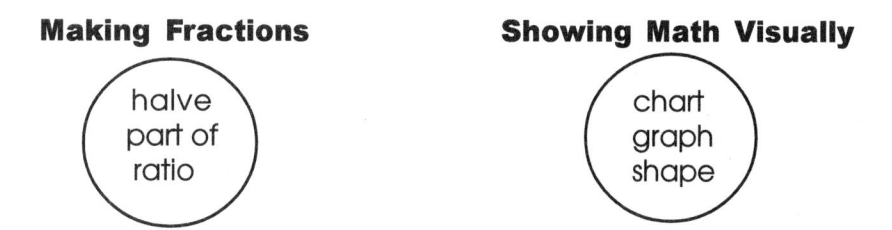

Making Fractions

(halve
part of
ratio)

Showing Math Visually

(chart
graph
shape)

After students have formed their groups, Amira works with them to develop a few generalizations about thinking algebraically. Generalizations range from the general (*Algebra requires figuring out what kind of thinking you need to use before you solve a problem*) to the specific (*In algebra you need to be able to show mathematical ideas in visual formats like graphs and charts*).

Over the course of the year, as students' exposure to new kinds of problems increases, Amira and the students revise their generalizations and expand their groups by adding words to old groups and creating new groups to accommodate new understanding. Throughout the process, Amira reminds her students to be flexible in their thinking; students are encouraged to "play" with the groupings, to feel free to put the same terms in different groups, and to look for ways to merge and combine small groups into larger ones.

Developing an Inductive Learning Lesson

To develop an Inductive Learning lesson, follow these seven steps:

Step 1
Identify from the text or unit key terms or sets of mathematical expression that demonstrate key concepts. Try to mix the familiar with the unfamiliar.

Step 2
Model the group-and-label process.

Step 3
Break students up into small groups and ask them to review the terms or expressions and then organize them into meaningful groups.

Step 4
Instruct students to create a simple label for each group that explains what the words or expressions in the group have in common. *Remember: Words and terms can go in more than one group.*

Step 5
Work with students to use their groups to make two or three generalizations about the topic.

Step 6
Ask students to collect information over the course of the lesson or unit that supports or refutes their generalizations.

Step 7
Build in time for reflection, self-assessment, and practice so students learn how to group and label on their own.

Inductive Learning: Observable Student Behaviors

When running an Inductive Learning lesson, you should help students pay attention to their overt operations as well as their covert thinking processes. This is best done through the use of focusing questions.

Overt Behavioral Objectives	Covert Behavioral Objectives	Focusing Questions (General)
Examining	Review information; recall items from prior knowledge	What do you see? hear? read? What did you notice?
Grouping data	Notice relationships; search for common attributes	Which of these do you think belong together? Why do you think A, B, and C go together?
Labeling groups	Synthesize common characteristics; generate word or phrase; compare, evaluate for appropriateness	What would be a good name for this group? Why do you think _____ would be an appropriate label?
Subsuming items under other labels; labels under more inclusive labels	Notice hierarchies and relationships not noted before; name or label the hierarchies or relationships	Which of these items now under one label would also belong under another label? Why do you think _____ belongs under _____ ?
Suggesting different ways of grouping, labeling, and subsuming items based on other relationships	Actively search for and explore new ways of organizing	Which of the items belong together for entirely different reasons? Why do you think _____, _____, and _____ belong together? Are there any possibilities we haven't explored?

Note to teacher: *The sample lesson that follows is designed to help students start to discover the different patterns for factoring polynomials. Each polynomial expression in the activity falls into one of four patterns.*

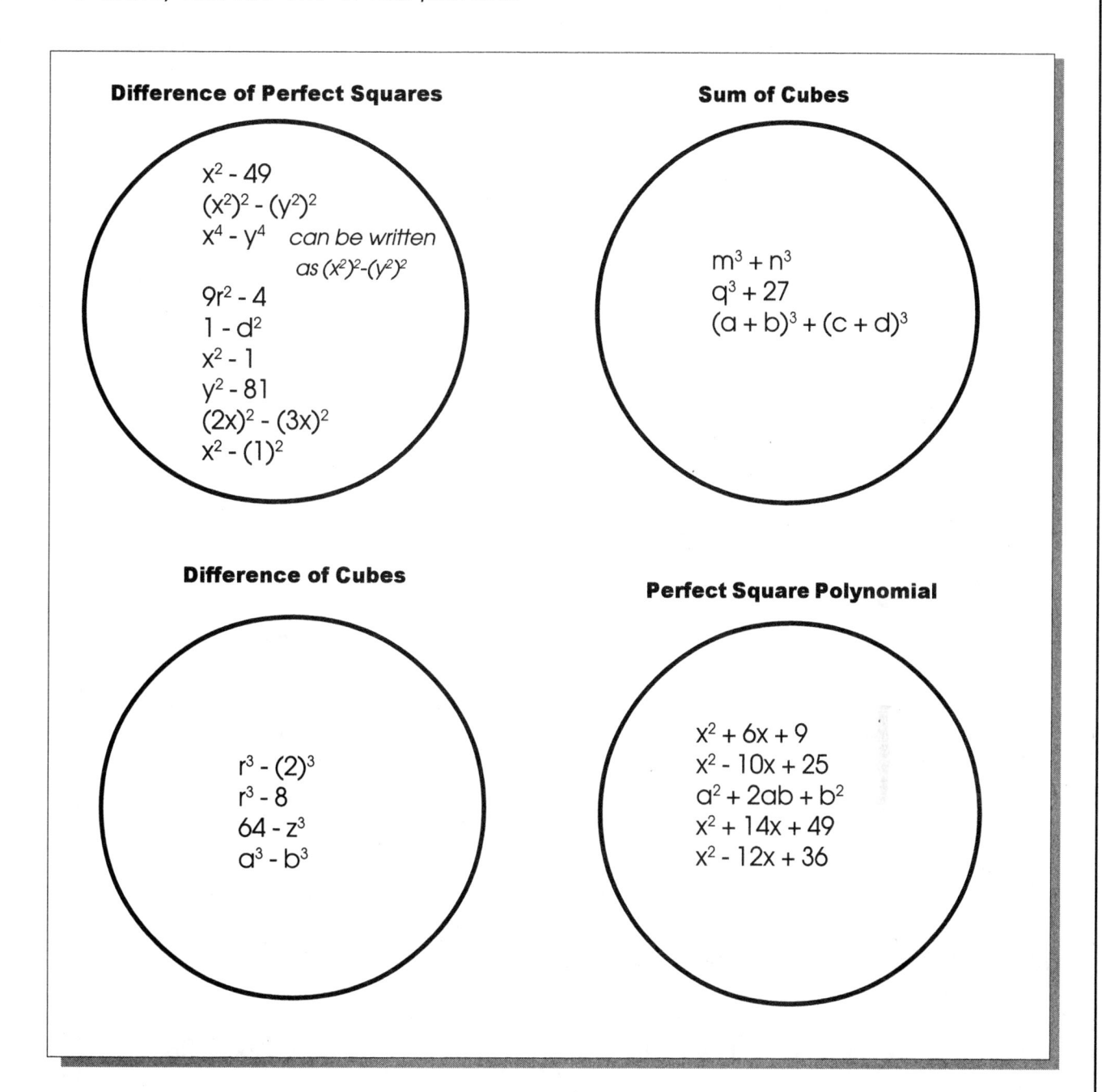

Difference of Perfect Squares

$x^2 - 49$
$(x^2)^2 - (y^2)^2$
$x^4 - y^4$ can be written as $(x^2)^2-(y^2)^2$
$9r^2 - 4$
$1 - d^2$
$x^2 - 1$
$y^2 - 81$
$(2x)^2 - (3x)^2$
$x^2 - (1)^2$

Sum of Cubes

$m^3 + n^3$
$q^3 + 27$
$(a + b)^3 + (c + d)^3$

Difference of Cubes

$r^3 - (2)^3$
$r^3 - 8$
$64 - z^3$
$a^3 - b^3$

Perfect Square Polynomial

$x^2 + 6x + 9$
$x^2 - 10x + 25$
$a^2 + 2ab + b^2$
$x^2 + 14x + 49$
$x^2 - 12x + 36$

Of course, students may well group their data in other ways, and their labels will likely be far less technical. It is suggested that several students be asked to read their groups. Make no quality judgments at this time. Instead, compare and contrast the groupings. As you move deeper into the unit on polynomials, students will revise their groups (as well as their generalizations) in light of new learning. Thus, students are actively engaged in constructing the big picture, which is far more conducive to deep understanding than simply asking them to memorize new information.

INDUCTIVE LEARNING

Student Activity

Featured math concept: **Introduction to Factoring Polynomials**

Student Name: _____

Directions:

Examine the expressions scattered over the page below. On the following page, write the expressions that seem similar to each other (or related in some way) into a circle. Then, stop and look at the circle. What do all of the items in the circle have in common? Use what they have in common to give the circle a "title." Place the title in the box under the circle.

Continue to place the expressions in the circles. You may use expressions more than once. Try to be creative. Don't simply find the most obvious similarities. Discover as many as you can. Create another page of circles if you run out of space on the given page.

$9r^2 - 4$

$x^2 + 6x + 9$

$x^2 - 49$

$r^3 - (2)^3$

$m^3 + n^3$

$1 - d^2$

$x^2 - 1$

$r^3 - 8$

$y^2 - 81$

$(a + b)^3 + (c + d)^3$

$q^3 + 27$

$x^4 - y^4$

$x^2 - (1)^2$

$(x^2)^2 - (y^2)^2$

$x^2 + 14x + 49$

$64 - z^3$

$x^2 - 12x + 36$

$x^2 - 10x + 25$

$(2x)^2 - (3x)^2$

$a^3 - b^3$

$a^2 + 2ab + b^2$

Page 128

INDUCTIVE LEARNING: *Introduction to Factoring Polynomials cont. ...*

Groups & Labels Organizer

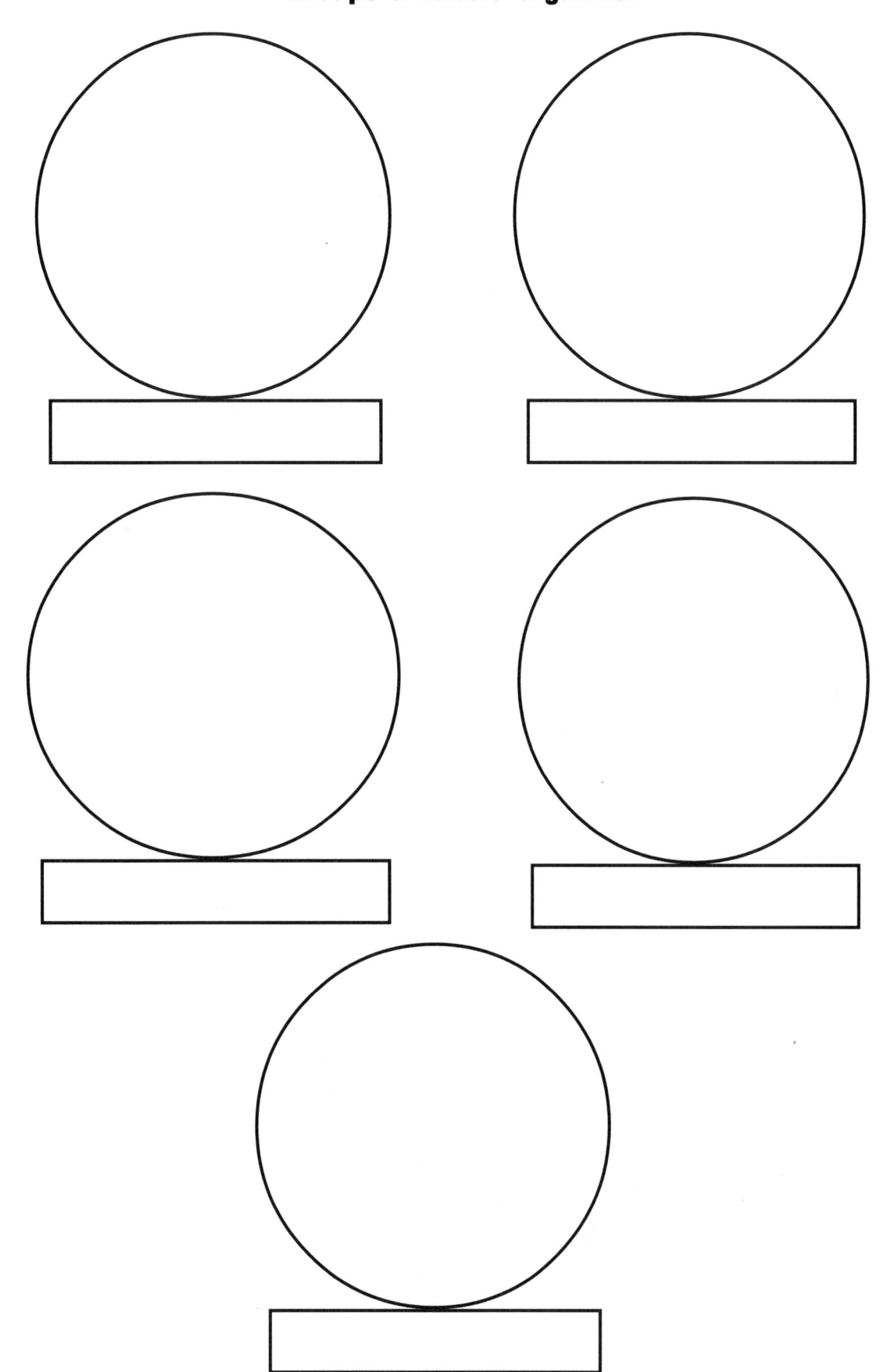

INDUCTIVE LEARNING: *Introduction to Factoring Polynomials cont. ...*

Generalization Organizer

Directions:
After you have developed your groups and labels, generate three or four generalizations. As you learn more about polynomials, collect evidence that supports or refutes each generalization in the appropriate column.

Evidence that Supports	Generalization	Evidence that Refutes

Mathematics, Styles, and Strategies
DIVERGENT THINKING

In too many cases, the mathematics classroom is a place where problems and questions have only one answer. The teacher has the answer and the students' job is to work to find out what that answer is. Day in and day out, teachers assign problems and only accept exact and predetermined answers in return. If a student's answer varies from the teacher's answer, the student is wrong. In this environment, many students build a dislike for mathematics. Mathematics should not be taught in a way that chokes out enthusiasm and differences in thinking. While there certainly is a place for exactness in mathematics, there is also a place in for creativity, imagination, and inventiveness. It is easy to forget that all the mathematics we teach was at one time new and inventive thinking. With this in mind, it is important to understand that the excitement associated with new mathematics and inventive thinking can be present in all students' math experiences since, at any given grade level, the mathematics they learn is new to them.

Through the Divergent Thinking Strategy, the spirit of creativity, imagination, and inventiveness can easily be incorporated in today's math classrooms. The essence of Divergent Thinking is diversity in thinking, problem solving, and solutions. How many different 3-digit numbers can be formed using the digits 7, 0, and 4? What might some of them be? Can you find the measures of a right triangle whose area equals 20 square units? How can the theorem "If a right triangle is isosceles, then the measure of either acute angle is 45 degrees" be proved? Through the Divergent Thinking Strategy, students can learn to appreciate and celebrate differences in thinking and creativity in mathematics.

Developing a Divergent Thinking Activity
Contrary to the belief of many, the field of mathematics lends itself extremely well to differences in thinking and creative expression. Developing a Divergent Thinking activity is as easy as asking your students to "find a way" rather than "telling them the way." For example, in the study of polygons and area, most students are taught to use the formula A = .5ap to find the area of a regular polygon. To implement a Divergent Thinking activity, the instructor might provide students with a regular polygon and simply ask them to work with a partner and develop their own plan for finding the area of the polygon. Through the Divergent Thinking activity, students will generate some interesting methods for finding the area of a regular polygon. The responses of students will serve as a powerful bridge between what students already know and the A = .5ap formula.

A Divergent Thinking activity can also be developed by breaking through the traditional walls of mathematics and inviting your students to explore the possibilities of math concepts in creative applications. Some examples include developing a lottery game based on prime numbers, creating a company logo using geometric figures, or writing a story about families of numbers. The possibilities are endless. The example that follows describes how a student might think through a Divergent Thinking activity that challenges students to create a design by applying transformations to the graph of $f(x) = \sin(x)$.

Divergent Thinking: A Sample of a Student's Thinking

Math student Callie begins by studying the graph of f(x) = sin(x), $0 \leq x \leq \pi$ and uses a graphing utility to verify the graph of the function. After viewing the graph of f(x) = sin(x), Callie decides to re-enter the function using a broader domain. She arbitrarily selects the domain (-12, 12) and, after seeing that more of the graph of f(x) = sin(x) is shown, she recognizes that the endpoints of the graph are not on the x-axis. As a result, Callie continues to experiment with the domain. Eventually, she discovers that (-12.56, 12.56) will allow the endpoints of the graph to lie on the x-axis.

Next, Callie decides that she would like to expand vertically the humps of the sin curve. She continues her exploration by entering f(x) = ksin(x) for various values of k. Trial and error lead Callie to try k = 3, which produces the graph of f(x) = 3sin(x). Callie then decides to reflect the graph across the x-axis since the graphs of f(x) = 3sin(x) and its reflection would make a nice design. After further creative investigations, Callie chooses to rotate the image 90 degrees. In an effort to maintain pattern consistency, she reflects that image across the y-axis. Callie now has an interesting design, but feels compelled to do a little more. So, she rotates the image an additional 45 degrees. Again, to maintain pattern consistency, Callie reflect the new image across the line y = x. She continues with similar procedures to obtain design balance in all four quadrants.

It is important to note the rigorous mathematical thinking involved in a Divergent Thinking activity. Some teachers might mistakenly think that a Divergent Thinking activity means *only* fun and games. The example above shows the contrary. During the development of the design, the student dealt with such content as function notation, function domains, graphs of functions, and transformations. The skills involved in creating the design included creative experimentation, analysis, synthesis, and evaluation of the decisions and resulting graphs.

The point is, through the Divergent Thinking Strategy, mathematics teachers can instill fun and creativity into powerful learning activities.

Student Activity

DIVERGENT THINKING
Featured math concept: **Creative Function Designs**

Student Name: _____

Directions:
Almost all the visual beauty of our world can be attributed to mathematical and geometric patterns found in both nature and man-made designs. Most of man's creations, nature's creatures, trees, and flowers are symmetrical and include a variety of geometric patterns in their designs. In this activity, you will use the graphs of functions to create your own innovative design.

Student Challenge
Use the TI-92 graphing calculator and the Cartesian or polar function plotter to create a visual design which features multiple graphs of real number or polar functions. Polar graph designs are pleasing to the eye and often include spirals, multiple petal roses, symmetric graphs, and repeated transformations. Be prepared to share your design with the class and explain its mathematical features.

Student Activity / **REPRODUCIBLE**

DIVERGENT THINKING
Featured math concepts: **Geometric Shapes and Creative Thinking**

Student Name: _____

Directions:
Use a computer program or paper, pencil, and a geometry template to design your own floor plan or exterior house design using geometric shapes. A complete floor plan should include a scale drawing of all identified rooms, room dimensions, doors, walk throughs, light fixtures, patios, and decks. A complete exterior house design should be drawn to scale and include doors, windows, shutters, roof, gables, cornice, and decorative details. A sample exterior house design and first-floor plan are shown below.

Sample Exterior

Sample Floor Plan

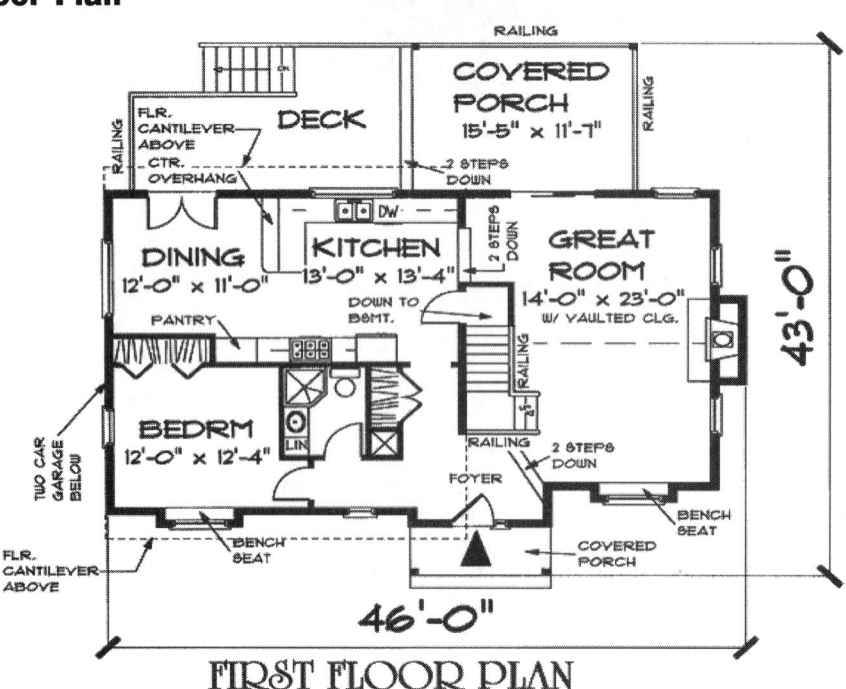

FIRST FLOOR PLAN

Page 134

DIVERGENT THINKING

Featured math concepts: **Reversibility and Computational Thinking**

Student Name: _____

Directions:
In mathematics, students are usually given a problem and asked to find the answer. Reversibility in thinking occurs when students are given an answer and asked to find a problem that produces that answer. Use reversibility in thinking to solve the following problems.

Problem 1

Let $a = \sqrt{2}$, $b = -4$, $c = \frac{3}{2}$, and $d = i$. Create an algebraic expression that includes a, b, c, and d, whose value is -20. Non-zero coefficients and exponents are allowed.

Problem 2

Create an equation of the form $y = a(x - h)^2 + k$ whose graph opens downward and is symmetric with respect to the line $x = 2$. Values for a, h, and k must not be equal to zero.

Problem 3

Find two complex numbers whose quotient is $4 + 2i$.

Problem 4

Find a quadratic equation whose solutions are $\frac{1}{2}$ and -4.

Problem 5

Find the dimensions of a square-base pyramid and sphere that have equal volumes.

Mathematics, Styles, and Strategies
ETCH-A-SKETCH

My grandmother always said, "If you want to remember something, write it down." While she had no formal training in education, she understood the important connection between writing and learning. The Etch-a-Sketch Strategy goes a step further by encouraging students to use their spatial intelligence to draw pictures or icons as the teacher speaks slowly. These icons represent their understanding of ideas communicated by the teacher. In order to draw the pictures, students must listen to the teacher carefully and interpret what they hear to form their own understanding. At the conclusion of the teacher's presentation, students share their drawings with their learning partners and try to guess what each other's symbols represent. After the students interact and discuss each other's ideas, the teacher leads a discussion of the ideas presented. After the discussion, the students complete a concept organizer activity. The Etch-a-Sketch Strategy can be used as an introduction to concepts or as a problem-solving tool that helps students visualize the problem situation.

Etch-a-Sketch (adapted from Siegel, 1984, and Brownlie, Close, & Wingren, 1990) takes advantage of students' natural inclination to create images during the learning process. Moreover, it helps them refine the skill so that it is focused on summarizing essential information. Working in conjunction with this nonlinguistic processing is the linguistic filtering of information as students discuss their images and convert them into the key ideas and details they contain.

Developing and Implementing an Etch-a-Sketch Activity
To develop and implement an Etch-a-Sketch activity, follow the steps on the next page.

Etch-a-Sketch for Problem Solving

1. Select a problem for students to solve.

2. Instruct your students to listen carefully as you slowly read the problem to them. As they listen, they should try to capture information relevant to the problem and determine what the problem is asking them to find. They should sketch pictures or icons that represent those details. Pause regularly so students have time to complete their sketches.

3. At the conclusion of the problem, ask all students to swap sketches with their learning partner. Each student should try to determine the meaning of his partner's sketches. Ask your students to share and discuss their interpretations of their partner's sketches.

4. After the time for sharing and discussing, ask your students to design a framework for solving the problem.

5. Lead your students in a class discussion of the information and ideas in the problem that you want your students to capture.

6. After the discussion, ask your students to solve the problem.

7. Conclude the activity by discussing students' solutions and reflecting on the problem-solving process.

Etch-a-Sketch for Learning and Understanding

1. Select or develop a passage that provides students with information you want them to know.

2. Instruct your students to listen carefully as you slowly read the passage to them. As they listen, they should try to capture the big ideas and sketch pictures or icons that represent those ideas. Pause regularly so students have time to complete their sketches.

3. At the conclusion of the passage, ask all students to swap sketches with their learning partner. Each student should try to determine the meaning of his partner's sketches. Ask your students to share and discuss their interpretations of their partner's sketches.

4. After the time for sharing and discussing, ask your students to record what they believe to be the main ideas and concepts.

5. Lead your students in a class discussion of the ideas that you intended them to capture.

6. After the discussion, ask your students to complete a concept activity.

7. Conclude the activity by discussing students' solutions and reflecting on the ideas and connections of the lesson.

Through the Etch-a-Sketch activity, students will develop a foundation of understanding that the teacher can build on with further instructional activities.

The example that follows provides a description of a sample problem for students to solve and a sample student sketch. More sample problems and passages can be found in the student activities that follow.

A Sample Etch-a-Sketch Activity

A Polygon Patio Problem

Dr. Albertson, who was a high school math teacher, had a friend Charles who worked in construction and home remodeling. One day Charles telephoned Dr. Albertson and asked him to help with the mathematical component of a construction project. Charles described the project as follows.

"The Jones family has a square patio in their backyard and wants me to build a treated-wood deck, in the shape of a regular hexagon, on top of the patio. The family wants two sides of the hexagonal deck to rest on two edges of the square patio and two vertex points to rest on the other two sides of the square. I need your help to determine the length of the edges of the hexagonal deck."

Dr. Albertson made some sketches and devised a problem-solving strategy. Work with your learning partner and do the same.

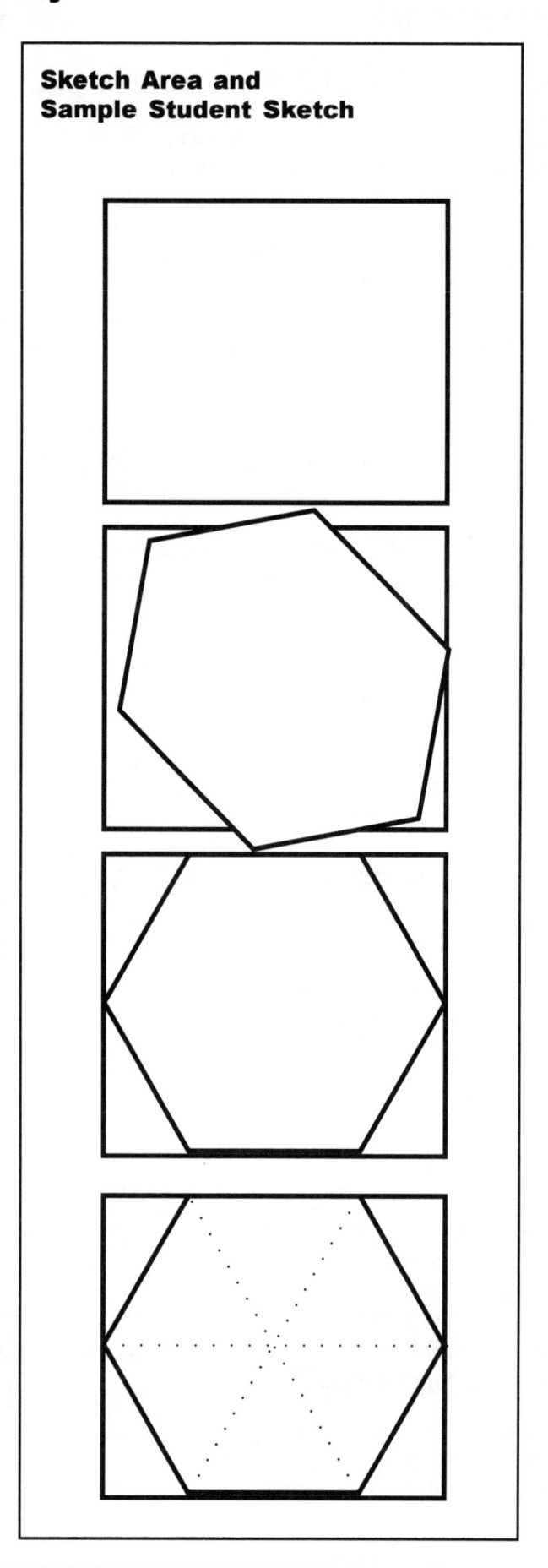

Sketch Area and Sample Student Sketch

ETCH-A-SKETCH

Student Activity

Featured math concepts: **Geometric Figures and Algebraic Representations**

Student Name: _____

Directions:

Read the following passage. During the reading, stop and draw sketches that remind you of the math concepts explained in the reading. Afterwards, share your sketches with your learning partner and explain how your sketches summarize your reading. Then, use your sketches to complete the concept organizer on the next page.

In geometry, a line is categorized as undefined, but characterized as being straight, infinite in opposite directions, and containing an infinite set of points. If a point is removed from a line, two half-lines remain. A half-line has no endpoint. If an endpoint is added to a half-line, it becomes a ray. Given any line and a point on the line, the set of points to one side of the point is called a half-line. Given any line and a point on the line, the set of points to one side of the point along with the point is called a ray. Given any line and two points on the line, the two points along with the points between the two points are called a line segment. A line segment has two endpoints.

The graph of $f(x) = mx + b$, for all real values of x, is a line. If $f(x) = mx + b$ is evaluated for $x \geq a$, for some arbitrary value 'a', the graph of $f(x)$ is a ray. If $f(x) = mx + b$ is evaluated for $x < a$, the graph of $f(x)$ is a half-line. If $f(x) = mx + b$ is evaluated for $a \leq x \leq b$, for two distinct arbitrary values 'a' and 'b', the graph of $f(x)$ is a line segment. If $f(x) = mx + b$ is evaluated for an arbitrary value $x = a$, the graph of $f(x)$ is a point. Virtually all sets of points in geometry can be represented by algebraic equations and inequalities.

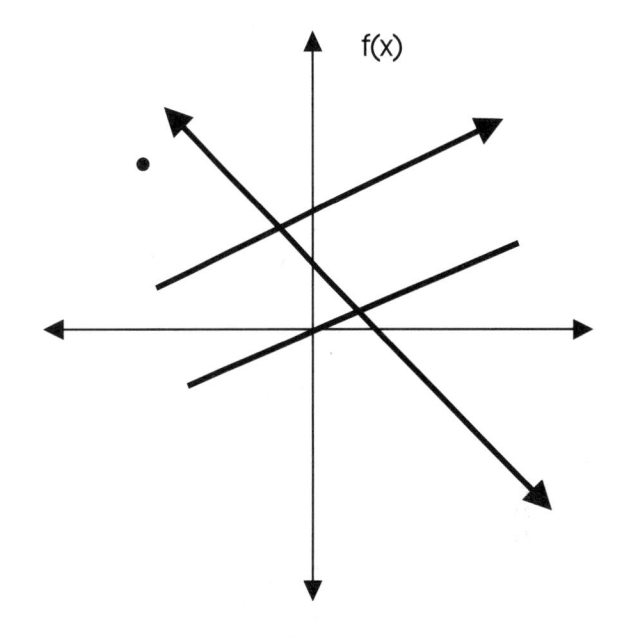

Sketch Area

Algebraic Representations of Geometric Figures

Draw line segments that connect the following names of figures with the matching equations and domain restrictions.

Ray	$\begin{cases} y = x, x \geq 4 \\ y = 2x - 4, x \geq 4 \end{cases}$
Point	$y = x - 4, x \leq 9$
Half-line	$y = .5x + 2, 1 \leq x \leq 6$
Line	$y = x + 6, x = 2$
Line Segment	$y = 2x + 5, x > 4$
Angle	$y = 2x + 1$, for all x

Which mathematical term describes the remaining parts of a line after an arbitrary point is removed from the line?
_____

Which mathematical term describes a point on a line and the set of points to one side of the given point?
_____

Find equations and domain restrictions for the figures shown below.

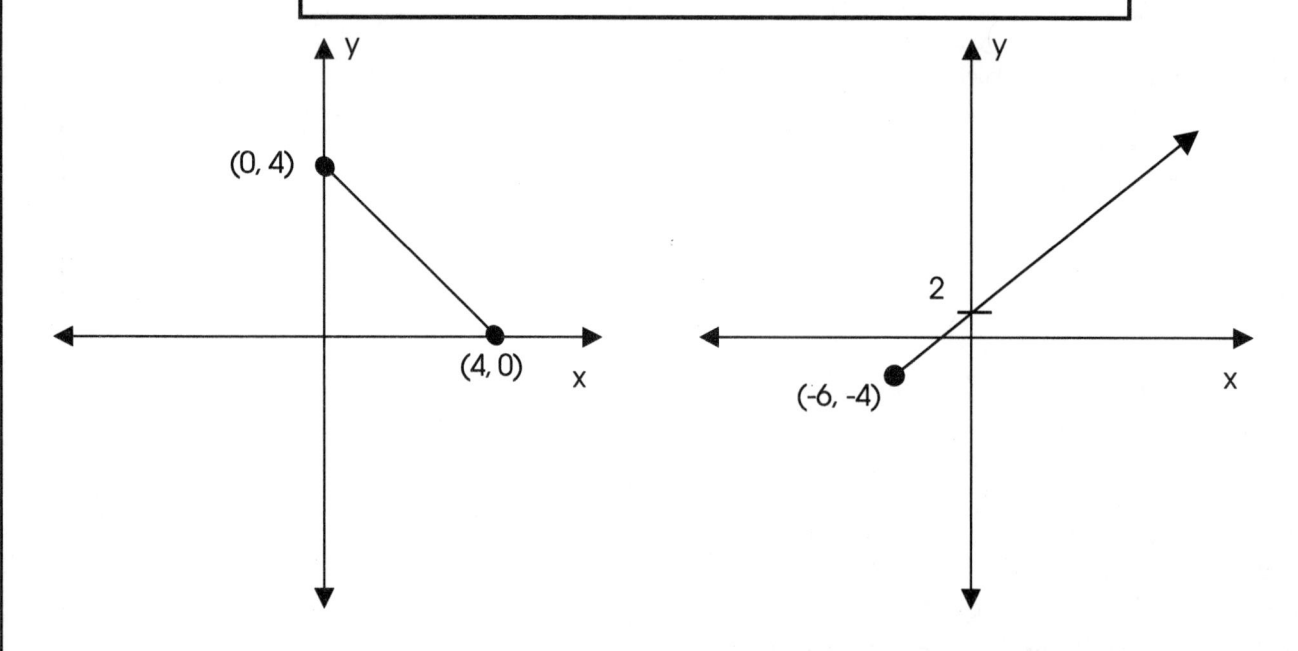

(0, 4)
(4, 0)

(-6, -4)
2

Explain the difference between a half-line and a ray.

Page 140

ETCH-A-SKETCH

Student Activity

Featured math concepts: **Algebra and a Nifty Card Trick**

Student Name: _____

Directions:
Read the following passage. During the reading, stop and draw sketches that remind you of the math concepts explained in the reading. Afterwards, share your sketches with your learning partner and explain how they summarize your reading. Use your sketches to help you solve the problem that follows.

Sketch Area

Andy likes to show his friends an interesting card trick. The trick involves making several stacks of cards, inviting an onlooker to choose any three stacks, and verifying an interesting mathematical relationship. Andy starts by dealing the first card from a shuffled deck of 52 poker cards and turning that card face up on the table. If the value of the card is less than 10, he counts and adds additional cards to that stack, face up, until he reaches the number 10. For example, if the first card Andy turns up is a 4, he adds 6 more cards to that stack as he counts 5, 6, 7, 8, 9, and 10.

The next card dealt starts a new stack. If a card starting a new stack has the value 10, no cards are added to that stack. The next card starts a new stack. Andy continues this process until no more completed stacks can be made. Andy asks a volunteer to choose any three of the completed stacks and turn them face down. Andy collects the rest of the cards and combines them with any cards that might have been left from the last incomplete stack. Andy shuffles the collected cards and deals out 19 cards face down. Then he generates a magic number by counting the number of cards left from the collected cards.

Andy reveals the magic number. "Why is that a magic number?" everyone asks. He asks the participant to turn up the top cards from the three turned-down stacks and add their values. Abracadabra! The sum of those three cards equals the magic number.

Use this information to solve the problem on the next page.

The Algebra Card Trick

This card trick described by your teacher must always work! This can be shown and proven using fundamental algebra concepts. Using your sketches and notes, work with a learning partner and follow the steps below to determine why this trick always works.

Step 1
Get a shuffled deck of playing cards and create the card stacks as described in your notes. Remember to turn three stacks over after all the stacks are made.

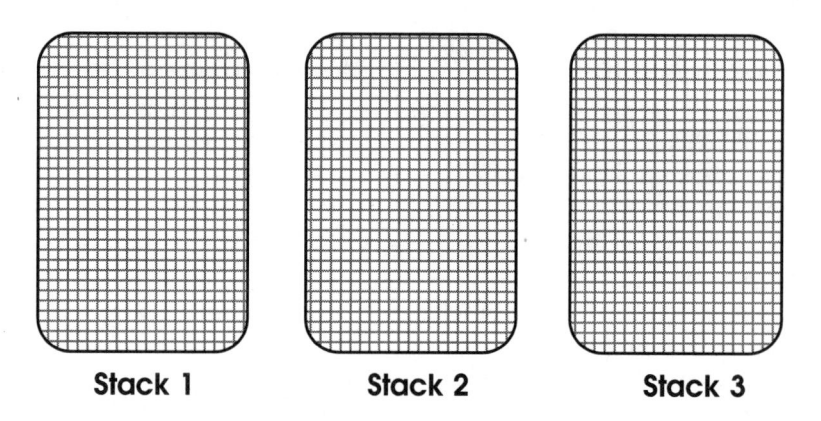

Stack 1   Stack 2   Stack 3

Step 2
Let n equal the value of the top card in any one of the three overturned stacks. (Before the stacks were turned over, n would have been the value of the card on the bottom of the stack.) Use the variable n and the number 11 to develop a simple formula that represents the number of cards in a stack with a top card with value n.

Step 3
Assign the variables n_1, n_2, and n_3 to the values of the top cards in stacks 1, 2, and 3. Use those variables and the formula from Step 2 to determine the number of cards in stacks 1, 2, and 3.

Step 4
Explain why the formula below represents the number of cards in the dealer's hands after all the cards, except those in Stack 1, 2, and 3, are collected by the dealer.

$52 - (11 - n_1) - (11 - n_2) - (11 - n_3)$

Step 5
Use the formula in Step 4 to explain why subtracting 19 cards from the remaining cards in the dealer's hands leaves the dealer with a number of cards equal to the sum of the values of the top cards in the stacks that were turned over.

Final number of cards in dealer's hands: $n_1 + n_2 + n_3$

Step 6
Perform the trick with a learning partner.

ETCH-A-SKETCH

Student Activity

Featured math concepts: **Geometric Figures and Algebraic Representations**

Student Name: _____

Directions:
Your teacher will read this passage to you. As it is read, use the sketch pad on the next page to draw sketches that correlate to the math concepts explained in the reading. Afterwards, share your sketches with your learning partner and explain how they summarize the reading. Then use your sketches to solve the geometry problems on the sketch page.

In the game of pool, the general object of the game is to drive the white cue ball into an object ball in a way that causes the object ball to roll into a pocket. A regulation size pool table is rectangular with length 9 feet and width 4.5 feet. A pool table has six pockets, four on the corners and two at the midpoints of the long sides.

In pool, a bank shot occurs when the cue ball drives the object ball into a cushioned rail and causes the ball to bounce (or bank) off the rail into a pocket. By the rules of geometry, a player who wants to bank a ball off a side rail and into a corner pocket can find the point of contact on the rail by using the following method.

1. Draw a perpendicular segment AB from the object ball to the rail you want to bank from. The point of intersection between the segment and the rail is Point B.

2. Draw segment BC from Point B on the rail to the center of the corner pocket you want the object ball to bank into.

3. Draw segment AD from the object ball to the center of the corner pocket adjacent to the pocket you want to bank into.

4. Draw a perpendicular line segment from the point of intersection of BC and AD to the rail you want to bank from. Call the point of intersection between this perpendicular segment and the rail point X. X marks the spot! This is the point you must bank into to pocket the object ball.

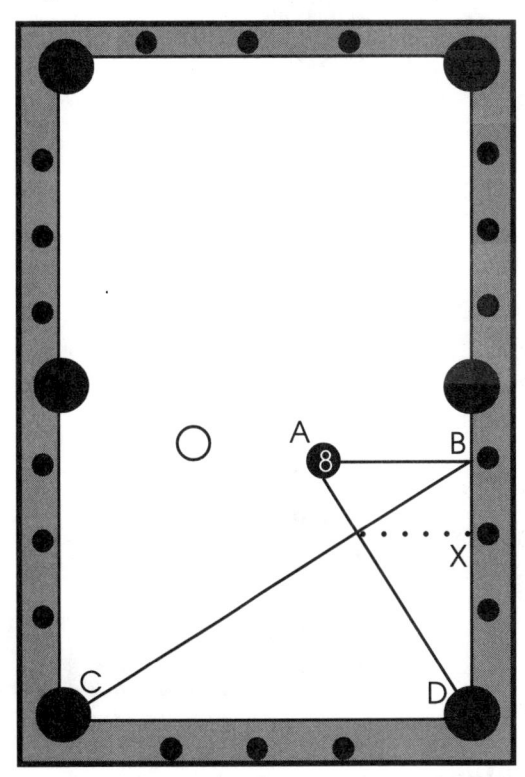

Student Problem
Work with a learning partner to compare sketches and determine the framework of a geometric argument or proof that will show that the path of the bank shot, angle AXC, will result in the object ball being pocketed in the corner pocket. To accomplish this, show that the angle AXB is congruent to angle CXD.

The Bank Shot Problem

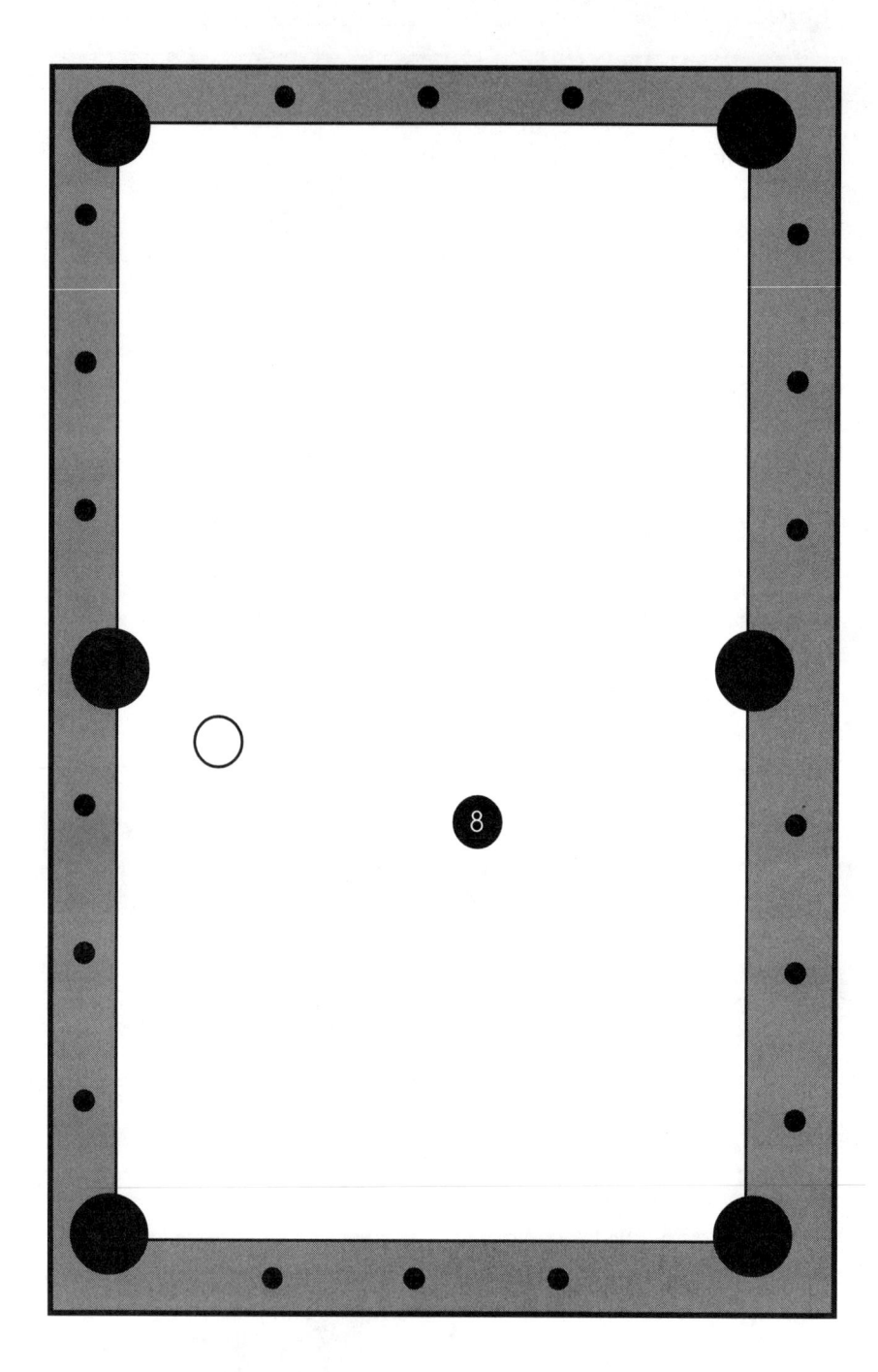

Problem 1
Use your Etch-a-Sketch notes to sketch the line segments and angles involved in determining the point on the rail where the object ball must come in contact to bank into the lower-left corner pocket.

Problem 2
Devise a geometric argument or proof to show why the method described in the Etch-a-Sketch activity works.

Mathematics, Styles, and Strategies
METAPHORICAL EXPRESSION

One of the greatest strengths of the field of mathematics is found in the variety of ways math can be used to model real-world problems and phenomena. Mathematics' strong correlation with the real world is due to the structure of mathematics itself. The structural essence of mathematics begins with a few definitions and assumptions and blossoms into an endless lineage of mathematical facts, processes, and consequences. In the Metaphorical Expression Strategy, based on the pioneering work of W. J. J. Gordon (1961), students engage in a metaphorical journey through math.

The inherent growth characteristics of mathematics and its greater connectivity make it extremely comparable to any real-world structure that begins small and progresses into a more complex system. As a result, many analogies can be found between mathematics and real-world phenomena. For example, the field of mathematics itself is often compared to a tree where each branch is like a major subject in math. The smaller branches that grow from the main branches are like math topics that are studied in a particular math subject. The Metaphorical Expression Strategy challenges students to think deeply about a specific math concept and discover and communicate an analogous relationship between the mathematics and real-world topics.

Developing a Metaphorical Expression Activity

Since mathematics correlates so well with the real world, students can be challenged to discover an analogous relationship between any two topics. If the purpose of the instructional activity is to improve students' understanding of mathematics, the real-world topic should be one that is well-known and understood by students. For example, the problem "Show how *radian* measure of angles and the unit circle is like the distance a wheel of a bicycle travels" is more effective than, "show how *radian* measure is like a stochastic process." Most students do not know anything about stochastic processes and, therefore, would not be able to make an analogous connection.

To challenge students' creative thinking process even further, you may allow them to choose (rather than providing them with) the item or analog they would like to compare to the given math concept.

Metaphorical Expression: Observable Student Behaviors

The power of the Metaphorical Expression Strategy is in the freedom of students' thoughts and expressions. The teacher should be careful *not* to promote *one right answer*. However, the fact that there is more than one right answer does not mean that every answer is as good as every other answer. When completing a Metaphorical Expression activity, students should be encouraged to:

1. be creative and flexible in their thinking;
2. be sure they understand the mathematics involved so they can find accurate and analogous relationships;
3. be comprehensive in their search for relationships; and
4. provide clear examples and evidence of the relationships they cite.

Metaphorical Expression: A Sample Problem-Solving Plan

Problem
Choose one of the phrases below and complete the Metaphorical Expression activity. Provide as much evidence as you can to support your reasoning.

- *Prime numbers in mathematics are like planets in the Universe because ...*
- *Polygons in mathematics are like constellations of the stars because ...*
- *Undefined terms, defined terms, assumptions, and theorems in geometry are like the theoretical aspects of space because ...*

Student's Response
Each student must first decide which topic is most exciting or promising for developing an analogous relationship. Let us assume that a student chooses to develop phrase two. Now the student should review/research polygons in mathematics and constellations of stars and take notes on the properties, characteristics, and components of both. By making connections between similar characteristics and by using creative thinking, the student should be able to find several analogous relationships between polygons and stars.

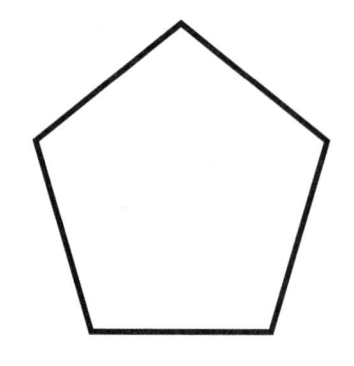

Pentagon   *Constellation Cepheus*   *Constellation Leo*

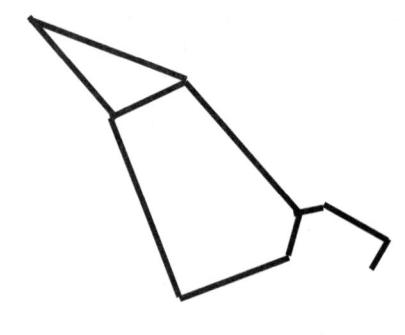

METAPHORICAL EXPRESSION

Student Activity

Featured math concepts: **Math and Music**

Student Name: _____

Directions:

While mathematics and music represent different fields of study, many of their components have a variety of things in common.

For example, in math a single digit represents a single number value. In music, a single note represents a single musical pitch.

5

As a point moves up and down the number line, the value of the number it represents becomes larger and smaller respectively. Similarly, in music, as notes move up and down the scale, the pitch of the sound they represent increases and decreases respectively.

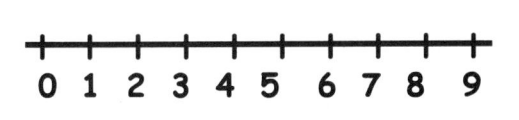

0 1 2 3 4 5 6 7 8 9

In mathematics, a greater number can be made by grouping two or more digits together. In music, two or more notes can be grouped to form a chord that, when played, generates a more powerful sound.

529

Student Challenge

Develop your own Metaphorical Expression that relates numbers to another phenomenon or choose one of the phrases below and complete the Metaphorical Expression activity. Provide as much evidence as you can to support your reasoning.

- *Digits and their multiples are like notes and octaves because ...*

- *A sheet of music is like a page of math problems because ...*

- *An instrument in music is like a calculator in math because ...*

METAPHORICAL EXPRESSION
Featured math concept: **Prime Factorizations**

Student Name: _____

Directions:
In most pockets of society, the term family usually refers to groups of related people that include brothers, sisters, parents, grandparents, aunts, uncles, and other relatives. In mathematics, families of numbers and shapes also exist because of the special relationships among the individual members of the families.

For example, the set of polygons in geometry is like a family because:
- all its members are related through the definition of a polygon
  (a closed figure made only of line segments)

- similar to an ordinary family, all the members of the polygon family have names
  (triangle, quadrilateral, pentagon, etc.)

- just as many families continue through future generations, the polygon family progresses infinitely

- in the real world, one's family is small compared to the entire population. Similarly, the polygon family is small compared to the entire population of math concepts and ideas.

Student Challenge
Develop your own Metaphorical Expression that relates prime factorization to another phenomenon or show how the prime factorization of a single number is like the family lineage of a single individual.

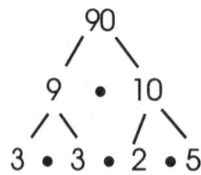

$$90$$
$$9 \cdot 10$$
$$3 \cdot 3 \cdot 2 \cdot 5$$

$$2 \cdot 3^2 \cdot 5$$

METAPHORICAL EXPRESSION

Featured math concepts: **Numbers and Space**

Student Name: _____

Directions:
While mathematics and outer space represent different fields of study, many of their components have a variety of things in common.

For example, in mathematics, space is the set of all points. In science, the universe consists of all of space and everything that is in it. In both the real world and mathematics, space is infinite. In mathematics, three-dimensional space can be coordinated with three real numbers axes that intersect at the origin or point (0, 0, 0). In the real world, the sun is the origin of our solar system. In mathematics, a point that represents a specific location in space is defined by an ordered triple (x, y, z). In the space of our universe, every star and planet known to man is identified by a name (Sun, Mercury, Venus, Earth, Mars, etc.).

Student Challenge
Develop your own Metaphorical Expression that relates prime numbers to a known phenomenon or choose one of the phrases below and complete the Metaphorical Expression activity. Provide as much evidence as you can to support your reasoning.

- *Prime numbers in mathematics are like planets in the universe because ...*

- *Polygons in mathematics are like constellations of the stars because ...*

- *Undefined terms, defined terms, assumptions, and theorems of geometry are like the theoretical aspects of space because ...*

Mathematics, Styles, and Strategies
MODELING AND EXPERIMENTATION

In its purest sense, the subject of mathematics is extremely abstract. Theoretically, what most people call numbers are only symbols that represent numerical ideas that have no tangible form. What most people commonly call lines are not really lines by mathematical definitions. In math, a line is a set of infinitesimally small points that cannot be seen. But in the real world, numbers can be modeled by groups of objects and lines can be modeled by graphical representations. Without the ability to model mathematics, the process of learning and understanding mathematics would be extremely difficult for all students.

Over the years, math educators have found new ways to model math concepts in the classroom. The list on the right shows some of the common manipulatives.

Through the Modeling and Experimentation Strategy, teachers can minimize the abstract nature of mathematics by allowing students to model math concepts with concrete manipulatives and draw conclusions through the process of experimentation.

Manipulatives used to Model Math Concepts

Place value	*Base ten blocks*
Addition process	*The Abacus*
Fractions	*Fraction rods*
Decimals	*Play money*
Integers	*2-sided counters*
Equations	*Balance scales, cups, counters*
Measurement	*Rulers, weights, scales*
Probability	*Containers and marbles*
Polynomials	*Algebra blocks*
Functions	*Function diagrams*
Graphs of functions	*Pattern plotters*
Geometry	*Graph paper*

Points to Remember When Developing and Implementing a Modeling and Experimentation Activity

• While the Modeling and Experimentation Strategy can help students learn and understand many math concepts and skills, this strategy is not suited for every math concept. For example, 2-sided counters can help students to understand the rules for combining integers, but can confuse students when used to teach the sign rules for multiplication and division. It is important to keep abreast of the realistic benefits of math modeling tools and not to force manipulatives in every situation.

• When deciding whether or not to implement a Modeling and Experimentation activity, the teacher should be convinced that the manipulatives represent the abstract components of the math concept very well. For example, a number line can serve as a good representation of whole numbers and fractions, whereas a textbook would not serve well as a model of a geometric plane (a plane is flat but has no thickness or boundaries).

• The Modeling and Experimentation activity should build a bridge between the concrete representations and the abstract understanding of the math concepts involved. For example, when balance, cups, and counters are used to model equations, the thinking involved in keeping the scales balanced is the same thinking required when applying the properties of equality in the equation-solving process.

MODEL AND EXPERIMENTATION

Student Activity

Featured math concept: **Solving Equations**

Student Name: _____

Introduction

A numerical equation is a mathematical statement that demonstrates equality between two numbers or number expressions.

The following are examples of numerical equations:

$$4 + 2 = 6$$
$$7 = 7$$
$$2 \cdot 5 = 8 + 2$$

A numerical equation is either true or false. The three examples above are all true. The equation 12 - 7 = 4 is an example of a false equation.

An algebraic equation is an equation that contains one or more variables. A variable is usually a letter that represents a known or unknown value.

The following are examples of algebraic equations:

$$4 + x = 8$$
$$2y - 4 = 6$$
$$2 \cdot z + 3 = 5$$

In the three algebraic equations, the variables x, y, and z represent unknown values. The process of finding the value of a variable that makes an equation true is known as solving the equation. Solving an equation requires mathematical knowledge and reasoning. The model described on the next page can help you understand the thought process involved in solving an equation.

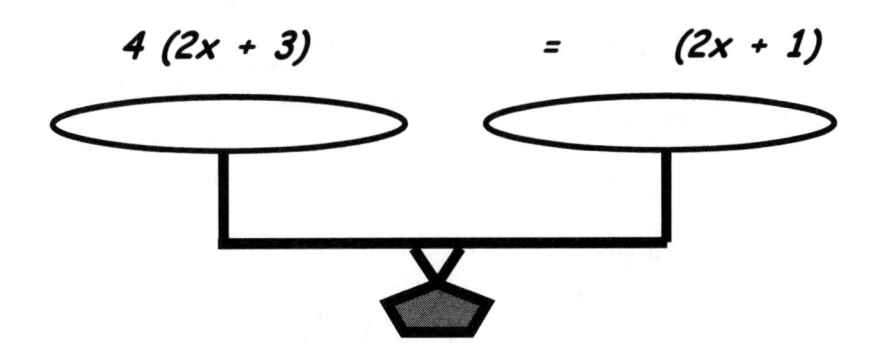

4 (2x + 3)   =   *(2x + 1)*

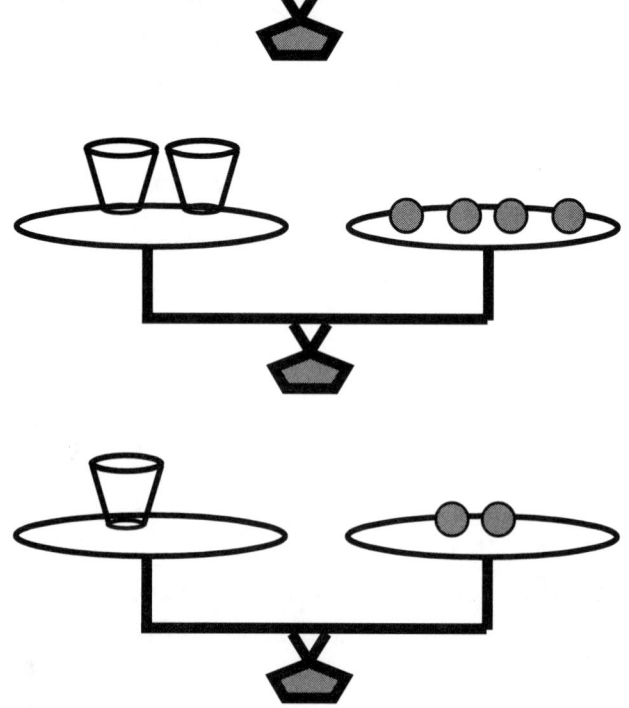

Modeling Algebraic Equations

Materials

- Five plastic medicine cups (or any small cups)
- Several two-sided counters
- Paper, pencil, ruler

Directions

- Use the paper, pencil, and ruler to draw a balance scale similar to the one above.
- Use the balance scale, paper cups, and two-sided counters to model an equation.
    - Paper cups represent variables (Upright +, Upside down -)
    - Quantities of two-sided counters represent positive and negative values (yellow +, red -). *See examples below.*
- Solve the equation using the following rules:
    1. Equal objects can be *added to* or *removed from* both sides of the scale.
    2. A *zero* can be added to or subtracted from any side of the scale. A *zero* consists of an equal number of red *and* yellow two-sided counters or an equal number of upright *and* upside down cups.
    3. Use rules 1 and 2 to reduce the problem to a simple model that can be solved using simple mental math.
    4. Check your solution using the original problem.

Example 1

Use the balance scale to solve
$2x + 4 = 8$

Solution

Step 1
Use the balance scale to model the equation.

Step 2
Remove 4 yellow counters from both sides of the scale.

Step 3
Use your mental math skills to reason that the value of the paper cup must be 2.

Step 4
Check the solution in the original equation.
$2 \cdot 2 + 4 = 8$

MODELING AND EXPERIMENTATION: Modeling Algebraic Equations *cont. ...*

Example 2
Use the balance scale model to solve
$2(x - 1) + 5 = 11$

Solution

Step 1
Use the balance scale to model the equation.

Step 2
Remove 2 zeros (◯●) from the left side of the scale.

Step 3
Remove 3 yellow counters from each side of the scale.

Step 4
Use your mental math skills to reason that the value of the paper cup must be 4.

Step 5
Check the solution in the original equation.
$2(4 - 1) + 5 = 11$

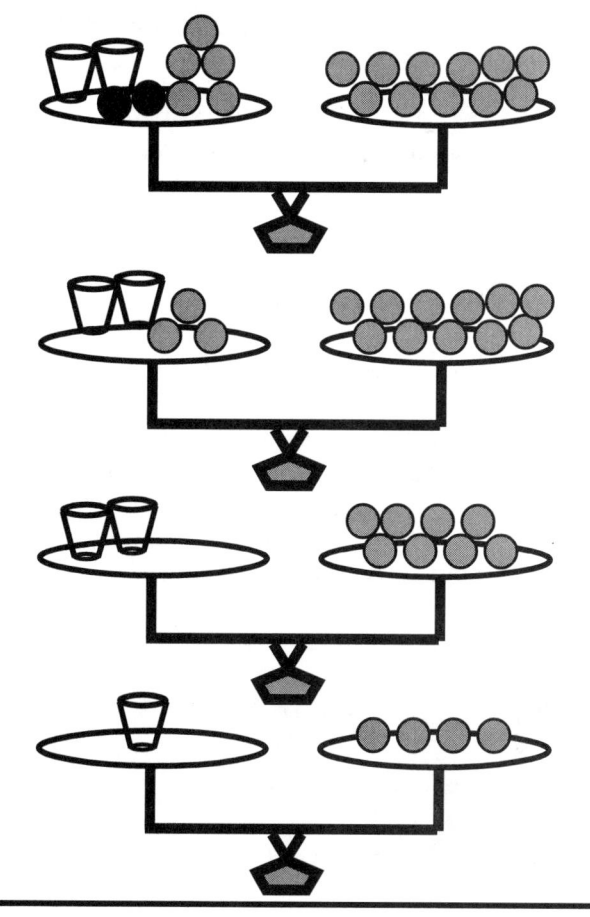

Example 3
Use the balance scale model to solve
$-x + 2 = 2x + 1$

Solution

Step 1
Use the balance scale to model the equation.

Step 2
Add a positive x to both sides to create a zero on the left side.

Step 3
Remove the zero from the left side of the scale and one yellow counter from both sides.

Step 4
Use your mental math skills to reason that the value of the paper cup must be $\frac{1}{3}$.

Step 5
Check the solution in the original equation.
$-\frac{1}{3} + 2 = 2 \cdot \frac{1}{3} + 1$

$1\frac{2}{3} = 1\frac{2}{3}$

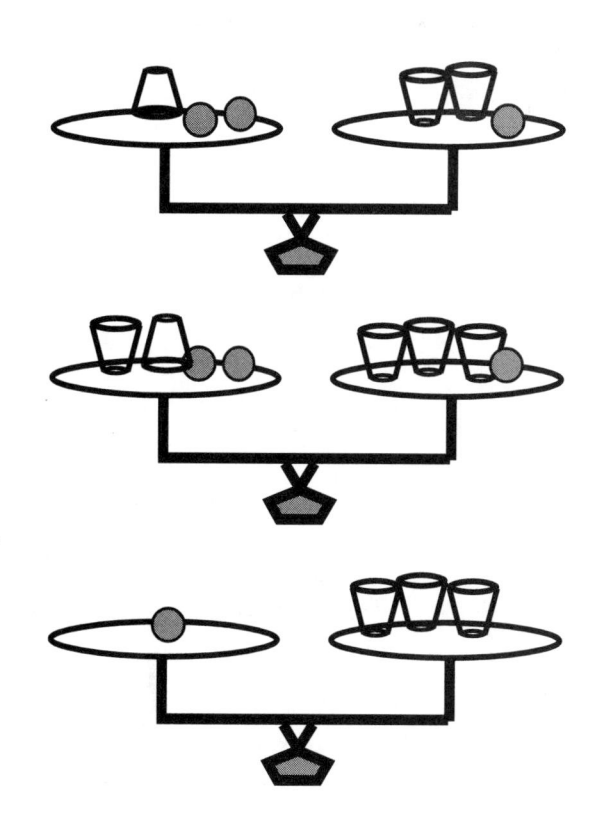

MODELING AND EXPERIMENTATION

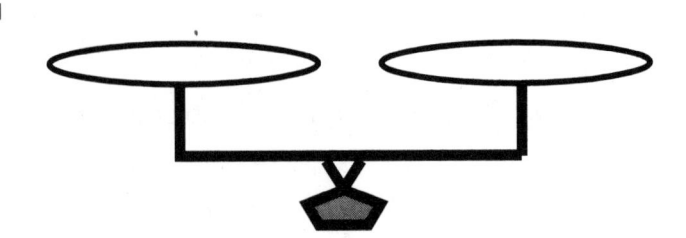

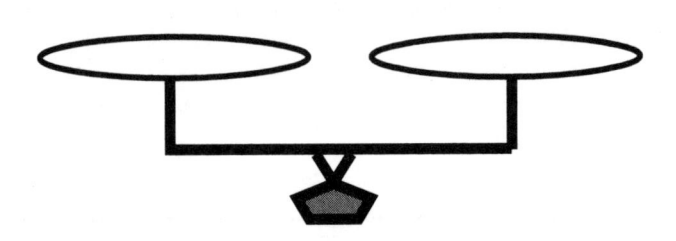

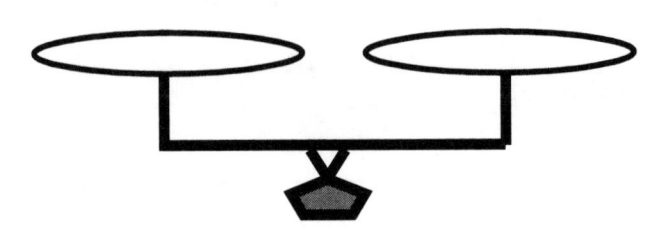

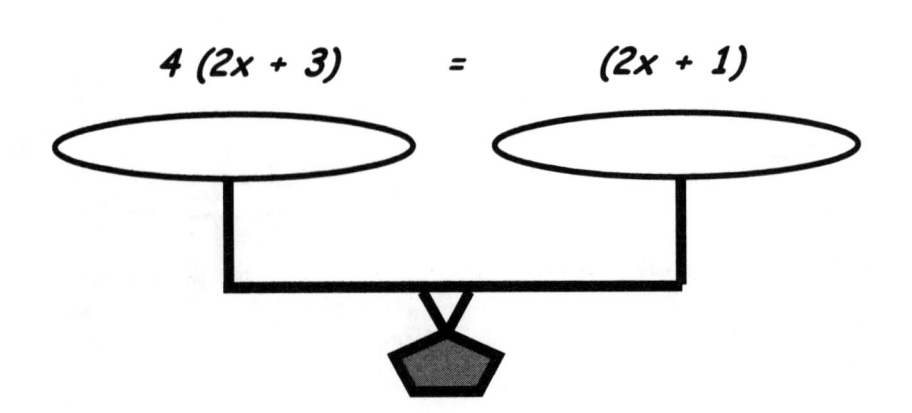

Featured math concept: **Solving Equations**

Student Name: _____

Directions:

Use paper cups, two-sided counters, and a balance scale to model and solve the algebraic equations below. Be sure to check your solutions in the original equations.

1. $2x + 6 - x = 12 + 3x$
2. $-x + 3 = -2x + -9$
3. $2(x - 1) = 10$
4. $x - 4 = x + 6$
5. $-4 + x = 2x + 10$
6. $-2 = 2(x + 2)$
7. $2 + x + 2x = 4x + 6$
8. $2x + 4 = 3x + 8$

$4(2x + 3) \quad = \quad (2x + 1)$

MODELING AND EXPERIMENTATION

Student Activity

Featured math concept: **Solving Equations**

Student Name: _____

Directions:

Use paper cups, two-sided counters, and a balance scale to model and solve the algebraic equations below. Be sure to check your solutions in the original equations.

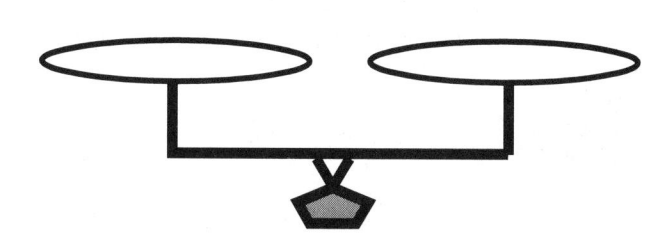

1. $2x + 6 - x = 12$

2. $7x + 4 = 2x + 14$

3. $2(x + 1) = 12$

4. $3x - 4 = x + 6$

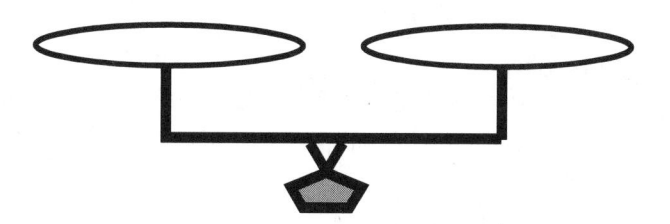

5. $4 - x = 2x + 10$

6. $8 = -2x + 2$

7. $2 - x + 2x = 2(x + 3)$

8. $2x + 4 = 5x + 13$

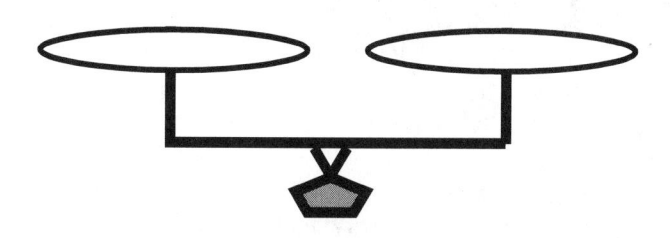

$4(2x + 3)$ = $(2x + 1)$

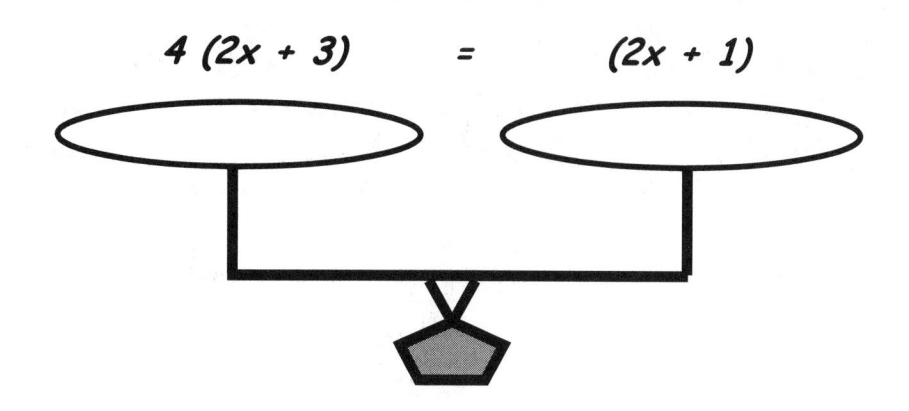

MODELING AND EXPERIMENTATION
Featured math concept: **Probability**

Student Activity

Student Name: _____

Directions:
The Miles Cereal Company is giving away pocket-sized sports trivia guides for baseball, football, basketball, swimming, track, and tennis. One trivia guide is included in each box of Energize cereal. The cereal boxes do not reveal the type of sports guide in each box. Therefore, when the customer purchases a box of cereal, he or she does not know which sports guide is enclosed until it is opened. Assuming that the sports guides are evenly distributed in any group of cereal boxes in any store, work with a partner and solve the following problems.

Problem 1
Based on the information above, if a customer purchases a box of Energize cereal, determine the probability that the customer will receive a track trivia guide.

Problem 2
If a customer purchases two boxes of Energize cereal, determine the probability that:
    a. the customer will receive two trivia guides for the same sport
    b. the customer will receive a tennis trivia guide and a baseball trivia guide

Problem 3
Work with your partner to hypothesize how many boxes of cereal a customer would have to purchase in order to collect all six sports trivia guides.

Problem 4
Conduct the following experiment. Let the numbers 1 - 6 on a single die represent the six different sports trivia guides. Use the act of rolling the die to model the concept of randomly selecting a box of cereal with a particular sports guide. Determine the number of rolls needed to roll all the numbers 1 - 6. Explain how this number might relate to Problem 3.

Problem 5
Within your classroom, compute the average of all the learning pairs' answers to Problem 4. How does the class average relate to the question posed in Problem 3?

MODELING AND EXPERIMENTATION
Featured math concept: **Exponential Growth**

Student Activity

Student Name: _____

Directions:
An exponential function is a function of the form $f(x) = a^x$, where a is a constant and x is a real-number variable. An exponential function behaves differently from a linear function, quadratic function, and trigonometric function.

Work with a partner and solve the following problems.

Problem 1
Tiny Tim loved to play with tin foil. He particularly enjoyed folding it and creasing it. One day, while folding and creasing his tin foil, he posed the following question to himself: "What if I had a super large sheet of tin foil and folded it in half 100 times ... how thick would it be?" Make an educated guess in terms of inches, feet, or miles.

Fold #	Thickness
0	1
1	2
2	4
3	8
4	16
5	32
6	64
7	128
8	256
9	512
10	1024 -> 1k
11	2k
12	4k
etc.	etc.

Problem 2
Assume that the original sheet of foil was 1mm thick. Complete the table below and use the round down method to find a quick approximation of an answer for Problem 1. When the table is complete, convert the 100th value to inches, feet, or miles.

Problem 3
Create a function of the form $f(x) = a^x$ to represent the thickness of the foil stack after x folds.

Problem 4
Use paper and pencil or a graphing utility to plot the graph of f(x) in Problem 3. Use the trace tool to approximate the value f(100).

Problem 5
Compare f(100) with your initial answer in Problem 2.

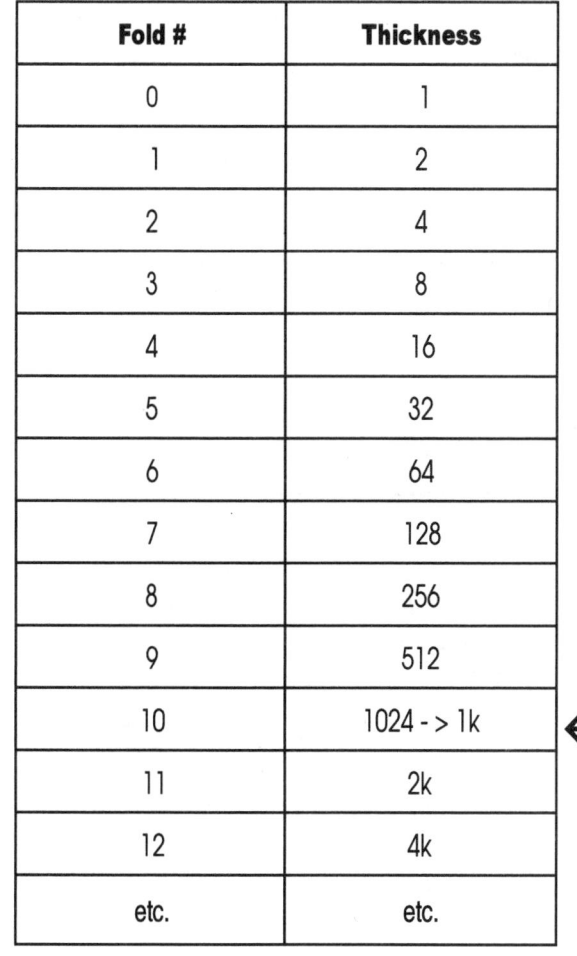

← Let k = 1000 and round 1024 down to 1k and use previous answers to continue the pattern. Round 1024k down to k^2. Continue the round down pattern to 100 folds.

Page **157**

Student Activity

MODELING AND EXPERIMENTATION
Featured math concept: **Combining Integers**

Student Name: _____

Directions:

Understanding the Rules of Combining Integers
Let the following shaded circles represent the members of two basketball teams, the Solids and the Shades. All the players shown will play, at the same time, in the game.

Problem 1
In terms of number of players, which team, if any, has an advantage in the picture below? State the team named followed by the number of excess players.

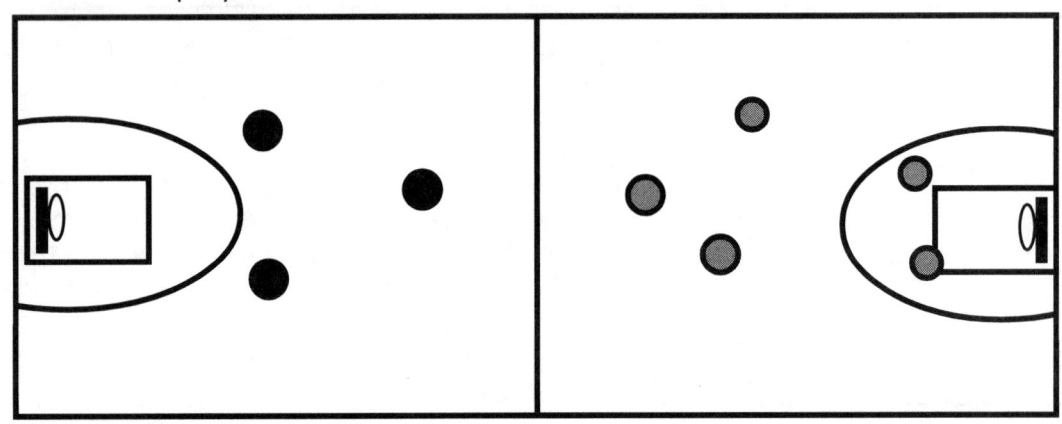

Problem 2
Which team, if any, has a player advantage in this picture? State the team name followed by the number of excess players.

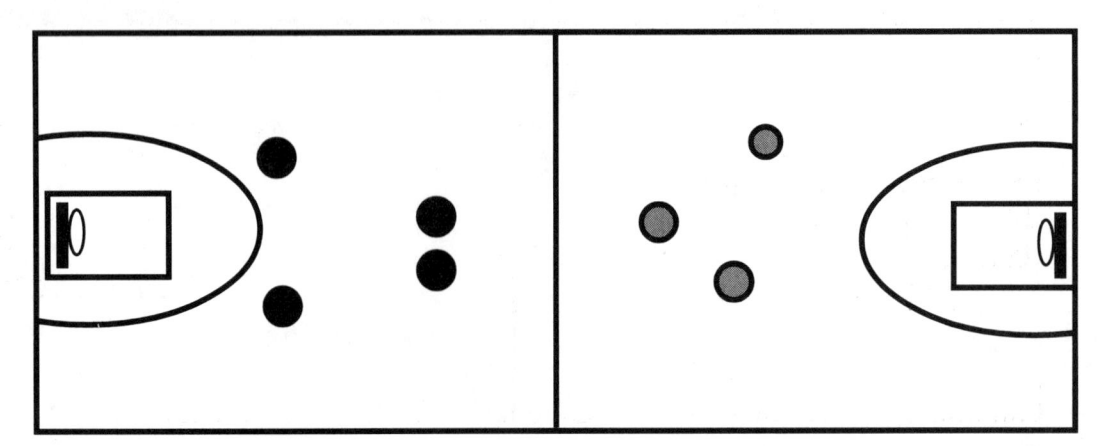

Continued on next page ...

MODELING AND EXPERIMENTATION: *Combining Integers* cont. ...

Note: If both teams have the same number of players, we will agree to respond to the question of advantage with the answer 0. If members of only one team show up for the game, we will agree to respond to the question of advantage by stating the team name followed by the total number of players who showed up for the game.

Problem 3
Which team, if any, has a player advantage in the picture below?

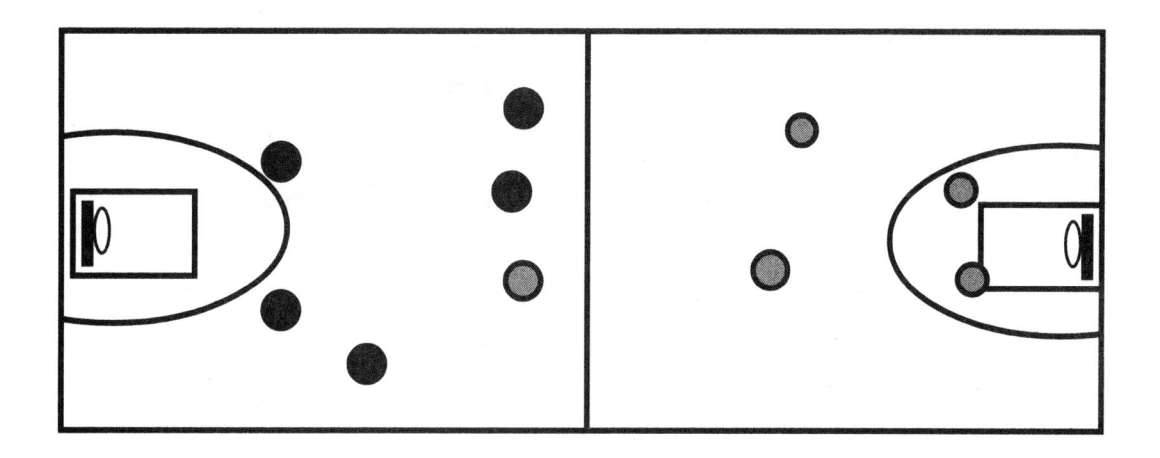

Problem 4
Which team, if any, has a player advantage in this picture? State the team named followed by the number of excess players.

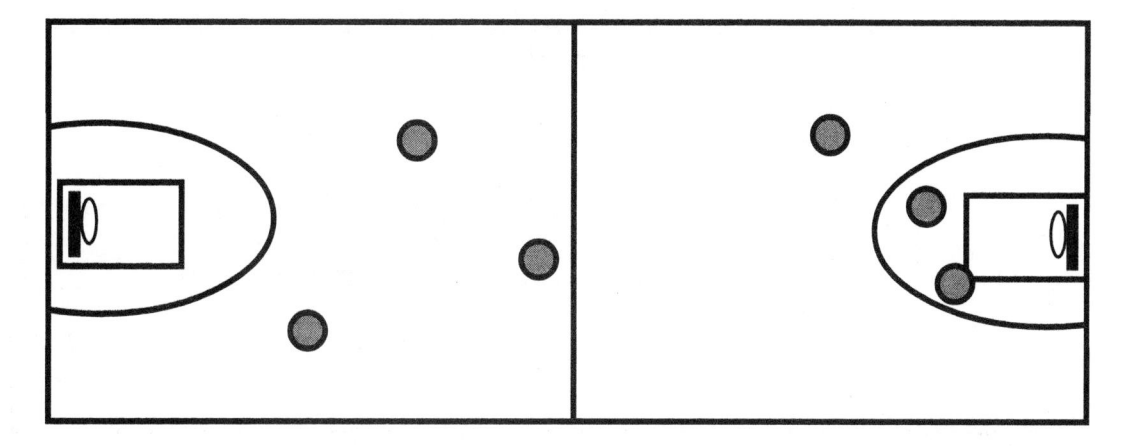

Continued on next page ...

MODELING AND EXPERIMENTATION: Combining Integers cont. ...

Making the transition from the basketball model to the math concept of combining integers.

When combining two integers with different signs, correlate the signs with the idea of opposing teams. Identify the sign whose associated number has an absolute numerical advantage. To combine the integers, state the sign of the number with the absolute advantage and the number which tells us how much the advantage is. Study the following examples.

$5 - 3 = 2$ (The positive team has the advantage by two.)

$- 6 + 10 = 4$ (The positive team has the advantage by four.)

$- 7 + 4 = -3$ (The negative team has the advantage by three.)

$- 3 - 2 = -5$ (The negative team has the advantage by five.)

$4 - 4 = 0$ (No advantage)

Problem 5
Simplify the following numerical expressions by combining the integers.

1. _____ 6 - 8

2. _____ -9 + 9

3. _____ -2 + 4

4. _____ 5 + 3

5. _____ -4 - 4

6. _____ -7 + 3

MODELING AND EXPERIMENTATION

Featured math concept: **Slope of a Line**

Student Name: _____

Directions:

Using Peg-boards to Develop an Understanding of Slope

In the linear equation model y = mx + b, the coefficient m is referred to as the slope. Let's investigate to see why.

Number three sets of five golf tees 1 - 5. Place one set of tees in the holes on the bottom row of a peg-board.

Problem 1
Let a multiplier m take on the value 1. Multiply the numbers on the golf tees by the multiplier m = 1. Move each golf tee vertically the number of holes equal to the product. Note the steepness or slope of the line formed by the golf tees.

Problem 2
Place a second set of golf tees in the holes on the bottom row. Now let the multiplier m have the value 2. Multiply the numbers on the golf tees by the multiplier m = 2. Move each golf tee vertically the number of holes equal to the product. Note the steepness or slope of the line formed by the golf tees. Compare the slope of the golf tees resulting from the slope m = 1 and m = 2.

Problem 3
Repeat Problem 2 with the third set of golf tees for m = 3.

Problem 4
Use graph paper or lattice paper to create a pencil/paper model of the peg-board problem. Draw a number line in the center of your paper. Use your pencil to simulate Problem 2 for the following values of m { 1, -1, 2, .5, -2, .25, -3, 3 }.

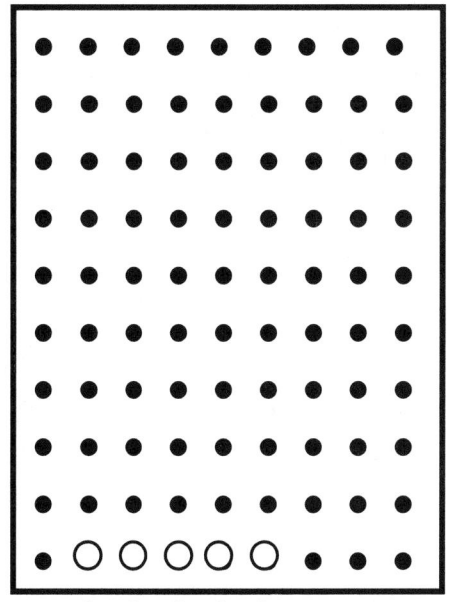

META-STRATEGIES

Integrated Mathematical Engagement
Knowledge by Design
Math Notes
Task Rotation
Do You See What I See?

Mathematics, Styles, and Strategies
INTEGRATED MATHEMATICAL ENGAGEMENT

On more than one occasion, a colleague of mine referred to mathematics as a foreign language. By definition, a foreign language is a language spoken, for the most part, outside one's country. Depending on one's perspective, the language of mathematics may not be considered common among people in our country. As a result, my colleague was somewhat justified in calling mathematics a foreign language.

The structures of mathematics and language have some commonalities. Both structures begin with simple units that serve as building blocks for bigger ideas. The field of mathematics has the unit digits 0 - 9, and the English language has the letters of the alphabet A - Z. Each unit digit represents a certain value, and each letter of the alphabet represents a sound. Digits in math can be grouped together in countless ways to represent numbers of greater value, and letters in language can be grouped together to form a variety of words. In mathematics the concept of digits gives way to more powerful concepts including operations on numbers, theorems, and entire fields of application and study. Similarly, in language arts, the concept of letters leads to more powerful concepts including words, phrases, sentences, paragraphs, and texts.

The connection between mathematics and language can be used to demonstrate the value of the Integrated Mathematical Engagement Strategy. Imagine if students who study a foreign language were strictly limited to the alphabet, vocabulary, and verb tenses, and never engaged in the actual communication process. Under those circumstances, students would experience great difficulty speaking, interpreting, and writing in that particular language. Similar results can occur in mathematics when students spend a great deal of time practicing first-level isolated skills and fail to engage in problems that integrate math concepts into more global and relevant problem-solving situations.

The purpose of the Integrated Mathematical Strategy is to engage students in rich problem-solving activities that require students to apply deeper understandings and make connections among several related math concepts. By thinking through the connections, applications, and rigorous meanings of math concepts, students will improve their knowledge and understanding of the fundamentals of math. The strength of the Integrated Mathematical Engagement Strategy is tied directly to the design of the problems in which students are engaged.

Developing an Integrated Mathematical Engagement Activity

There are three types of Integrated Mathematical Engagements. In a Type I Integrated Mathematical Engagement, teachers can pose problems that focus on mathematical applications of other math concepts. For example, students in the midst of studying functions might be asked to solve the following problem:

Type I Integrated Mathematical Engagement

Consider the rule r(x) = n where x is a positive integer and n is the number of proper factors that x has.

- a. Is r(x) a function? Why or why not?
- b. Find the value of r(20), r(12), and r(1).
- c. If r(x) is a function, is it a one-to-one function?
- d. Describe the range and graph of r(x) if x represents positive prime numbers.

In the Type I problem above, the function concept is applied to the concept of number theory, factors of numbers, and prime numbers. Students are challenged to extend their thinking and connect the fact that a positive integer has one and only one number of proper factors to the definition of function. As a result, this problem leads students to think more deeply about functions and factors of numbers.

In a Type II Integrated Mathematical Engagement, teachers can pose problems that feature a cumulative and global treatment of related math concepts. In another example with functions, students might be asked to solve the following problem:

Type II Integrated Mathematical Engagement

Consider the rule "double and subtract one." Use that rule to perform the following tasks.

- a. Construct a function diagram for the rule *square and add one*.
- b. Use set notation to display the domain represented in the function diagram.
- c. Use set notation to display the range represented in the function diagram.
- d. Write the ordered pairs represented by the function diagram as a relation.
- e. Write the inverse relation.
- f. Write the function rule using the letter f and function notation.
- g. Find the inverse equation f^{-1} and verify that it works.
- h. Plot the points from d and e on a coordinate plane.
- i. Sketch the complete and continuous graphs of f(x) and $f^{-1}(x)$ on a coordinate plane.
- j. Run the vertical and horizontal line tests on the graph of f.
- g. Explain the geometric relationship between the graphs of f(x) and $f^{-1}(x)$.

In this Type II engagement, students are challenged to demonstrate understanding of all the components of functions as they apply to one rule. In many math classes, each concept represented by the parts of this problem is treated as a daily topic. Students would only see the cumulative integration on the chapter review or chapter test. Through the Integrated Mathematical Engagement Strategy, students learn these concepts globally and quickly (one day in a block class and two days in a traditional class) and are quickly engaged in problem solving. As a result, students are challenged to understand the relationships and connectedness of otherwise seemingly disjointed ideas.

In a Type III Integrated Mathematical Engagement, teachers can pose problems that feature real-world applications and that require a wider scope of mathematical problem solving. In another example with functions, students might be asked to solve the following problem:

Type III Integrated Mathematical Engagement

Consider the following scenario. A swimming pool repair man charges $50 for a house visit plus $25 for each hour he spends at a person's house. Time is rounded to the nearest hour for the $25 per hour portion of the bill. In addition, swimming pool parts, filter parts, and chemicals are charged to the home owner at a cost that is 10% above the factory cost. While the service time charge is not taxed, the sum cost of parts and chemicals is taxed at 6%.

Work with a partner to create a cost function c(x, y) where x is the number of service minutes and y is the factory cost of parts. Use your function to determine the total cost to the home owner for a visit from the pool man that resulted in the following data.

Service Information
Service date	August 12, 2002
Service check-in time	9:22 a.m.
Service completion time	11:58 a.m.

Parts and Factory Cost
Vacuum hose	$29.00
Chlorinator assembly	$74.00

Chemicals and Factory Cost
50 pack of chlorine tablets	$39.00
25 pounds of soda ash	$21.00

In the Type III example above, students are introduced to functions of two variables and challenged to work with time, rounding, percent, and problem solving. Reinforcement problems can easily be generated by changing the service times, supplies, chemicals, and costs. Students can deepen their understanding of functions by connecting the formal definition of a function of one variable to the idea of a cost function dependent on two variables.

In summary, the Integrated Mathematical Engagement Strategy is a great way to engage your students in thoughtful problem solving and to deepen their understanding and retention of important math concepts. The student activities that follow include one of each type of Integrated Mathematical Engagements.

Student Activity

INTEGRATED MATHEMATICAL ENGAGEMENT
Featured math concept: **Properties of Numbers**

Student Name: _____

Directions:
In most high school math textbooks, the properties of numbers are defined as true for all real numbers. But what about other sets of numbers? Some interesting challenges result when the properties of numbers are tested for different sets of numbers.

For example, the closure property of addition of real numbers states that *for any two real numbers, the sum of those real numbers is also a real number*. If, instead of all real numbers, the closure property of addition was tested for all integer multiples of seven, would the property still hold?

Work with a learning partner and determine which properties listed below hold for the sets of numbers described in the problems below. Remember, for an identity property to hold, the identity element must be in the set in question. For the inverse properties to hold, the inverses must also be in the set in question.

Properties to Be Tested
- Closure for addition, subtraction, multiplication, and division
- Commutative for addition, subtraction, multiplication, and division
- Associative for addition and multiplication
- Distributive of multiplication over addition and subtraction
- Identity for addition and multiplication
- Inverse for addition and multiplication

Problem 1
The integer multiples of seven

Problem 2
The odd natural numbers

Problem 3
The set of prime numbers

Problem 4
The set of proper fractions (with integer terms)

Problem 5
The set of negative real numbers

INTEGRATED MATHEMATICAL ENGAGEMENT
Featured math concepts: **Functions and Logarithms**

Student Name: _____

Student Activity

Directions:

1. Complete the function diagram to the right and:

    a. Identify the domain elements
    b. Identify the range elements
    c. Write the function as a relation
    d. Write the inverse relation
    e. Find the inverse equation
    f. Plot the points from c
    g. Plot the points from d
    h. Use the function name f and write the ordered pairs from the function diagram in function notation
    i. State the geometric relationship between the graphs of f and g

    f: one-half log base two of x then add 1

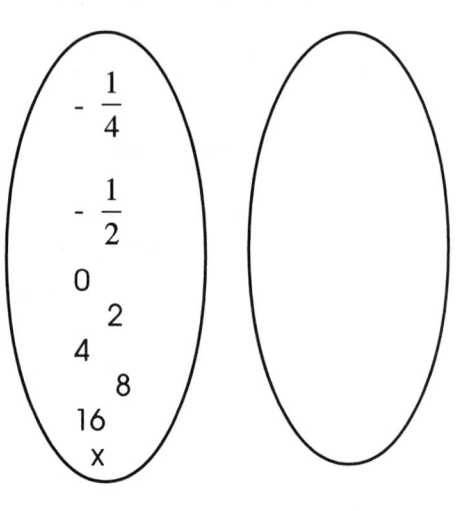

    $-\frac{1}{4}$, $-\frac{1}{2}$, 0, 2, 4, 8, 16, x

2. Sketch the graphs of

    a. $f(x) = 4 + \ln x$

    b. $f(x) = \ln(x - 5)$

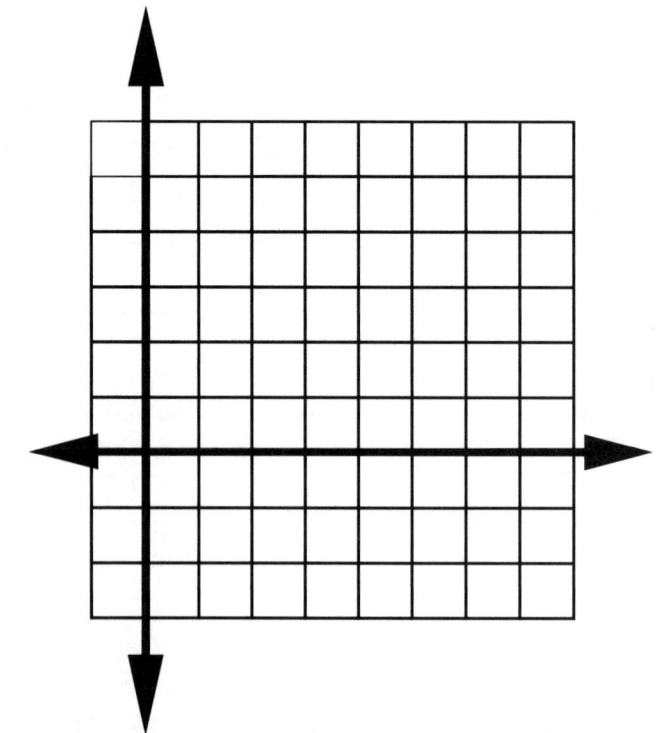

3. Simplify $\log_3(81)$

4. Solve $3^{(x+2)} = 18$ for x

Student Activity

INTEGRATED MATHEMATICAL ENGAGEMENT
Featured math concepts: **Architecture and Geometry**

Student Name: _____

Directions:
Work with a learning partner and solve one of the problems below. Be creative, accurate, and neat.

Problem 1
Use graph paper, ruler, and protractor or a computer drawing tool to design and draw the survey of a golf course with the following specifications.

a. The golf course must reside on a 150-acre rectangular tract of land that is twice as long as it is wide.
b. The course must contain a front set of nine holes and a back set of nine holes. Each set of nine holes must include exactly 2 par three holes, 2 par five holes, and 5 par four holes.
c. From the longest tees, the sum total of course play will be 6600 yards.
d. A maximum of two dog-leg right holes and two dog-leg left holes are allowed on each set of nine holes.

Problem 2
Use graph paper, ruler, and protractor or a computer drawing tool to design and draw a floor plan of a house with the following specifications.

a. The floor plan will consist of 2500 square feet of heated living space if it is a ranch and 3500 square feet of heated living space if it is a two-story house.
b. If the house is a ranch it will include three bedrooms, a den, a formal living area, a dining area, a kitchen, two and one-half baths, and appropriate closets and hallways.
c. If the house is a two story it will include four bedrooms, a den, a formal living room, a dining room, a kitchen, four baths, and appropriate closets, hallways, and stairs. (A possible bonus room can be included upstairs.)
d. Markings for windows, doors, light fixtures, electrical outlets, and ceiling fans must be included.

Mathematics, Styles, and Strategies
KNOWLEDGE BY DESIGN

The Knowledge by Design Strategy engages students in the thinking processes associated with designing a new and improved product. The strategy is adapted from the work of David Perkins (1986), who argues that when students learn to see the structure or design in what they are learning, their abilities to think both creatively and analytically improve dramatically.

During a Knowledge by Design activity, students in the math classroom are required to analyze or describe a given math concept or tool, consider and communicate its purpose, discuss and report its advantages and disadvantages, and determine how the concept or tool can be improved. By engaging in these four tasks, students will explore concepts deeply and develop their thinking in all four learning styles.

Developing a Knowledge by Design Activity
To develop a Knowledge by Design activity, select a specific object, term, figure, theorem, or algorithm in math and present it to your students as the object of the learning activity. Allow your students to work with a learning partner. Assign the following four tasks to the learning pairs. Maintain a reasonable time limit (approximately 10 minutes each) for each task.

1. Develop a precise description of the concept or tool.
2. Determine the purpose and value of the concept or tool.
3. List the advantages and disadvantages of the concept or tool.
4. Create ideas on how the concept or tool can be improved.

The teacher may choose to facilitate a class discussion on the students' findings between each stage. When all four stages of the activity are complete, a summary can be provided along with further related instructions.

A Sample Knowledge by Design Activity

The following Knowledge by Design activity asks middle school math students to analyze and improve the *variable equation used to represent the slope-intercept form of a linear equation*. The four student tasks in the activity are displayed in a two-by-two chart. The students would be asked to work in learning pairs as they discuss and answer the four Knowledge by Design questions. Sample student responses are shown below.

Analyzing and Improving the Variable Representation of the Slope-Intercept Form of a Linear Equation

Describe the components of the equation $y = mx + b$	**What is the purpose of the equation $y = mx + b$?**
• It is an equation with two variables; m is the slope. • b is the y-intercept. • The graph of the solution of $y=mx+b$ is a line. • x and y are the ordinates of points on the line. • The solution set is infinite.	• To provide a symbolic descriptor of the line. • To provide a tool for generating ordered pairs of points on the graph. • To standardize the algebraic representation of a geometric line.
What are the pros and cons of the equation $y = mx + b$? p • The slope and y-intercept can quickly be identified. p • Ordered pairs can quickly be generated using this equation. p • Since the equation is solved for y, it can easily be typed into a graphing utility. c • The constants m and b do not seem to correlate with the words slope and intercept.	**How can the $y = mx + b$ equation be improved?** • Perhaps use the symbol s for slope instead of m. • Perhaps use the symbol i for y-intercept instead of b. • Perhaps underline or box the letters x and y since they are the true variables.

KNOWLEDGE BY DESIGN

Student Activity

Featured math concept: **Use of a Calculator**

Student Name: _____

Directions:

Today, most people have access to a calculator. Perhaps your have your own calculator, or at least access to one, for your math class. What kind of calculator do you use? Is it a four-function calculator, a scientific calculator, a fractions calculator, or a graphing calculator? The questions that follow will ask you and your learning partner to analyze your calculator and make suggestions for improving it. Answer the questions and be prepared to discuss your results with the class.

Describe the present features of your calculator.	What is the purpose of your calculator in this class?
Discuss possible arguments for and against using a calculator in school.	How can your calculator or use of it be improved?

Student Activity

KNOWLEDGE BY DESIGN

Featured math concepts: **The Complex Numbers and the Imaginary Unit i**

Student Name: _____

Directions:

In the study of higher-level mathematics, students must deal with a special class of numbers called Complex Numbers. The questions that follow will ask you and your learning partner to analyze Complex Numbers and make suggestions for improving them. Answer the questions and be prepared to discuss your results with the class.

Describe the Complex Numbers and the Imaginary unit i.	What is the purpose of Complex and Imaginary Numbers?
Discuss possible advantages and disadvantages of the class of numbers known as the Complex Numbers.	How can the Complex Numbers or use of them be improved?

Student Activity

KNOWLEDGE BY DESIGN

Featured math concepts: **Probabilities and Games of Chance**

Student Name: _____

Directions:
Probability is studied in high school and college. The laws of probability form the basis of many games of chance. The questions that follow will ask you and your learning partner to analyze the lottery, if your state has one, or another game of chance that you are familiar with. Answer the questions and be prepared to discuss your results with the class.

Describe the components of your state's lottery game or other game of chance. Include the rules of the game and what a player must do to win.	**What is the purpose of this game?**
Discuss possible advantages and disadvantages of the way this game of chance is played.	**How can this game be improved?**

Mathematics, Styles, and Strategies
MATH NOTES

Mathematical word problems, despite their prominence on state and national tests, still prove one of the most difficult and frustrating types of problems for most students. Unlike other math problems, word problems require reading and math skills, and their difficulty often brings out the impulsive side in students: Rather than taking the time to figure out what the problem is asking them to do, students often leap towards a solution. The Math Notes Strategy uses a special notetaking technique that helps students analyze and break down word problems so that they can develop an effective problem-solving plan. Math Notes also teaches students how to draw on all five essential components of mathematical reasoning, as defined by Sternberg (1999):

- The ability to identify a problem
- The ability to represent a problem, mentally or visually
- The ability to formulate strategies for solving the problem
- The ability to plan before problem solving
- The ability to assess one's own work and process

Developing and Implementing a Math Notes Lesson

Developing a Math Notes lesson is as simple as selecting a word problem or set of word problems that you would like students to focus their attention on. Implementing the lesson in the classroom means coaching students through six steps (at right), which make an excellent classroom poster.

Before asking students to practice using the strategy on their own, it is a good idea to model Math Notes by working through each of the steps using a sample problem. Be sure to "think aloud" by verbalizing your internal thinking process ("*Okay, let's see ... one way to model this problem might be to ...* "). Record your work on the board or an overhead. You might consider modeling the strategy using the problem and completed organizer found on the following page.

Set up the problem by listing the facts and determining what information is irrelevant and what information is missing from the problem.

Organize your thinking by asking: "What question needs to be answered?" and "Are there any hidden questions that need to be answered?"

Look for ways to represent the problem either physically or visually, or both.

Verbalize your thinking by listing, in words, the steps you will take to solve the problem.

Execute the steps and solve the problem.

Reflect on your solution and check your work by asking, "Is the math done correctly?" "Does my solution answer the question asked?" "Does my answer make sense?"

Building a Math Notes Notebook

As students practice working with the Math Notes technique and learn to apply it independently, have them keep a notebook of all the problems they have solved using the Math Notes Strategy. This notebook can become a significant reference for students when they encounter new problems. By referring to their notebooks, students can look for problems that have similar patterns to the new problems they are trying to solve, and they can adapt problem-solving strategies from models they have used before.

Sample Problem and Organizer

At 11:00 pm eastern time, a jet leaves Cheyenne for Pittsburgh traveling at 600 mph. One hour later, at midnight eastern time, a different jet leaves Pittsburgh for Cheyenne, traveling at 700 mph. Jet 1 travels at 10,000 feet and Jet 2 travels at 12,000 feet. The distance between Pittsburgh and Cheyenne is 1427 miles. Find the time when the two jets will pass each other.

The Facts

What are the facts?
- Jet 1 leaves at 11:00 pm
  Jet 2 leaves at 12:00 pm
- Jets travel towards one another
- Distance from Cheyenne to Pittsburgh is 1427 miles
- Jet 1 travels at 10,000 feet
  Jet 2 travels at 12,000 feet

What is missing?
- Distance jets will have traveled when they meet
- Equation d = rt
  (distance = rate • time)

What is irrelevant?
- The elevation of the planes is irrelevant

The Steps

1. Set up the equation:
   $d_1 + d_2 = 1427$
   $r_1 t + r_2(t-1) = 1427$
   $600t + 700(t-1) = 1427$

2. Solve equation:
   $1300t - 700 = 1427$
   $t = 1300 \overline{)2127}$
   $t \approx 1.64$ hours

3. Convert time into standard form:
   $1.64 \approx 1$ hour, 38 minutes

4. Add 1 hour, 38 minutes to starting time (11:00).

5. Answer the question:
   Planes will pass each other at 12:38 am.

The Question

What is the problem asking?
- At what time will the two planes meet?

What are the hidden questions?
- If $d_1 = r_1 t$ and $d_2 = r_2 t$, when will $d_1 + d_2 = 1427$ miles?

Visualization

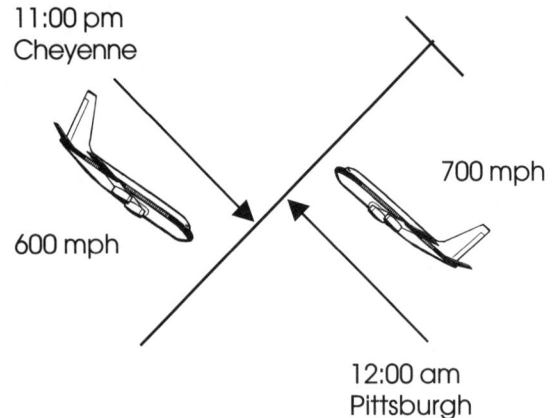

11:00 pm
Cheyenne

600 mph

700 mph

12:00 am
Pittsburgh

The Solution

1. $600t + 700(t-1) = 1427$
2. $1300t - 700 = 1427$

        $t = 1300 \overline{)2127}$

        $t = 1.64$ hours

3. $1.64 \approx 1$ hour and 38 mins.
4.   11:00 pm + 1 hr., 38 mins. = 12:38 am
5.   Planes will pass each other at 12:38 am

MATH NOTES

Student Activity

Featured math concept: **Problem Solving**

Student Name: _____

Directions:
Solve each of the problems below, following the steps in Math Notes (SOLVER). Record your notes on the Math Notes organizer on the next page.

Problem 1
Mr. James is going to pour a concrete slab for his new camper, tow vehicle, and dog pen. The slab will have the shape and dimensions of the diagram shown below. The concrete costs $62 per cubic yard and weighs approximately 20 lbs. per cubic foot. The slab will be four inches thick. Find the cost of concrete for the project. (Round your answer to the nearest $50.)

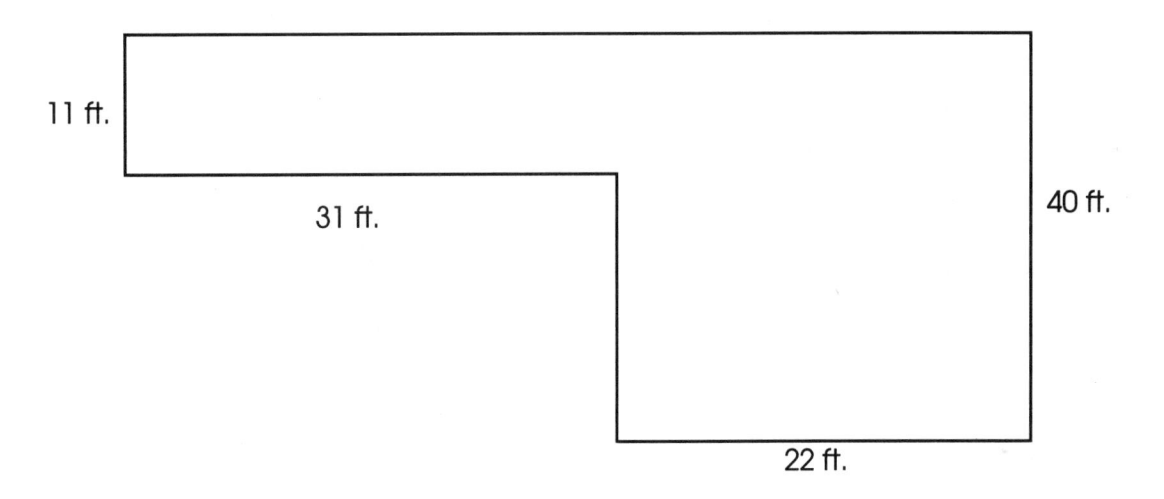

11 ft.
31 ft.
40 ft.
22 ft.

Problem 2
Amy's horse Lucky weighs 1200 lbs. and trots at a rate of 10 feet per second. Kristine's horse Kit weighs 1400 lbs. and canters at a rate of 25 feet per second. If Amy starts to trot her horse around a 1 mile track at 10:15 am and Kristine starts to canter her horse around the same track at 10:20 am, what time will Kit catch up with Lucky? Assume that both horses start their run at the same position on the track, and that the horses will trot and canter long enough for one horse to catch up with the other. When Kit catches up to Lucky, how far will each horse have run?

Math Notes Organizer

The Facts

What are the facts?

What is missing?

What is irrelevant?

The Steps

What are the steps we can take to solve the problem?

The Question

What question needs to be answered?

Are there any hidden questions that need to be answered?

Visualization

How can we represent the problem visually or physically?

The Solution

Mathematics, Styles, and Strategies
TASK ROTATION

During a unit on fractions, if each student were asked to do one of the following mathematical tasks, which one would each student choose to do?

Problem 1
Use the rules of fractions to perform the following operations. Simplify your answers.

$$3\frac{1}{2} + 2\frac{1}{4} \qquad 4\frac{1}{4} - 1\frac{1}{4} \qquad 2\frac{1}{2} \times 4\frac{1}{5} \qquad 4\frac{1}{2} \div 2\frac{1}{4}$$

Problem 2
Let the bold figure to the right represent one whole. Working with a learning partner, use graph paper and shading to show that:

$$2\frac{1}{4} + 1\frac{1}{2} = 3\frac{3}{4}$$

Problem 3
The algorithm for dividing two fractions is as follows: To divide two fractions, rewrite the first fraction, invert the second fraction, and multiply the two fractions together. Study this algorithm and figure out why this procedure works.

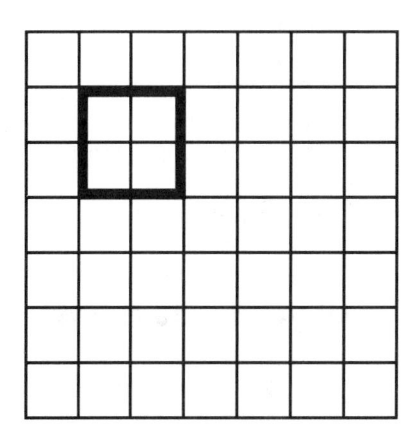

Problem 4
Create a fraction problem that, on the surface, appears to be complex but simplifies to a very simple answer (like 0 or 1). Be prepared to share your creation with the class.

The choice of each student would likely be dependent on each student's *learning style*. Learning styles are based on the groundbreaking work of Carl Jung (1923), who discovered that the way people take in information and make decisions about the importance of that information develops into personality types. They are also based on the work of Kathleen Briggs and Isabel Myers (1962/1998), who elaborated on Jung's work to develop a comprehensive model of human differences made famous by their Myers-Briggs Type Indicator®. Using the Silver-Strong learning style model (Silver, Hanson, 1998), which synthesizes the work of Jung and applies it to teaching and learning, we can see four distinct styles of math students. These four styles are summarized on the following page.

Of course, no one has just one style. Mathematical styles are not fixed categories that make one person a Mastery learner and another an Interpersonal learner. Throughout our lives and in various situations, we use all four styles to solve problems posed by various situations. But it is also true that most of us develop familiarity and strength in one or two styles, and we tend to be weaker in one or two other styles. This means that learning styles are the key to motivating students and helping them experience the joys of success. The trick is to help students capitalize on their strengths by accommodating their dominant styles while encouraging them to stretch and grow in their weak styles. No strategy achieves this effect better than Task Rotation (Silver, et al., 1996).

WHAT IS YOUR MATH LEARNING STYLE? WHAT ARE YOUR STUDENTS' STYLES?

THE FOUR TYPES OF MATH STUDENTS*

Mastery Math Students ...

Want to ... learn practical information and set procedures

Like math problems that ... are like problems they have solved before and that use algorithms to produce a single solution

Approach problem solving ... in a step-by-step manner

Experience difficulty when ... math becomes too abstract or when faced with non-routine problems

Want a math teacher who ... models new skills, allows time for practice, and builds in feedback and coaching sessions

Interpersonal Math Students ...

Want to ... learn math through dialogue, collaboration, and cooperative learning

Like math problems that ... focus on real-world applications and on how math helps people

Approach problem solving ... as an open discussion among a community of problem solvers

Experience difficulty when ... instruction focuses on independent seatwork or when what they are learning seems to lack real-world application

Want a math teacher who ... pays attention to their successes and struggles in math

Understanding Math Students ...

Want to ... understand why the math they learn works

Like math problems that ... ask them to explain, prove, or take a position

Approach problem solving ... by looking for patterns and identifying hidden questions

Experience difficulty when ... there is a focus on the social environment of the classroom (e.g. on collaboration and cooperative problem solving)

Want a math teacher who ... challenges them to think and who lets them explain their thinking

Self-Expressive Math Students ...

Want to ... use their imagination to explore mathematical ideas

Like math problems that ... are non-routine, project-like in nature, and that allow them to think "outside the box"

Approach problem solving ... by visualizing the problem, generating possible solutions, and exploring among the alternatives

Experience difficulty when ... math instruction is focused on drill and practice and rote problem solving

Want a math teacher who ... invites imagination and creative problem solving into the math classroom

---

*If you are interested in finding the learning styles of your math students, we suggest using the **Math Learning Style Inventory for Secondary Students**. A sample of the **Math Learning Style Inventory** is included in Appendix A of this book.

Developing a Task Rotation Activity

In order to develop a Task Rotation activity, the teacher must understand the four learning styles. Additionally, the teacher must be able to pose questions about a given concept in all four styles. The four questions in the example at the beginning of this introduction are representative of the four learning styles.

Problem 1 says, *"Use the rules of fractions to perform the following operations. Simplify your answers"* and asks students to apply the operations on fractions algorithms. Since the rules are straightforward, students can work independently without discussion, manipulatives, or creative/divergent thinking. This task is well suited for a student with a dominant *Mastery* learning style.

Problem 2 says, *"Let the bold figure to the right represent one whole. Working with a learning partner, use graph paper and shading to show that $2\frac{1}{4} + 1\frac{1}{2} = 3\frac{3}{4}$."* It allows students to work together and use graph paper as a model for adding mixed numbers. This task is well suited for a student with a dominant *Interpersonal* learning style.

Problem 3 says, *"The algorithm for dividing two fractions is as follows: To divide two fractions, rewrite the first fraction, invert the second fraction, and multiply the two fractions together. Study this algorithm and figure out why this algorithm works."* This problem challenges students to think deeply about the division algorithm and to use their understanding of fractions and division to determine why this simple rule works. This task is well suited for a student with a dominant *Understanding* learning style.

Problem 4 says, *"Create a fraction problem that, on the surface, appears to be complex, but simplifies to a very simple answer (like 0 or 1). Be prepared to share your creation with the class."* It enables students to be inventive and creative. Even though the task requires students to think critically about processes needed to perform operations on fractions, the nature of the task will result in different answers from different students. This task is well suited for students who have a dominant Self-Expressive learning style.

In summary, to develop a Task Rotation activity, identify a math concept for students to learn and develop four problems, questions, or tasks that are representative of the four styles.

Implementing the Task Rotation Activity

The Task Rotation activity can be presented to students in four quandrants or as a series of four successive questions. In a Task Rotation math activity, the teacher can ask all students to solve all four learning style questions or make one question mandatory and let students choose one or two of the remaining three.

Mastery	Interpersonal
Understanding	Self-expressive

Mastery

Interpersonal

Understanding

Self-expressive

TASK ROTATION

Student Activity

Featured math concept: **Working with Polynomials**

Student Name: _____

Directions:

In this Task Rotation, you will be asked to think in various ways about polynomials. Complete the four tasks below. When you have completed all four tasks, reflect on your work. Which task was easiest for you? Which was hardest? Which did you like best? Which did you like least?

Mastery Task

Perform the following operations on polynomials:

1. $(-2x^2 + 3x - 7) + (8x^2 - 9x - 2)$
2. $(x^2 + 7x + 12) \div (x + 3)$
3. $(x^2 - 6x + 12) - (2x^2 - 4x - 4)$
4. $(x^2 + x + 2)(x - 2)$

Interpersonal Task

Work with a learning partner.

a. Find the perimeter and area of the rectangle below. Write your answers as polynomials.

(rectangle with length $x^2 + 2x + 2$ and width $x + 4$)

b. If $x = 2$, find the length and width of the rectangle. Use the length and width to find the perimeter and area of the rectangle. If 2 is substituted for x in your answers from 'a', do you think the polynomial versions of perimeter and area should match your answers from 'b'? Discuss with your partner, then solve to see if they are equal.

Understanding Task

Use the diagram below to explain why $(x + 2)(x + 4) = x^2 + 6x + 8$

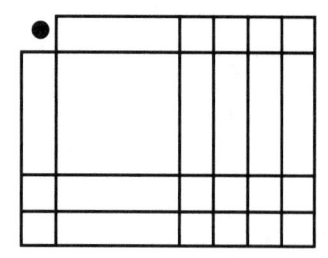

Self-Expressive Task

Create a geometric figure with dimensions that are polynomials of x with degree two. Choose your polynomials so the perimeter and area are both multiples of 10 when x takes on a whole number value greater than 1.

Page 182

Student Activity

TASK ROTATION
Featured math concepts: **Parallel Lines and Congruent Angles**

Student Name: _____

Directions:
Solve the problems in the Mastery category below. Check your answers with your learning partner's answers. Then work with your learning partner and solve two of three Interpersonal, Understanding, and Self-Expressive problems.

Mastery Challenge

In the figure to the right, line l is parallel to line m. The measure of angle 1 equals 35 degrees. Find the measures of the other angles.

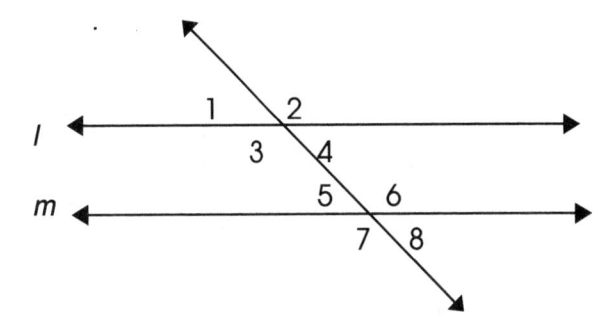

Interpersonal Challenge

Working with a partner, use a straight edge to draw a parallelogram that is not a rectangle. Label the four angles A, B, C, and D. Apply the theorem *If two parallel lines are cut by a transversal, consecutive interior angles are supplementary*, by identifying all pairs of angles that are supplementary. Use a protractor to measure the angles and verify that your identified pairs of angles are supplementary.

Understanding Challenge

In the figure to the right, $\overline{DE} \parallel \overline{AC}$. Use the *alternate interior angles theorem* and triangle ABC to prove that the sum of the interior angles of any triangle is 180 degrees. (Hint: Use the fact that line DE is a straight angle.)

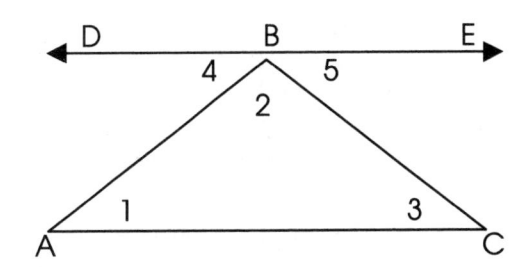

Self-Expressive Challenge

In geometry two lines are parallel if they are in the same plane and never intersect. It is possible to creatively extend the idea of parallelism to people. Two people might be said to be parallel if they live in the same state but never come in contact. Work with a learning partner and create five extensions of the concept of parallelism to the real world.

		TASK ROTATION
Student Activity		Featured math concepts: **Integers and Perfect Squares**
		Student Name: _____

Directions:
Work with a learning partner to perform the Mastery challenge below. Then, work with your learning partner and solve two of three Interpersonal, Understanding, and Self-Expressive problems.

Mastery Challenge
Memorize the following perfect squares. Be prepared to demonstrate your knowledge on a quiz of the perfect squares 1 - 20.

$1^2 = 1$	$5^2 = 25$	$9^2 = 81$	$13^2 = 169$	$17^2 = 289$
$2^2 = 4$	$6^2 = 36$	$10^2 = 100$	$14^2 = 196$	$18^2 = 324$
$3^2 = 9$	$7^2 = 49$	$11^2 = 121$	$15^2 = 225$	$19^2 = 361$
$4^2 = 16$	$8^2 = 64$	$12^2 = 144$	$16^2 = 256$	$20^2 = 400$

Interpersonal Challenge
Work with a learning partner and use lattice paper or a geoboard to model each of the perfect squares below. For each number, create a square whose side length is equal to the square root of the perfect square. Count the number of unit squares in each square.

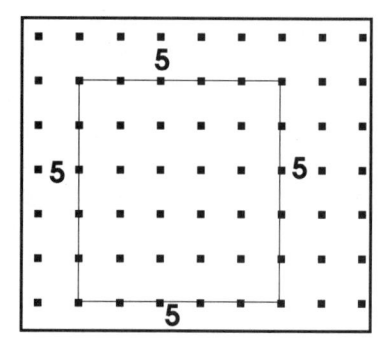

25   16   9   49   1   4

Understanding Challenge
In mathematics, the square of a number x is $x^2 = x \cdot x$. The cube of a number x is $x^3 = x \cdot x \cdot x$. To multiply x^2 and x^3 you add the exponents ($x^2 \cdot x^3 = x^5$). Why is this true? Why don't you multiply the exponents? Determine and explain the rule for dividing two numbers with the same base but different exponents.

Self-Expressive Challenge
In mathematics, the term *square* indicates *exponent two* and the term *cube* indicates *exponent three*. The reason these terms are used is because the area of a square with side length x is x^2 and the volume of a cube with side length x is x^3. Work with your learning partner to create or invent a new math term for another power. Share your creation with the class along with the thinking process that resulted in the development of your new term.

Mathematics, Styles, and Strategies
DO YOU SEE WHAT I SEE?

As state and national standards are emphasizing problem-solving skills, teachers are faced with the prospect of developing a skill-based curriculum without cutting into content. To do this effectively, teachers need strategies that:

- are easy to implement;
- require little planning and marking time and cause no major disruptions in existing programs;
- allow them to reach all students so that those with lower proficiency aren't left behind;
- are aligned with state tests and designed to develop the skills identified in state standards;
- require students to engage in in-depth thinking as well as more routine forms of thought; and
- provide manageable opportunities for teachers to diagnose problems and provide coaching.

Do You See What I See? (Strong & Silver, 1998) was designed in response to these classroom needs and as a powerful technique for helping students to slow down and make a plan before solving a problem. Indeed, one of the most common blocks on new math achievement tests is not forgetting basic math rules, but impulsive problem solving. Students decide quickly what a problem wants and how to solve it. By using the Do You See What I See? Strategy, you can help students become more careful, planful, and powerful problem solvers.

Sample of a Problem Suitable for Do You See What I See?

To build his 10th-graders' problem-solving skills, Mr. Wheatley uses Do You Hear What I Hear? in conjunction with math word problems like this one, which is part of his unit on linear equations:

In economics, supply shows the quantity of items that the company is capable of producing at various prices. Demand shows the number of pairs of sneakers consumers desire at various prices. Demand is generally a negatively sloped line, while supply is positively sloped. Price is placed on the y-axis and the quantity is placed on the x-axis. You can think of price and quantity as coordinate pairs, where quantity is the x-coordinate and price the y-coordinate. Profit is maximized where supply and demand intersect.

1. What price should SlamDunk Sneakers charge per pair, and what quantity should they produce in order to maximize their profits? Supply and demand schedules are as follows:

price ($)	demand
100	0
80	400
60	800
40	1200
20	1600
0	2000

price ($)	supply
100	1000
80	800
60	600
40	400
20	200
0	0

2. The government has suddenly imposed a $1 tax on sneakers. A tax can be visually depicted as a parallel shift to the left of the supply curve by the amount of the tax. Determine the new optimal price and quantity.

Implementing Do You See What I See?

Phase 1: Comprehending the Problem
- Devote one class period a week to exploring complex and non-routine problems connected with current or past math topics (Problem-Solving Friday).
- Read the problem aloud twice to your students.
- During the first reading ask students to take notes on the relevant information.
- During the second reading ask them to create a sketch representing the problem using numbers or letters (but no words) where appropriate.

Phase 2: Developing a Problem-solving Plan
- Provide students with a written version of the problem and ask them to revise their notes. Make sure students do not solve the problem yet.
- Create small collaborative groups (3 - 4 students) and ask the teams to share their information and then:
  Define what the problem is asking for; develop a plan to solve the problem; but do not solve the problem.

Phase 3: Exploring Different Approaches
- As students work, circulate, listening to and observing student approaches. Ask questions but do not attempt to provide answers or hints. Select two or three students with different approaches to lay out their plans to the class while the class questions and critiques.

Phase 4: Revising and Publishing
- Assign the problem for homework. Students need to solve the problem and submit a written justification for their approach. Have students do three problems like this a month, and ask them to select their best effort each month. Have students meet in editor/response groups to revise and publish their work. Mark only the one published piece.

Often, teachers will create posters that hang in the room for the entire year as a way of reminding students how they should attack problems. For example, one group of teachers created the poster below for their students:

PROBLEM-SOLVING FRIDAY

You know you know how to solve a problem when you know how to ask and answer these questions:

What does the problem say? (make notes)

What's relevant and what's not and why? (be clear about your reasons)

What does the problem look like? (diagram it)

What's my plan for solving it? (first, next, then, finally)

How would I explain it to someone who had never solved a problem like this?

References

Adler, M. (1982). The paideia proposal: Rediscovering the essence of education. *American School Board Journal, 169(7),* 17-20.

Brownlie, F., Close, S., & Wingren, L. (1990). *Tomorrow's classrooms today: Strategies for creating active readers, writers, and thinkers.* Markham, Ontario, Canada: Pembroke.

Briggs, K. C., & Myers, I. B. (1998). Myers-Briggs Type Indicator ®, Form M. Palo Alto, CA: Consulting Psychologists Press. (Original work published 1962)

Bruner, J. (1968). *Toward a theory of instruction.* New York, NY: Norton.

Gardner, H. (1983). *Frames of mind: The theory of multiple intelligences.* New York: Basic Books

Gardner, H. (1999). *Intelligence reframed: Multiple intelligences for the 21st century.* New York: Basic Books

Gordon, W. J. J. (1961). *Synectics.* New York, NY: Harper and Row.

Jensen, E. (1988). *Teaching with the brain in mind.* Alexandria, VA: Association for Supervision and Curriculum Development.

Johnson, D. W., & Johnson, R. T. (1999). *Learning together and alone: cooperative, competitive, and individualistic learning.* Boston, MA: Allyn & Bacon.

Jung, C. (1923). *Psychological types.* (trans. H. G. Baynes). New York: Harcourt, Brace.

Marzano, Robert J., Pickering, Debra J., & Pollock, Jane E. (2001). *Classroom instruction that works.* Virginia: Association for Supervision and Curriculum Development.

Mosston, Muska. (1972). *Teaching: from command to discovery.* Belmont, CA: Wadsworth Publishing Co.

Mullis, I.V.S., Owen, G.H., & Phillips, G.W. (1990). *America's challenge: Accelerating academic achievement (a summary of findings from 20 years of NAEP).* Princeton, NJ: Educational Testing Service.

Perkins, D.N. (1986). *Knowledge as design.* Hillsdale, NJ: Lawrence Erlbaum Associates.

Siegel, M. G. (1984). *Reading as signification.* Doctoral dissertation, Indiana University, Bloomington.

Silver, H. F., & Hanson, J. R. (1998). *Learning styles and strategies* (3rd ed.). Woodbridge, NJ: Thoughtful Education Press.

Silver, H. F., & Hanson, J. R., Strong, R. W., & Schwartz, P. B. (1996). *Teaching styles and strategies* (3rd ed.). Woodbridge, NJ: Thoughtful Education Press.

Slavin, R.E. (1987). *Cooperative learning: Student teams. What research says to the teacher.* Washington, DC: National Education Association.

Slavin, R.E. (1991). *Student team learning: A practical guide to cooperative learning (3rd edition).* Washington DC: National Education Association.

Sousa, D. (1995). *How the brain learns.* Virginia: National Association for Secondary School Principals.

Sternberg, R.J. (1999). The nature of mathematical reasoning. In L.V. Stiff & F.R. Curcio (Eds.), *Developing mathematical reasoning in grades K-12: 1999 Yearbook.* Reston, VA: National Council of Teachers of Mathematics.

Strong, R.W., & Silver, H.F. (1998). *Simple and deep: Factors affecting classroom implementation and student performance.* Unpublished research.

Suchman, J. R. (1966). *Developing inquiry.* Chicago: Science Research Associates.

Taba, H. (1971). *Hilda Taba teaching strategies program.* Miami, FL: Institute for Staff Development.

Answers and Solutions to Selected Problems

Page 26

Quiz 1
1. sinx cos y − cosx siny
2. cosx cosy − sinx siny
3. $\frac{1}{2}(\sin(x+y) + \sin(x-y))$
4. $\frac{\tan x + \tan y}{1 - \tan x \tan y}$
5. sinx cosy + cosx siny

Quiz 2
1. sinx cosy + cosx siny
2. cosx cosy + sinx siny
3. $\frac{1}{2}(\cos(x-y) + \cos(x+y))$
4. $\frac{\tan x - \tan y}{1 + \tan x \tan y}$
5. cosx cosy − sinx siny

Quiz 3
1. cosx cosy + sinx siny
2. $\frac{\tan x + \tan y}{1 - \tan x \tan y}$
3. $\frac{1}{2}(\sin(x+y) + \sin(x-y))$
4. $\frac{\tan x - \tan y}{1 + \tan x \tan y}$
5. $\frac{1}{2}(\cos(x+y) + \cos(x-y))$

Quiz 4
1. $\frac{1}{2}(\cos(x+y) + \cos(x-y))$
2. cosx cosy + sinx siny
3. $\frac{1}{2}(\sin(x+y) + \sin(x-y))$
4. $\frac{\tan x - \tan y}{1 + \tan x \tan y}$
5. $\frac{1}{2}(\cos(x-y) + \cos(x+y))$

Quiz 5
1. sinx cosy + cosx siny
2. cosx cosy + sinx siny
3. $\frac{1}{2}(\sin(x+y) + \sin(x-y))$
4. $\frac{\tan x + \tan y}{1 - \tan x \tan y}$
5. sinx cosy − cosx siny

Page 27

Quiz 1
1. a+b = b + a
2. (ab)c = a(bc)
3. a+0 = a
4. ab ∈R
5. $a \cdot \frac{1}{a} = 1$

Quiz 2
1. a+0 = a
2. ab ∈R
3. a(b + c) = ab + ac
4. ab = ba
5. (ab)c = a(bc)

Quiz 3
1. (a + b) + c = a + (b + c)
2. a(b − c) = ab − ac
3. a+b = b +a
4. a + 0 = a
5. a • 1 = a

Quiz 4
1. ab = ba
2. (a + b) + c = a + (b + c)
3. a • 1 = a
4. a + b ∈R
5. a + −a = 0

Quiz 5
1. a(b + c) = ab + ac
2. a + b = b + a
3. a + b ∈R
4. ab ∈R
5. a • 1 = a

Page 28

Quiz 1	196	441	121	576	324	361	529
Quiz 2	144	441	196	625	289	169	484
Quiz 3	256	529	225	484	196	289	576
Quiz 4	361	400	225	529	361	256	441

Page 31

1. $\dfrac{1}{\sqrt{2}}$ 2. $\dfrac{1}{\sqrt{2}}$ 3. $\dfrac{1}{2}$ 4. $\dfrac{\sqrt{3}}{2}$ 5. 1   6. 1

Problem 1.
$$(\csc x + \cot x)(1 - \cos x) = \sin x$$
$$\left(\dfrac{1}{\sin x} + \dfrac{\cos x}{\sin x}\right)(1 - \cos x) = \sin x$$
$$\dfrac{1}{\sin x} - \dfrac{\cos x}{\sin x} + \dfrac{\cos x}{\sin x} - \dfrac{\cos^2 x}{\sin x} = \sin x$$
$$\dfrac{1}{\sin x} - \dfrac{\cos^2 x}{\sin x} = \sin x$$
$$\dfrac{1 - \cos^2 x}{\sin x} = \sin x$$
$$\dfrac{\sin^2 x}{\sin x} = \sin x$$
$$\sin x = \sin x$$

Problem 2.
$$\cos^4 x - \sin^4 x = \cos 2x$$
$$(\cos^2 x + \sin^2 x)(\cos^2 x - \sin^2 x) =$$
$$1(\cos^2 x - \sin^2 x) =$$
$$1(\cos 2x) = \cos 2x$$

Problem 3.
$$\left(\dfrac{1 + \dfrac{\sin x}{\cos x}}{1 - \dfrac{\sin x}{\cos x}}\right)^2 =$$

$$\left(\dfrac{\dfrac{\cos x + \sin x}{\cos x}}{\dfrac{\cos x - \sin x}{\cos x}}\right)^2 =$$

$$\left(\dfrac{\cos x + \sin x}{\cos x} * \dfrac{\cos x - \sin x}{\cos x}\right)^2 =$$

$$\dfrac{\cos^2 x + 2\sin x \cos x + \sin^2 x}{\cos^2 x - 2\sin x \cos x + \sin^2 x} =$$

$$\dfrac{1 + 2\sin x \cos x}{1 - 2\sin x \cos x} =$$

$$\dfrac{1 + \sin 2x}{1 - \sin 2x}$$

Page 32   Warmup   1. 5/6   2. 19/15   3. 7/20   4. 1/6   5. 71/10   6. 1

Problem 1. 9   Problem 2. 81/4   Problem 3. 1764/25

Page 37

1. <u>Function-</u> is a correspondence between a first set, called a domain, and a second set, called a range, such that to any member of the domain, there corresponds exactly one member of the range.
<u>Ordered Pair-</u> a pair of numbers in a particular order; the coordinates of a point in a plane.
<u>Graph-</u> a geometric representation of the solution set of an equation or inequality; a set of points whose values are representative of a mathematical relationship

2. <u>Parabola-</u> a graph of a quadratic function that can be described by an equation of the form:
$f(x) = ax^2 + bx + c$, where a does not equal 0.
<u>Translation-</u> the composite of two reflections over parallel lines; Sliding a figure in a plane.
<u>Reflection-</u> For a point A which is not on a line M, the reflection image of A over M is the point B if and only if m is the perpendicular bisector of line AB. For a point A on a plane M is A itself. A flip across a line.

3. a. moved along the y-axis 2 units
   b. moved along the y-axis 4 units
   c. moved two spaces to the right along the x-axis
   d. moved 4 spaces to the left along the x-axis
   e. broadens (widens) the parabola
   f. reflects the graph across the x-axis
   g. the graph is translated 2 spaces to the right and 2 spaces up
   h. reflects the graph across the x-axis and translates it 4 spaces along the y-axis

Page 39   1. x = 5   2. a = 22   3. x = 80   4. b = 6.71   5. y = 20   6. all numbers

Page 41   1. x = 11   2. x = .1   3. x = 1   4. x = 3/4

Page 65   yes: 8, 24, 0, 3, 15   no: 5, 2, 7, 20, 16   Multiples of three or Perfect Squares – 1

Page 66   yes: 4, 16, 1, 8, 2   no: 3, 20, 35, 14, 12   Factors of 16
           yes: 4, 12, 42, 60, 6   no: 13, 10, 64, 40, 15   Numbers between twin primes (tweeners)

Page 67   Number of diagonals are odd

Page 70   1. Each edge ≈ 8.6 inches   2. V_{left} = ≈ 303 cubic in.   3. ≈ 1182

Page 71   There is no missing dollar. The cook has $25, the waitress has $2, each of the three salesmen has $1. $25 + $2 + $3 = 30. (In the story, three men contributing $9 each already accounts for the $27 (cook + waitress). When the story refers to '*plus the $2 the waitress has*', that's the error in the story.)

Page 72   1. $2\sqrt{2}$; $8\sqrt{5}/5$
           2. $(3 + \sqrt{15}, 4 + \sqrt{15})$
           3. $((-1 + \sqrt{21})/2, (3 + \sqrt{21}/2)$

Page 73 1A) $y = -\sqrt{3}x$, $x \in [-1,0]$
$y = \sqrt{3}x + 2\sqrt{3}$, $x \in [-1,0]$
$y = 0$, $x \in [0,2]$
$y = \sqrt{3}x - 2\sqrt{3}$, $x \in [2,3]$
$y = -\sqrt{3}x + 4\sqrt{3}$, $x \in [2,3]$
$y = 2\sqrt{3}$, $x \in [0,2]$

B) P = 12
A = $6\sqrt{3}$

C) L = $2\sqrt{3}$
W = 2

D) P = $4\sqrt{3} + 4$
A = $4\sqrt{3}$

2A) shaded: (4,0), (6,0), (7,$\sqrt{3}$), (6, $2\sqrt{3}$), (4, $2\sqrt{3}$), (3, $\sqrt{3}$)
partially shaded: (0,0), (2,0), (3, $\sqrt{3}$), (2, $2\sqrt{3}$), (0, $2\sqrt{3}$), (–1, $\sqrt{3}$)

2B) $y = -\sqrt{3}(x-4)$, $x \in [3,4]$
$y = \sqrt{3}(x-4) + 2\sqrt{3}$, $x \in [3,4]$
$y = 0$, $x \in [4,6]$
$y = \sqrt{3}(x-4) - 2\sqrt{3}$, $x \in [6,7]$
$y = -\sqrt{3}(x-4) + 4\sqrt{3}$, $x \in [6,7]$
$y = 2\sqrt{3}$, $x \in [4,6]$

Page 74   1a. 190   b. 4950   c. 2550   d. 15050

Page 75   1. $\sqrt{2}$ 2. $\sqrt{3}$ 3. $\dfrac{\sqrt{6}}{2}$ 4. rectangle   5. $\sqrt{2}$
6. triangle VYS

Page 76   p: true   q: false   r: false   Logical Statement: True

Page 79

Number of Rods	S.A	Volume
1	88	40
2	140	80
3	192	120
4	244	160
5	296	200
n	36 + 52n	40n

Page 81

Number of Rods	S.A.	Volume
1	88	40
2	136	80
3	184	120
4	232	160
5	280	200
n	40 + 48n	40n

Page 82   b. 34, 55, 89, 144, 6765   c. $x_{n+1} = x_n + x_{n-1}$

Page 84   Given: Triangle ABC is isosceles and segment BD is perpendicular to segment AC

Prove: Triangles BDA and BDC are congruent

1. $\angle A \cong \angle C$ 　　　　　　　　　　1. Base angles of an isosceles triangle are congruent
2. $\angle BDA$, $\angle BDC$ are right angles　　2. Perpendicular lines form right angles
3. $\angle BDA \cong \angle BDC$　　　　　　　　3. Right angles are congruent
4. $\overline{BD} \cong \overline{BD}$　　　　　　　　　　　4. Reflexive property
5. Triangles BDA and BDC are congruent　　5. AAS

Page 85   Polygons

Page 86   Proof by induction

Page 99   1. 9   2. 5   3. 1   4. 12   5. 12   6. 3   7. 18   8. 15   9. 14 ; **COLLINEAR**

Page 114   Problem 2 $2x + 2$;   the number of factors of x; $x^3 - 3$

Page 135   Problem 1. $[(2a^2)(4c) + b]i^2$ Problem 2. $y = 2(x-2)^2 + 4$
           Problem 3. $(4 + i)$ and $\left(\frac{7}{10} - \frac{1}{10}i\right)$ Problem 4. $x^2 + 3\frac{1}{2}x - 2 = 0$
           Problem 5. sphere: r = 3 and pyramid: s=6 and h=3

Page 140   1. half-line   2. ray   3. $y = -x + 4$, $0 \leq x \leq 4$; $y = x + 2$, $x \geq -6$
           4. A ray has an endpoint, a half line has no endpoint

Page 154   1. x = -3   2. x = -12   3. x = 6   4. no solution   5. x = -14
           6. x = -3   7. x = -4   8. x = -4

Page 155   1. x = 6   2. x = 2   3. x = 5   4. x = 5   5. x = -2
           6. x = -3   7. x = -4   8. x = -3

Page 157   Problem 3. $f(x) = 2^x$

Page 160   1. -2   2. 0   3. 2   4. 8   5. -8   6. -4

Page 167 Problem 1. Closure for addition, subtraction, multiplication, Commutative for addition, multiplication, Associative for addition, multiplication, Distributive, Identity for addition, Inverse for addition
Problem 2. Closure for multiplication, Commutative for addition and multiplication, Associative for addition, multiplication, Distributive, Identity for multiplication.
Problem 3. Commutative for addition, multiplication Associative for addition, multiplication, Distributive
Problem 4. Closure for multiplication, Commutative for addition, multiplication, Associative for addition, multiplication, Distributive, Identity for addition, Inverse for addition.
Problem 5. Closure for addition, Commutative for addition and multiplication, Associative for addition, multiplication, Distributive

Page 168 3. 4   4. .63093

Page 177 Problem 1: $950
Problem 2: 10:23:20 a.m.   5000 ft

Page 182 Mastery
1. $6x^2 - 6x - 9$
2. $x + 4$
3. $-x^2 - 2x + 16$
4. $x^3 - x^2 - 4$

Interpersonal
A) $P = 2x^2 + 6x + 12$
   $A = x^3 + 6x^2 + 10x + 8$

B) Yes they are P = 32 and A = 60

Self Expressive
A square with side length $10x^2$.

Page 183
1. 35   5. 35
2. 145 6. 145
3. 145 7. 145
4. 35   8. 35

Understanding
  The sum of angles 2, 4, and 5 equal 180 degrees (straight angle). Angle 4 equals angle and angle 5 equals angle 3 (alternate interior angles). By substitution, angles 1, 2, and 3 add to 180 degrees. These angles represent the interior angles of any triangle.

The First Learning Style Inventory for Math Students!

NEW!
MATH LEARNING STYLE Inventory™

for Secondary Students
Grades 6 - 12

A **Self-Scoring Tool** for Secondary Students to Identify Their Preferred Learning Styles in Mathematics

Based on Carl Gustav Jung's Theory of Psychological Types

© 2003 Thoughtful Education Press, LLC. All rights reserved. No part of this publication may be reproduced in any manner whatsoever without the written permission of Thoughtful Education Press, LLC.

Developed by Harvey F. Silver, Edward J. Thomas, and Matthew J. Perini

What Kind of Problem Solver Are *You*?

Math is all about problem solving. But not all students and not all mathematicians solve problems in the same way. In fact, even though your textbook might tell you otherwise, there are many different ways to solve math problems. Your own preferences as a problem solver can tell you a lot about how your mind works and how you learn best.

So, how do you go about solving problems in math? Let's conduct a little experiment to find out. Read "The Canoe Problem" below. When you feel ready, use the workspace to solve "The Canoe Problem." But here's the twist: As you are getting ready to solve the problem and as you are doing the work of problem solving, try to look and listen in on your own mind. What is it doing? What is it saying? How is it attempting to solve the problem?

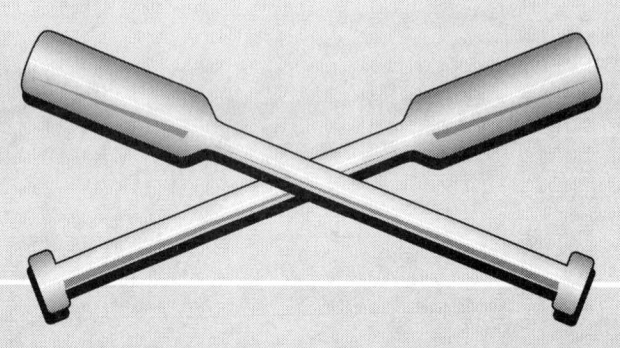

The Canoe Problem
Nineteen campers are hiking through Acadia National Park when they come to a river. The river is moving too rapidly for the campers to swim across. The campers have one canoe, which fits three people. On each trip across the river, one of the three canoe riders must be an adult. There is only one adult among the nineteen campers. How many trips across the river will be needed to get all of the children to the other side of the river?

Now take a look at the next page and how four different students solved "The Canoe Problem." As you read each student's description, think about how much (or how little) each student reminds you of yourself as a problem solver.

How Four Different Students Solved "The Canoe Problem"

Maria

Well, the first thing I did was gather up the facts quickly: 19 campers, 1 canoe, 3 people per canoe, etc. Then – don't think this is crazy – I used a piece of paper to stand for the boat, with one red pen on it to stand for the adult and two blue pens on it to stand for the children. Using actual objects to simulate the problem really helps me – it makes it easier to grasp the problem.

To solve the problem I moved step-by-step from beginning to end. First, I took the facts I gathered up and set them up carefully on paper. Then, I used basic math to get my answer of 17 trips across the river. Finally, I double checked my calculations to make sure I had done my math correctly.

Giovanni

I was very happy when the teacher said we could work with a learning partner. For me, the best way to learn math and solve problems like this one is to talk. I really like it when the teacher comes around and asks me how I'm doing, and I also like when I can work with friends and share my ideas. The best ideas seem to come when people are talking or working together. Anyway, what I really liked about today's learning partnership with Jody is that we didn't just get the answer to the problem right and wait around. We also talked about how we solved the problem and what we might do next time to improve as problem solvers.

Tanisha

I find that problems like this one often have hidden questions or little tricks in them that aren't always so obvious. For example, some people missed the fact that every time 2 children get across the river, that's 2 trips across – one there and one back. By looking at the hidden question, I saw the pattern to the problem pretty quickly: 2 out of 18 children get to the other side for every 2 trips across river. That means it will take 18 trips to get all 18 children across. But here's another little trick: On the last trip, they only need to go one way and not back again. So the answer's actually 17.

Anyway, once I figured out the answer, I checked to make sure it made logical sense and that it answered the question posed by the problem. In both cases, it did.

Al

I need to see the problem in my head. I closed my eyes and actually pictured the river and saw the 18 kids and the 1 adult with that 1 canoe. Then, I generated possible answers by sort of playing with the problem, trying different things out. When I do a problem like this, I try out different ways to solve it. Sometimes, I come up with more than one solution. For this problem, I came up with 9 and 17 as possible answers, so I explored each one to see which one worked. That's how I came up with 17.

Sometimes, I like to imagine cool twists or variations that would make the problem more interesting. For example, what if the boat held only a certain amount of weight and all the campers' weights were given? Then we would have to find the best way to load the boat on each trip.

What we do as problem solvers is closely related to the way we learn. Everyone learns, but we don't all learn in the same way. The differences in how people learn are called **learning styles.** You can see your style in the way you talk, the way you think, and the way you solve problems. Some students, like Maria, solve math problems using step-by-step procedures. Others are like Tanisha. These students prefer to find patterns and discover hidden questions. Students like Al are drawn to problems that are unique and love to speculate on the possible solutions. For students like Giovanni, there's no better way to solve a challenging math problem than by discussing it with friends and fellow students. Which of these students sounds most like you?

On the next page you will find the beginning of the *Math Learning Style Inventory.* It is designed to help you and your teacher understand how you learn best when it comes to math. Follow the directions and enjoy yourself.

This is not a test, so relax and answer honestly.

What Kind of Problem Solver Are You?

The **Math Learning Style Inventory** is a learning tool that provides you and your teacher with information on which learning styles you prefer the most and which you like the least when it comes to math. This information will help you and your teachers make better decisions about learning and teaching.

The **Math Learning Style Inventory** is not a test. There are no right or wrong answers. If you're having trouble with a word, phrase, or idea, please ask your teacher for help.

Directions for Responding

The **Math Learning Style Inventory** is made up of twenty-two numbered statements about your preferences as a math student, followed by four choices, lettered A, B, C, and D. All you have to do is rank the choices in the order in which you prefer them. Use the following point system to rank your choices:

- Give your first, or favorite, preference ....5 points
- Give your second preference ....3 points
- Give your third preference ....1 point
- Give your fourth, or least favorite, preference ....0 points

Remember to assign a different number of points (5,3,1,0) to each of the four choices in each set. Do not make ties.

1. **When it comes to math, I want to:**
   - A. Learn practical information and set procedures.
   - B. Know why the math I learn works.
   - C. Use my imagination to explore mathematical ideas.
   - D. Learn math through dialog and collaboration.

2. **When I encounter a difficult problem, I tend to:**
   - A. Look for any "tricks" or hidden questions.
   - B. Visualize the problem in my head.
   - C. Let how I'm feeling dictate what I do.
   - D. "Roll up my sleeves" and get right to work.

3. **A math classroom should:**
   - A. Encourage spontaneity and curiosity.
   - B. Be a place where learning math is fun.
   - C. Be focused on helping students remember important math procedures.
   - D. Be a place where I can make and validate my own conclusions.

4. **I would prefer a math teacher who is:**
   - A. Friendly and cares about me.
   - B. Organized and rewards hard work.
   - C. Knowledgeable and respects my ideas.
   - D. Enthusiastic about math and uses creative methods to teach.

5. **I like math problems that are:**
   - A. Similar to problems that I've encountered before and that I can use a procedure to solve.
   - B. Challenging and require me to think my way through them.
   - C. New and interesting and that require me to experiment to find a solution.
   - D. About real life.

© 2003 by Thoughtful Education Press, L.L.C. All rights reserved.
Reproduction of this instrument by any process is unlawful without the written permission of Thoughtful Education Press, L.L.C.

6. **I tend to lose interest in math when:**

   - **A.** The teacher doesn't explain the rationale behind learning what we're learning.
   - **B.** We practice the same things over and over again, with little variety or choice.
   - **C.** I can't see how what we're learning is connected to people's lives.
   - **D.** I can't remember the steps I need to follow to solve the problem.

7. **I would prefer to:**

   - **A.** Write a short story about a mathematical concept.
   - **B.** Work with a group to perform a skit that shows how math helps people solve their problems.
   - **C.** Report on the life of a famous mathematician.
   - **D.** Research and take a position on a controversial topic, such as: *Was math discovered, or was it invented?*

8. **I will work hard when:**

   - **A.** My teacher appreciates my effort.
   - **B.** I know how to do the work.
   - **C.** I understand why the math I'm learning is important.
   - **D.** I get a chance to apply math in my own creative way.

9. **I would say that problem solving is mostly about:**

   - **A.** Applying step-by-step procedures.
   - **B.** Asking questions and discovering patterns.
   - **C.** Generating possible solutions and exploring among the alternatives.
   - **D.** Sharing ideas and collaborating with fellow learners.

10. **A great math classroom is like:**

    - **A.** A courtroom, where I get to explain and defend my ideas.
    - **B.** A laboratory, where I get to experiment and try out new things.
    - **C.** A book club, where I get to discuss my learning with my teacher and fellow classmates.
    - **D.** A sports practice, where I get to fine tune my skills before they count.

11. **My ideal math teacher would:**

    - **A.** Allow me to use my imagination and creativity.
    - **B.** Allow ample time for discussion and small group work.
    - **C.** Show me exactly what I need to know and give me time to practice.
    - **D.** Challenge me to think on my feet.

12. **The best kinds of math assignments:**

    - **A.** Encourage teamwork and involve the whole class.
    - **B.** Let me practice what I already know.
    - **C.** Ask me to use data to prove something.
    - **D.** Have interesting "twists" that make them unique.

13. **It's hardest for me to focus when:**

    - **A.** There's too much abstraction and not enough time for practicing skills.
    - **B.** There's too much group work and not enough independent thinking.
    - **C.** There's too much routine work and not enough that's new and interesting.
    - **D.** There's too much independent seat work and not enough cooperative work.

14. Show me a square, a rectangle, and a triangle, and I'll show you:
- A. The similarities and differences between the three shapes.
- B. A cool design that uses all three shapes.
- C. Which shape is my personal favorite.
- D. How to find the area and perimeter of each shape.

15. In math class, the most important thing is:
- A. Being able to think "outside the box."
- B. Sharing my successes and struggles with my teacher so I can see how to improve.
- C. Calculating and computing accurately.
- D. Learning how to think and reason for myself.

16. A great problem solver in math:
- A. Is never afraid to consult with fellow problem solvers.
- B. Has a great memory for formulas and procedures.
- C. Plans out his/her problem-solving strategies in advance.
- D. Will look at a problem from a variety of perspectives.

17. No math classroom should be without:
- A. Clear guidelines and expectations.
- B. Some good, healthy debate.
- C. A variety of activities and the chance to choose those that interest me.
- D. Lots of interaction and hands-on learning that involves everyone.

18. I learn best when my math teacher:
- A. Asks thought-provoking questions and lets me think for myself.
- B. Uses interesting problems to teach new concepts.
- C. Encourages me and my classmates to share our ideas.
- D. Gives me immediate feedback on how I'm doing.

19. I would prefer to demonstrate what I know about a math concept by:
- A. Doing a creative project.
- B. Reflecting on my learning in a journal.
- C. Completing a worksheet or taking a quiz.
- D. Conducting further research and writing an essay.

20. I get most anxious in math class when:
- A. I don't see how what I'm learning relates to me.
- B. I encounter open-ended problems that don't have clear answers or procedures for solving them.
- C. There's more focus on working in groups than there is on learning content.
- D. I'm not able to visualize what I'm learning in my head.

21. I would prefer to learn a new math concept by:
- A. Listening to a teacher lecture and taking notes.
- B. Comparing and contrasting the new concept with another concept that's related to it.
- C. Using a metaphor/simile to develop a new perspective on the concept (e.g., *Factors are like a family tree because…*).
- D. Playing a math game.

22. I like math problems best when they:
- A. Ask me to use logic to solve a challenging problem and explain my thinking. (See Problem A on page 6.)
- B. Challenge me to use math creatively. (See Problem B on page 6.)
- C. Involve real-life situations and problems people commonly face. (See Problem C on page 6.)
- D. Ask me to find correct answers. (See Problem D on page 6.)

22. (continued)

(Sample math problems)

Problem A

You are given eight golf balls. Seven of the golf balls have the exact same weight, but one ball is slightly lighter (you cannot feel the difference). You have a balance scale, but can only make two weighings. How can you find the lighter ball in only two weighings? Explain.

Problem B

In geometry, two lines are parallel if they are in the same plane and never intersect. Take the mathematical concept of parallel lines and apply it to non-mathematical situations or objects. For example, two people might be said to be parallel if they live in the same town but never come in contact with one another. Think of at least three new examples of things that are, figuratively speaking, parallel. Be sure to explain how each example can be considered parallel.

Problem C

As class social chairperson, you ordered 256 T-shirts for your class. After checking the number of shirts carefully and placing them into the storeroom, you tell the section leaders to each pick up 1/4 of the shirts to distribute to their class section.

Tanya arrives first and takes 1/4 of the shirts. Later, Matt arrives and takes 1/4. During lunch, Rich stops by and picks up 1/4. Finally, just before the final bell, Nicky takes 1/4 of the shirts.

The next morning, you are surprised when Matt, Rich, and Nicky tell you that they don't have enough shirts. You can't figure it out – you know you ordered 256 shirts. Then you discover some shirts are still in the storeroom. Matt, Rich, and Nicky tell you they all followed your instructions.

What happened? How many shirts are still in the storeroom and how many do you need to give to Matt, Rich, and Nicky?

Problem D

Use divisibility rules to determine if the first number is divisible by the second number.

1. 1075; 5
2. 699; 3
3. 385; 6
4. 117; 3
5. 3242; 3
6. 2002; 6
7. 13,766; 3

Determining Your Results

DIRECTIONS FOR SCORING THE INVENTORY

This part is a little tricky. In order to get a score for each of the four learning styles, you will need to transfer the points from the inventory you just completed onto the scoring grid below. To do this, you will write the score you gave to each choice in the box next to the corresponding letter.

For example, look at your four responses to Question 1 on page 3 of the inventory. What number did you give Choice **A**? On the grid below, write that number in the white box next to **A** in Row 1. What number did you give Choices **B, C,** and **D** for Question 1? Write those numbers in the white boxes next to **B, C,** and **D** in Row 1. Then, do the same for Questions 2 - 22: Transfer your points from the inventory onto the grid by writing them in the white boxes next to the corresponding letters. But notice that the letters on the grid rotate. Not all the letters in Column 1 are **A's**, not all the letters in Column 2 are **B's**, and so on. **Be extra careful when transferring your points from the inventory onto the grid,** so that your score will be accurate. When you have transferred all your scores, compute the totals for each column.

Question Number	Mastery Choices		Understanding Choices		Self-Expressive Choices		Interpersonal Choices	
1	A		B		C		D	
2	D		A		B		C	
3	C		D		A		B	
4	B		C		D		A	
5	A		B		C		D	
6	D		A		B		C	
7	C		D		A		B	
8	B		C		D		A	
9	A		B		C		D	
10	D		A		B		C	
11	C		D		A		B	
12	B		C		D		A	
13	A		B		C		D	
14	D		A		B		C	
15	C		D		A		B	
16	B		C		D		A	
17	A		B		C		D	
18	D		A		B		C	
19	C		D		A		B	
20	B		C		D		A	
21	A		B		C		D	
22	D		A		B		C	
Totals								

© 2003 by Thoughtful Education Press, L.L.C. All rights reserved.
Reproduction of this instrument by any process is unlawful without the written permission of Thoughtful Education Press, L.L.C.

What Does All This Mean?

When it comes to learning math, there are really four distinct learning styles. These four math learning styles are described below. After you have read all four descriptions, write your scores from the previous page in the appropriate style box. Do you agree with your scores?

Mastery Math Students

Want to... learn practical information and procedures

Like math problems that... are like problems they have solved before and that use set procedures to produce a single solution

Approach problem solving... in a step-by-step manner

May experience difficulty when... math seems too abstract or when faced with open-ended problems

Learn best when... instruction is focused on modeling new skills, practicing, and feedback and coaching sessions

Interpersonal Math Students

Want to... learn math through dialog, collaboration, and cooperative learning

Like math problems that... focus on real-world applications and on how math helps people

Approach problem solving... as an open discussion among a community of problem solvers

May experience difficulty when... instruction focuses on independent seat work or when what they are learning seems to lack real-world application

Learn best when... their teacher pays attention to their successes and struggles in math

---

Maria is a **Mastery Math Student** (see page 2).

Tanisha is an **Understanding Math Student** (see page 2).

My **Mastery** Score: ___
My **Interpersonal** Score: ___
My **Understanding** Score: ___
My **Self-Expressive** Score: ___

Giovanni is an **Interpersonal Math Student** (see page 2).

Al is a **Self-Expressive Math Student** (see page 2).

Understanding Math Students

Want to... understand why the math they learn works

Like math problems that... ask them to explain, prove, or take a position

Approach problem solving... by looking for patterns and identifying hidden questions

May experience difficulty when... there is a focus on the social environment of the classroom (e.g., on collaboration and cooperative problem solving)

Learn best when... they are challenged to think and explain their thinking

Self-Expressive Math Students

Want to... use their imagination to explore mathematical ideas

Like math problems that... are non-routine, project-like in nature, and that allow them to think "outside the box"

Approach problem solving... by visualizing the problem, generating possible solutions, and exploring among the alternatives

May experience difficulty when... math instruction is focused on drill and practice and rote problem solving

Learn best when... they are invited to use their imagination and engage in creative problem solving

---

© 2003 by Thoughtful Education Press, L.L.C. All rights reserved.
Reproduction of this instrument by any process is unlawful without the written permission of Thoughtful Education Press, L.L.C.

What Does My Math Learning Style Profile Look Like?

Different kinds of problems and different kinds of classrooms call for different kinds of thinking. All students rely on all four learning styles to help them learn mathematics. However, we all tend to develop strengths so that one or two styles may be much easier for us to use than the others. The deepest and best understanding of how you learn mathematics will come when you build a Math Learning Style Profile, which shows your preferences for all four learning styles.

Building a Math Learning Style Profile is easy. To build yours, take your point totals for each style from the bottom of page 7 and chart them on the profile graph below. For each style, mark the score along the diagonal line in the appropriate style box. For example, if you had a total of 63 points for your Mastery score, you would make a mark along the diagonal line roughly halfway between the 50-mark and the 75-mark in the Mastery box. Repeat this process for each of the four styles. Once you have made your four marks, connect all four dots with straight lines to create a four-sided polygon. This figure represents your math learning profile and shows you, at a glance, which styles are your strongest and which need extra attention.

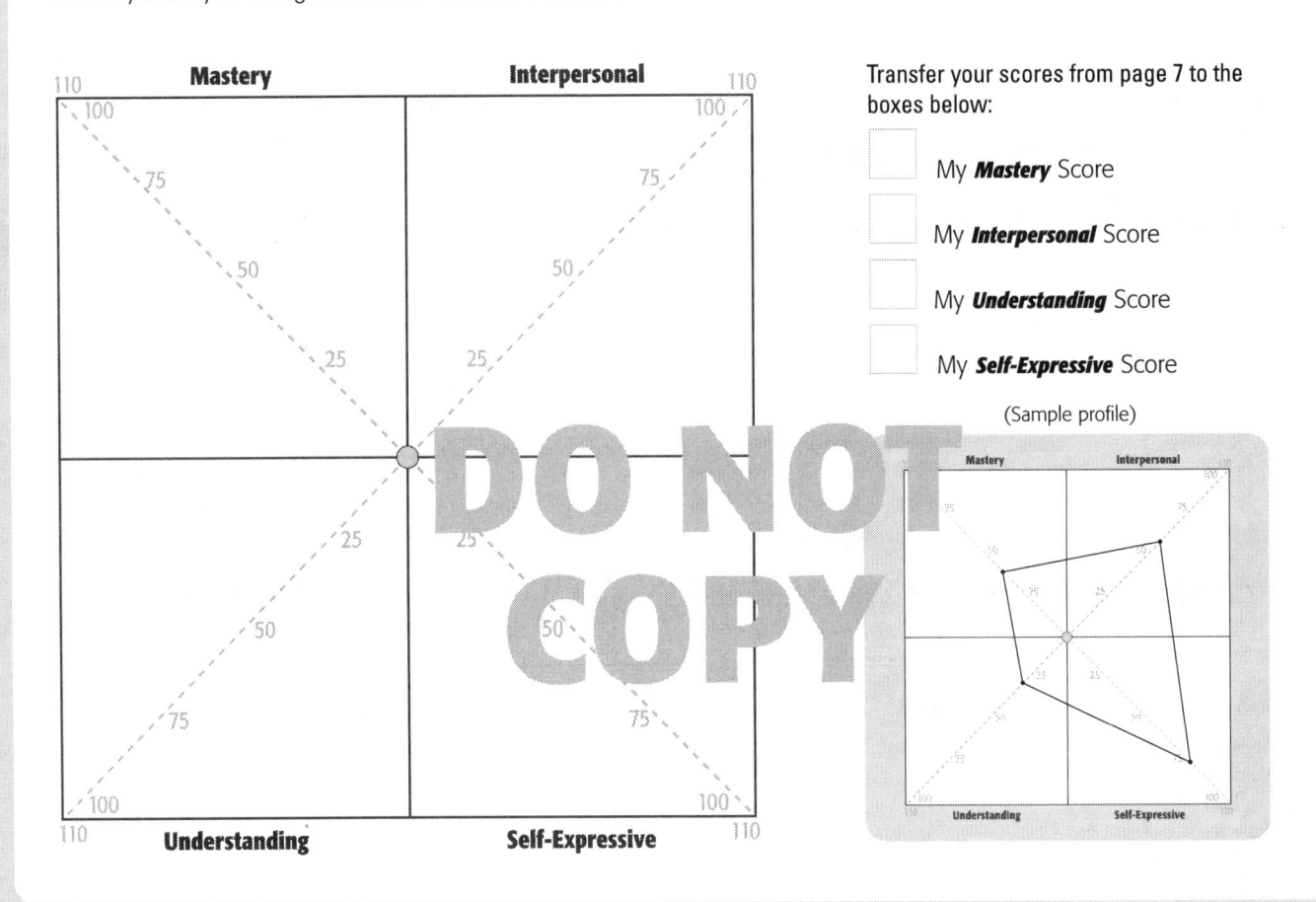

Transfer your scores from page 7 to the boxes below:

☐ My **Mastery** Score

☐ My **Interpersonal** Score

☐ My **Understanding** Score

☐ My **Self-Expressive** Score

(Sample profile)

Understanding Your Comfort Level

90	–	110	:	A very strong preference; almost total comfort when using this style
65	–	89	:	Comfortable when using this style
40	–	64	:	Moderately comfortable when using this style
20	–	39	:	Little comfort when using this style
0	–	19	:	A very weak preference; uncomfortable when using this style

© 2003 by Thoughtful Education Press, L.L.C. All rights reserved.
Reproduction of this instrument by any process is unlawful without the written permission of Thoughtful Education Press, L.L.C.

Reflecting on My Math Learning Style Profile

Now that you have built your own personal Math Learning Style Profile, it's time to think about your results and to reflect on how your new knowledge about yourself can affect your learning in math.

How is your learning style profile reflected in your work as a math student?

Were there any significant differences between your impression of yourself as a learner and your actual results from the Math Learning Style Inventory?

If so, can you account for these differences?

How can your awareness of your Math Learning Style Profile be an asset to you?

All learning styles can and should be developed so that we become more complete learners. What style(s) would you like to develop and why? How will you do this?

27 effective research-based, classroom-tested strategies

The Ideal Tools for Differentiating, Targeting and Succeeding at Math Instruction

New! Styles and Strategies for Teaching Mathematics
by Ed Thomas

Today's math teachers hear many calls: higher standards, differentiation, real-world applications, non-routine problem solving, the list goes on and on. Math teacher, professor, and researcher Ed Thomas shows us that building the 21st-Century math classroom means answering two crucial questions:

- Which research-based strategies are most effective for delivering math instruction?
- How can math teachers address the various needs of their students and still meet today's demanding standards?

With 27 research-based, classroom-tested instructional strategies; a sensible plan for learning-style-based differentiation; and dozens of ready-to-use reproducible lessons, *Styles and Strategies for Teaching Mathematics* will show you how to build the 21st-Century math classroom today.

#HSM001 Styles and Strategies for Teaching *High School* Mathematics (208 pages) $29.95
#MSM001 Styles and Strategies for Teaching *Middle School* Mathematics (208 pages) $29.95

"This book is the ideal tool for differentiating and targeting math instruction. Whenever student achievement data identifies specific learning gaps, this book is my go to reference. It has taught me how to become a better problem solver and how to help teachers help all students in our math classrooms."

— *Jody Hoch*
K-12 Director of Mathematics
Rush-Henrietta Central School District, NY

Save $35.00 *Plus get a FREE Portfolio Bag!*

The Math Learning Style Inventory (MLSI)

Differentiation poses a special challenge in math. Yet we know that if we fail to pay attention to students' needs, interests, and styles, their learning will suffer.

The *Math Learning Style Inventory* is the first learning style instrument designed specifically for math students. Built around the six most important variables to student success in math, the MLSI includes:

- an interactive student's introduction to learning styles in math
- a self-scoring 88-item instrument
- a visual representation of the student's learning profile
- a reflection activity that helps students maximize learning assets and minimize weaknesses

Use the MLSI to build individual and classroom profiles, and bring your math instruction to the next level now.

#MLSI01 (Grades 6-12) . . $5.00 (call for quantity discounts!)

The Math Differentiation Kit
Includes:
- **30** *Math Learning Style Inventories*
- *Styles and Strategies for Teaching Mathematics*
  208 pages (please specify Middle or High School version)
- User's Manual
- Durable nylon carry-all portfolio

#MDK01H (High School) $129.95
#MDK01M (Middle School) $129.95

Buy the Whole KIT and Save!

order now! 800-962-4432

Thoughtful Education Press • 227 First Street • Ho-Ho-Kus, NJ 07423 • www.silverstrong.com